William Henry Withrow

A Canadian in Europe

William Henry Withrow

A Canadian in Europe

ISBN/EAN: 9783743373051

Manufactured in Europe, USA, Canada, Australia, Japa

Cover: Foto ©Andreas Hilbeck / pixelio.de

Manufactured and distributed by brebook publishing software (www.brebook.com)

William Henry Withrow

A Canadian in Europe

BEING

Sketches of Travel

IN

FRANCE, ITALY, SWITZERLAND, GERMANY, HOLLAND
AND BELGIUM, GREAT BRITAIN AND IRELAND.

BY

WILLIAM H. WITHROW, M.A.

ON THE MER DE GLACE.

Toronto:
ROSE-BELFORD PUBLISHING COMPANY.
WILLIAM BRIGGS, KING STREET EAST.

MDCCCLXXXI.

Entered according to Act of the Parliament of Canada, in the year one thousand eight hundred and eighty, by HUNTER, ROSE & Co., in the Office of the Minister of Agriculture.

TO

MR. JOHN MACDONALD,

IN MEMORY OF

A PLEASANT MEETING IN EDINBURGH,

AND OF

GREAT KINDNESS RECEIVED,

This Book

IS INSCRIBED

WITH THE HIGHEST REGARD,

BY

The Author.

PREFACE.

THE chief charm of foreign travel is, I think, the pleasant memories it bequeaths. I have endeavoured in the following pages to communicate some degree of the enjoyment and profit derived from a hurried run through the old historic lands of Europe. If any, who may favour me with their attention, find half as much pleasure in reading this book as I have found in writing it, I shall consider it very successful. The substance of these chapters was contributed, without any idea of their permanent embodiment in book form, to a Monthly Magazine, of which the writer has editorial charge. But the favour with which they were received seemed to indicate that even another book of travel might not be beyond the endurance of the human mind; and, at the request of many friends, they have been revised and expanded to their present form. Through the liberality of the publishers the book is more copiously illustrated than any previous Canadian volume of the sort, and I doubt not that the admirable engravings will more than make up for any lack of interest that the text may exhibit

W. H. W.

TORONTO, October 22, 1880.

CONTENTS.

CHAPTER I.
PAGE.

Getting one's Sea Legs—Sunday Service—In a Gale—The Giants' Causeway—Liverpool—First ride in England—London—Hyde Park—Smithfield—City Road Chapel—Fleet Street—St. Paul's —Westminster Abbey.. 17-34

CHAPTER II.

France—Through Normandy—Rouen—Gothic Art—Jeanne d'Arc— French Politeness—Paris—Tragic Memories of the Place de la Concorde—The Louvre—Old Masters and Modern Paintings— Versailles—Musée de Cluny—Père Lachaise—The Parks—Napoleon's Tomb—Morality and Religion—Paris from a Balloon 35-57

CHAPTER III.

Italy—First view of the Alps—Mont Cenis Tunnel—Italian Manners—Turin—Capuchin Monks—Genoa—Its Palaces—Pisa—Its "Leaning Miracle"—Early Art—The Misericordia—The Hunger Tower.. 58-71

CHAPTER IV.

Rome—The Forum—Its Utter Desolation—The Colosseum—The Jews' Quarter—Ancient Baths—High Mass at St. Peter's— Grave of Shelley—Scene of St. Paul's Martyrdom—In the Catacombs—Their Testimony—Their Structure—Their Chambers—Their Art and Epitaphs—The Appian Way—Roman Tombs and Columbaria—Mammertine Prison—The "Holy Stairs" —Pantheon—Harlequin on an Emperor's Grave—Pincian Hill— A "Model Family"—Art in Rome—Angelo and Raphael—The Vatican—Up the Tiber—Tivoli—Falls of Terni—Orte—Assisi.. 72-114

CHAPTER V.

Italian Landscape—Peasant Life—Naples—Strange Sights—Lazaroni—Street Scribes—Virtuous Donkeys—In the *Grotto del Cane*

—At "Puteoli"—Temple of Serapis—Adventure in the Sibyl's Grotto—At Cumæ—Baja and its Memories—Glories of the Bay of Naples—Capri—The Blue Grotto—A Midnight Ride—Up Vesuvius—"Hangers On"—A Steep Climb—In the Crater—Molten Lava—Pompeii—Old Roman Life—Pathetic Relics—Ancient Art—Degradation of Woman—The Gospel in Italy....115-141

CHAPTER VI.

Ride to Florence—Its Heroic Memories—The Duomo—Giotto's Tower—The Baptistery—Its Gates and Mosaics—Santa Croce—Art in Florence—Boboli Gardens—San Marco—Memories of Savonarola — The "Angelic Brother" — Bologna—Its Leaning Towers—Ferrara—Blind Credulity.............................142-155

CHAPTER VII.

Venice—Its Past and Present—Sunset on the Grand Canal—Oriental Character of People—Historic Pigeons—The Glories of St. Mark's—Sunset from the Campanile—Doge's Palace—Bridge of Sighs—The Arsenal—The *Bucentaur*—On the Rialto—Venetian Superstition—The Gondola—A Methodist Chapel—The Lido—Verona—Milan—The Cathedral—Memories of Borromeo, St. Ambrose, Augustine—Da Vinci's "Last Supper"..............156-176

CHAPTER VIII.

The Italian Lakes—Sunset on Como—Isola Bella—Beauties of Maggiore—My First Alpine Climb—Peasant Life—A *Diligence*—Over the Alps—Hospice at Summit—The Devil's Bridge—Quaint Swiss Inn—St. Gotthard Tunnel—Memorials of Tell—Lake of Uri—Tell's Chapel—Up the Righi—The Highest Hotel in Europe—Magnificent Mountain Prospect—Lucerne—The "Dance of Death"—Thorwaldsen's Lion—Organ Concert................177-200

CHAPTER IX.

Through the Unterwald—Swiss Politeness—Brünig Pass—Meiringen—Illuminated Falls—Over the Alps Afoot—The Bernese Oberland—Alpine Echoes—In an Ice Grotto—Climbing Mount Männlichen—View from the Summit—The Jungfrau—An Avalanche—Lauterbrunnen—The Staubach—Interlaken—Giessbach Falls—Bernese Costume — The Gemmi Pass — Baths of Leuk—A Strange Custom...201-218

CHAPTER X.

Adventures on Mule Back—Gorge of the Trient—The Tête-Noire—A Swiss Hotel—*Table d'Hôte*—The *Mer de Glace*—A Perilous Pass—Mont Blanc—*Crétins*—Geneva and its Memories—In Calvin's Church—The Rhone and Arve—Castle of Chillon—Lausanne—Fletcher Memorial—Freiburg and its Organ............219-236

CHAPTER XI.

The City of the Bear—The Bears' Den—The Alpen-Glow—Basle—A " Graceful Amenity "—Falls of the Rhine—Through the Black Forest—Quaint Costumes—Strassburgh—The Minster—Mass for the Dead—German Domination—Heidelburg—Its Ruined Castle—The Great Tun—Students' Fête......................237-253

CHAPTER XII.

Worms—Luther's Monument and Memories—Mayence—Frankfort—The Jews' Quarter—Their Persecutions—The Kaiser-Saal—Art Treasures—Luther-House—Down the Rhine—" Sweet Bingen "—Character Studies—The Legend of the Mouse Tower—Robber Castles—The Lurlenberg—Song of the Sirens—Coblentz—The " Broad Stone of Honour"—The " *Wacht am Rhein* "—Drachenfels—Legend of Rolandsbogen—Bonn 254-272

CHAPTER XIII.

Cologne—Its Minster—Legend of Ursula—The Three Kings—Aix-la-Chapelle—Tomb of the Great Charles—The Netherlands—Brussels, Another Paris—Historic Sites—Hôtel de Ville—The Mad Painter—Antwerp—Rubens—His " Descent from the Cross "—Matsys—" The Beautiful Wild Chimes "............273-281

CHAPTER XIV.

Holland—Dutch Characteristics—A Kermis—Vanity Fair Outdone—Dutch Manners—Dutch Art—A Night of Terror—Delft—The Hague—Its Galleries—Leyden—Haarlem—The " Venice of the North "—Rembrandt at his Best—The Bible House—Jews and Germans—Ghent—The Bell Roland—The Beguinage—Bruges—A Mediæval Pageant—From the Belfry—Ostend—England.....282-296

CHAPTER XV.

London Again—Greenwich Palace and Park—A Bibulous People—The Tower and its Tragic Memories—The Heart of London—Cheapside—St. Paul's—The Temple—Whitehall—The Abbey—The Tombs of the Kings—Westminster Palace—England's Uncrowned King—Up the Thames—Chelsea—Fulham—Putney—Staines 297-312

CHAPTER XVI.

English Lawns—Windsor Castle—Its Historic Memories—State Apartments—View from Tower—The Royal "Mews"—Eton College—What makes a Gentleman—Richmond—Claremont—By Father Thames—Zion House—Kew Gardens......... 313-326

CHAPTER XVII.

Hampton Court—Bushy Park—The Maze—Historic Chambers—Raphael's Cartoons—Oxford—Christ Church—An Ancient Servitor—The Bodleian—" Maudlin "—Strange Customs—St. Mary's Church—Martyr Memories—" Taking Mine Ease in Mine Inn "—Stratford-on-Avon-Shakespeare's Grave—His Boyhood's Scenes—His Birthplace—Warwick Castle—Drive to Kenilworth—The Wizard's Spell—Mervyn's Bower—Coventry—Rugby—Harrow—Sydenham..327-352

CHAPTER XVIII.

Cambridge—The Fen Country—Peterborough—York and its Minster—Ut Rosa Flos Florum—The East Coast—Edinburgh—Old St. Giles—Memorials of Knox—His House—The Castle—Holyrood—Memorials of Mary—Ancient Wynds—The Covenant Stone—Calton Hill—Musings at Melrose—The Spell of Poetry—Abbotsford—Sterling Castle—The Trosachs Pass—Fair Ellen's Lake—Loch Lomond—Glasgow—St. Mungo's Shrine—Staffa and Fingal's Cave—Belfast—Irish Humour—A Bad Harvest—The Boyne Water—Dublin—A Preposterous Statue—Home Rule—The " Jolting Car "—Through Wales—Chester—Its Walls and Rows—Home Again..353-376

A CANADIAN IN EUROPE.

CHAPTER I.

At Sea—Liverpool—London.

A VISIT to Europe had been for years the dream of my life. To a denizen of this new continent, the monuments and institutions of the past, as seen in the Old World, possess a fascinating interest. In the hoary minsters and crumbling classic fanes, in the many places consecrated by heroism or by song—by the martyr's or the patriot's blood, or by the poet's lyre—one beholds a crystalized history which thrills the soul with a presence and a power before unimagined. And of all the lands in the world our hearts turn with deepest interest to Great Britain and her sister isle, "the mother of us all," the birthplace of liberty, the vanguard of the world's civilization. Next we turn to the early cradle-land of Empire, the City of Rome, with its memory-haunted ruins, and to the nations and peoples which have sprung from its decay. The arts and monuments of mediæval and modern Europe, and the sublime or lovely landscapes of its grandest or softest scenes are also of intense and imperishable interest, and in turn engage our attention.

In fulfilment of my long-cherished purpose, on the 23rd of May, 1879, I left the good city of Toronto. In four and twenty hours I reached the ancient capital, Quebec. The grand old fortress sat proudly on its throne of rock, the royal standard fluttering gaily in the breeze in honour of the Queen's birth-day.

Towards evening, a tender took the passengers on board the good ship "Dominion," Captain Bouchette, master, of the Dominion Steamship line. To one sailing in an ocean steamer for the first time, the arrangements on shipboard are of much interest. What strikes one most is the economy of space, together with the precautions against danger and means adopted to secure steadiness and safety —the small port-holes, with their iron shutters, the firmly-lashed tables and seats, the swinging shelf for glasses, etc., all ominous suggestions of the effects of stormy weather.

The sail down our noble St. Lawrence is very pleasant, giving good views of the Falls of Montmorenci ; the island of Orleans ; Grosse Isle, the quarantine station, where lie the remains of many a poor immigrant; and of the bold north-shore. Soon we are out in the Gulf, and our good ship feels the effects of the rollers from the Atlantic. The breakfast-table of the second day is a crucial test. More than one countenance becomes

" Sicklied o'er with the pale cast of thought ; "

and the ladies, without exception, retire to finish their meditations in the solitude of their state-rooms. Locomotion becomes difficult on deck, and passengers make strange lurches in trying to make their way about. The high lands of the south shore of the Gulf are covered with snow, as are also those of Newfoundland; and quite a snow-storm occurs on the 27th of May. As we cross the Grand Banks of Newfoundland we thread our way through a fleet of vessels engaged in the cod-fishery. Our steam whistle and fog-horn keep up a continuous warning, and a sharp look-out is maintained for their lights amid the darkness. Next day two ice-bergs, one a huge and triple-towered snowy mass, a quarter of a mile long and a hundred and thirty feet high, come into view and pass slowly astern. Strange lonely birds also appear and accompany us far out to sea, and some all the way across the Atlantic.

The most striking impression as we sail on day after day is one of the littleness and loneliness of man in the midst of this immensity of waters. On every side swings the far horizon, unbroken by a single object. Around us roll and toss, like a chained giant tugging at his fetters, the tumultuous waves of the multitudinous seas,—

"Vast-heaving, boundless, endless and sublime."

Still across the trackless main, in spite of adverse winds or waves, the good ship finds, to the destined port, her unerring way. I never appreciated so much the beauty and fidelity of the description, in the one hundred and seventh Psalm, of God's wonders in the deep, as when read at sea.

After a few days, old Ocean smooths his rugged front.

His billows ripple with a thousand smiles. The tables again are filled. The passengers promenade the deck, or group in wind-sheltered and sunny spots. The ship's library is ransacked. The setting of the sails, the changing of the watch, casting the log, taking the sun's altitude, and exchanging signals with a passing vessel, excite their lively interest. Everybody affects nautical language. It is no longer noon, but "eight bells." We do not go to bed, but " turn in ;" and " Ay, ay, sir!" does duty for an affirmative response.

On Sunday morning at half-past ten the ship's bell tolls for service. The officers who are off duty, dressed in their best blue jackets, with the passengers muster in the cabin. At the head of the long dining-table is placed a cushion covered with the Union Jack, which serves as a reading-desk and pulpit. The beautiful service of the Church of England is read, every body joining heartily in the responses. The comprehensive petitions of that service, with its form of prayer for those at sea, for all who travel by land or water, and the prayer to be used during a storm, are realized with fresh power. Then follows a short and practical sermon, with special references to our needs as voyagers together over life's solemn main. Keble's exquisite " Sun of my soul," and Lyte's pathetic "Abide with me, fast falls the eventide," have a new charm as sung amid the restless tossing of the main and the hoarse roaring of the billows.

As we neared the Irish coast a heavy easterly gale set in as if to baffle our efforts to reach the " Isle of Saints."

The "white horses" raced past our vessel, and the sea smote with tremendous shock her iron bulwarks, and then rose high in the air in a column of spray and drenched the deck. With close-reefed sails the good ship forged her way in the very teeth of the gale, mounting up, up on the waves as it would climb the skies, and then sinking down, down into the hollow of the seas, producing a sensation of deadly qualm in those of the passengers who were affected by the awful *mal de mer*. At the dining-table one has an excellent opportunity to study the law of hydrostatics by observing the efforts of his soup to maintain its level notwithstanding the oscillations of the ship. This being rocked in the cradle of the deep, as one lies in his berth, rolled from side to side with now his feet and then his head pointing to the stars, is a rather queer sensation. It is rather difficult, too, to walk the deck when it keeps sinking away from you, as though the bottom had fallen out of everything, or rising up like a hill under your foot. And through all the storm the fearless seagulls on tireless wing skim the waves and soar and circle around the ship, the very poetry of motion. With scarce a motion of the wing they beat up against the wind, then glide down its yielding slope, ascending and descending— like the angels of the patriarch's vision,—the invisible stars of heaven. Sometimes they sit brooding on the stormy wave that breaks into foam all around them, as quietly as if brooding on their nest on the shore; and they will fly so close that we can see the form of their beak and the colour of their eyes.

STEAMSHIP "DOMINION."

At length the blue hills of Old Ireland come in view, and a welcome sight they are to eyes weary with the unbroken sweep of the far horizon. The first land seen is the north-west coast of Donegal. Behind a bold and rocky shore are seen, rolling away in purple billows, the Derryveagh Mountains, some peaks of which rise to the height of over two thousand feet. They are not crowned with trees like our hills in Canada, but with a beautiful green sward, through which the naked rock at times breaks forth, rising in sharp peaks and rugged crags.

Before evening we came abreast of the entrance to Lough Foyle, with its thrilling memorials of the siege of Londonderry. About sunset we passed in full view of the Giant's Causeway, where, according to the veracious legend, "Fin McCoul," an Irish giant, cast up a highway across the Channel that a Scotch giant might walk across in order to have a trial of strength between them. Fin was of course victor; but he generously allowed his beaten adversary to settle in Ireland; so there being no longer any necessity for the Causeway, it was allowed to be washed away by the action of the waves. Its remains, however, may still be seen for the confutation of the sceptical. At Fingal's Cave, in Scotland, and on the Irish coast, the tombs of the respective giants are also pointed out; and what better proof can one ask than that?

> "Dark o'er the foam-white waves,
> The Giants' pier the war of tempest braves;
> A far-projecting, firm basaltic way
> Of clustering columns, wedged in close array,

> With skill so like, yet so surpassing art,
> With such design, so just in every part,
> That reason pauses, doubtful if it stand
> The work of mortal or immortal hand."

In the purple gloaming, which here lasts far into the night—we are six hundred miles north of Toronto—we passed within half a mile of the noble cliff of Fair Head, rising five hundred feet in the air, with remarkable columned rocks, known as the Giant's Organ; and looming on the left was the Mull of Cantyre, in Scotland.

The Irish Sea was tranquil as a sea of glass, as we passed the Isle of Man, and twenty miles from Liverpool took on board our pilot. Keen was the interest to hear what had been happening in the great world from which, ten days before, we had been cut off, and the newspapers were eagerly scanned and discussed. A score of ocean steamers were gliding out on ebb-tide as we entered the Mersey, and beheld its seven miles of docks and its forest of masts. From the turbid condition of the river it is evident that "The quality of Mersey is not strained."

The busy aspect of the scene forcibly recalls the description of a local bard:

> "Behold the crowded port,
>   Whose rising masts an endless prospect yields,
>   With labour burns, and echoes to the shout
>   Of hurried sailors, as they hearty wave
>   Their last adieu, and loosening every sail,
>   Resign the speeding vessel to the wind."

Liverpool bears little of the impress of antiquity. The splendid public buildings that we see, the palace-like hotels, the crowded and busy streets are all of comparatively recent construction. It has more the air of New York or Chicago, than that of an Old World town. The famous St. George's Hall, the Exchange, the City Hall and especially the massive warehouses and miles on miles of docks give a striking impression of its commercial greatness.

It was Whitsuntide when I landed, and the streets were crowded with holiday visitors, many of them of a decidedly bucolic appearance. The knee-breeches, smock frocks and flaming neck-ties of the rustic yokels, and the " Dolly Varden " dresses, bright ribbons and blooming cheeks of the country lasses were just like the pictures that Leech and Dickens give us with pencil and pen. The Walker Art Gallery was visited, I was told, by 24,000 persons in two days. This ministry of art in the æsthetic education of the people must be very salutary.

Few things in Liverpool pleased me more than a visit to the new Temperance Coffee-house just opened. It is a handsome stone building, on the main street. Inside it is elegantly painted and frescoed. Up stairs are rooms with handsome pictures and panelled walls, marble-topped tables, and a luxurious bar, with huge burnished tea and coffee urns. To test the food furnished I ordered coffee and a large bun—both excellent,—for which I paid one penny ! There are thirty-seven of these Temperance Coffee-houses in Liverpool, under the same Limited Liability Company. They pay a profit of ten per cent., and I believe will yet be the solution of the drink question in England—the greatest social problem of the age.

Taking the Midland Railway for London next day, I

passed through some of the finest scenery in England; through the celebrated Peak of Derbyshire, and down the beautiful valley of the Derwent. The memories of that first ride through this dear old historic land will never be effaced—the soft-rounded hills, the lovely vales, the stately parks and mansions, the quaint farmsteads and granges, the red-tiled or straw-thatched cottages, the ivy-grown churches, the fields cultivated like a garden, and the hawthorn hedges in full bloom—just as we see them all in Birket Foster's pictures. In traversing Bedfordshire, I passed many places hallowed by the footprints of the immortal dreamer, John Bunyan; Finchley Common, where he spoke bold words on behalf of religious freedom; Luton, where he spread the glad tidings of free salvation, and censured what he believed to be iniquities of priestcraft; Dallow Farm, in a loft of which he took refuge when pursued because of the truths he had spoken; the Village of Elstow, in which he was born, and where in his reckless youth he had led a dissolute life; Elstow Church, a venerable pile, the notes of whose bells had often been wafted on the air as he pulled the ropes; and then Bedford, where he was imprisoned, and within the walls of the old gaol wrote "The Pilgrim's Progress to the Celestial City."

On this gentle pastoral scenery of the still-flowing Ouse, with its many windings, its pollards, and its moated granges, his eyes have often gazed; and from that soft green sward he may have taken his description of "Bypath

WESTMINSTER BRIDGE.

Meadow." Was his "Vanity Fair," I wonder, copied from the London of his day?

I reached London at the St. Pancras Station, the largest in the world, with its vast sky of glass and palatial hotel, and was driven in a "Hansom," but not handsome, cab—an odd-looking two-wheeled gig, in which the driver sits aloft behind the hood—to a quaint old hotel in a pleasant square filled with trees, in Bloomsbury—the scene of the Gordon riots. The somewhat formal air of its great breakfast-room, the neatness of the table service, the respectful attentions of the servants, the clean and comfortable chambers, the quiet home-like feeling of the house were a pleasant contrast to the splendid cheerlessness of an American caravansary.

My first walk is up Oxford Street to Hyde Park. It is a fine day, and the world of fashion is abroad—handsome carriages, high-stepping horses, liveried and silk-stockinged footmen—some with their hair powdered white as snow. The broad acres of the Park, with its stately trees, its soft green turf, its moving throngs, make as pretty a picture in the afternoon light as one need wish to see. Here flows a ceaseless stream of open carriages containing the flower of the English nobility, enjoying their afternoon drive. There is probably no such collection of beautiful ladies and exquisite toilets in the world—fair, fresh English faces, with a delicate bloom, fine-cut profile, an air of high-born culture, and an indefinable but unmistakable tone and refinement acquired through generations of hereditary descent. Beside the carriage drive is a promenade and a row of chairs—in places four rows—for the less aristocratic portion of the community; and the fair faces were by no means confined to the carriage people.

Parallel with this fashionable drive runs the Rotten Row—derived, say the antiquaries, from *route du roi*, or royal road—the favourite resort of fair equestrians, and their gallant attendants; and a pretty sight it is to see the elegant and accomplished riders, and the curvettings of their spirited and high-bred horses.

One of the strongest impressions felt in London is that of its wealth and its poverty, its greatness and its misery, the immense differences of rank, the luxury of the rich, the wretchedness of the poor. Poverty is everywhere apparent, notably in the itinerant venders of toys, trinkets, combs, pencils—almost anything for a penny; and, in the poorer regions, the wayside stalls for cheap food—pigs' feet, tripe, and the like. I noticed these especially at the great Smithfield market, with its memories of the martyrs, where the cries of the chapmen and venders vociferously seeking custom were bewildering.

From Smithfield I visited a spot dear to the heart of every Methodist the wide world over—City Road Chapel, the mother church of Methodism. It seems to bring one nearer to the springs of Methodism to stand in the old pulpit in which its early fathers preached; to sit in Wesley's chair; to see the room in which he died; the study, a very small room, in which he wrote many of his books; the very time-worn desk at which he sat; and then to stand by the grave in which he is buried. In the old parsonage I saw the teapot, of generous dimensions, from which Wesley used to regale the London preachers every Sunday. On one side was the verse beginning "Be present at our table, Lord," and on the other, the words " We thank Thee, Lord, for this our food," etc. At his grave I plucked an ivy leaf as a memento of the visit. Near by rest the ashes of Clarke, Benson, and other fathers of Methodism. In the Bunhill Fields Cemetery, on the opposite side of the street, I visited the graves of probably the three most widely-read writers in the English or in any language, John Bunyan, Isaac Watts, and Daniel Defoe.

To walk down Fleet Street transports one back to the reign of Good Queen Anne, and further. One would scarcely be surprised to meet the burly figure of Dr. Johnson walking down the street, carefully touching certain stones by the wayside, and if he missed one, going back and beginning over again. I patronized a barber shop, which the owner announced on his sign was a former palace of Henry VIII. In the old timbered ceiling, his monogram is still seen, and some of the old furniture is preserved. I visited Dick's Tavern at Temple Bar; and the Cheshire Cheese Inn, in Wine Office Court, built in 1400, where Johnson, Goldsmith, Boswell, Richardson, Garrick, and the rest of their goodly fellowship were wont to hold their Olympic symposia. Of the Bar itself, on which the heads of rebels used to be impaled, only a fragment remains.

In the afternoon I visited the Spring Exhibition of the Royal Academy of Arts, in their noble rooms at Burlington House. The collection was of great excellence—the finest specimens of recent British art. It was a treat to hear the fine-flavoured English that was spoken, especially by ladies, with a purity of intonation not common in Canada, and to receive the high-bred courtesies which were graciously accorded to every inquiry. I had heard that the English were cold and repellant in their manners to strangers. I found them the very reverse; cheerfully giving every information in their power, and even putting themselves to inconvenience to do so.

My first Sunday in England was a red-letter day. I had the privilege of visiting two of the grandest temples of Protestant Christendom. The first glimpse of the mighty dome of St. Paul's made my heart leap. But a closer inspection of the building is disappointing. It is blackened with London smoke and corroded with the gases in the air, so that parts are covered with a whitish incrustation like nitre. Within, the dome is vast and solemn, and the view down the nave is awe-inspiring, but to me it conveys no religious impression. " Gothic architecture," says Ruskin, "confesses Christ; classic architecture denies Christ." The sentiment is extreme, but to me it expresses the difference between St. Paul's and Westminster Abbey. In the latter the clustering shafts springing toward the sky, and the groined arches leaping from their summit and supporting the sky-like vault overhead, must kindle in the coldest nature a religious aspiration.

Then it is hoary with the associations of at least eight hundred years. I saw the crumbling effigies in the cloisters of the Norman Abbots, from A. D. 1068–1214. The pious hands that carved the fret-work I beheld had mouldered to dust eight hundred years ago.

A full choral service was rendered—the sublime anthems pealing through the vaulted aisles, as they have for so many centuries. The retention of so much of the old Roman liturgy in the Anglican services is an illustration of the conservative tendency that characterizes the English treatment of all ancient institutions. And all around were England's mighty dead, laid to rest in this great Walhalla of the nation—her kings and warriors, and statesmen; and mightier than they, her kings of thought and literature—the anointed priests and sages and seers of the "Poets' Corner," in which I sat. And I felt that in all this, though a stranger from over-sea, I was not an alien, but that I shared the inheritance in those spirit-stirring memories of the English-speaking race throughout the world; and tears of deep and strong emotion filled my eyes.

Dean Stanley, the greatest of all the deans of the venerable abbey, whom, most of living men, I longed to hear, preached the sermon. It being Trinity-Sunday, he discoursed on the text, "In the name of the Father, and of the Son, and of the Holy Ghost." He is a little old gentleman, wears a skull cap, and has an indistinct utterance, but the sermon was one of the most impressive I ever heard. He reminded us that five hundred years ago, that very day, the eighth of June, Edward the Black Prince died, the knight of the Holy Ghost; and exhorted us in the name of the blessed Trinity to be faithful soldiers of the Holy Cross. The painted light that streamed through the crimson and purple robes of the apostles and prophets in the great rose window grew fainter and fainter; and before the service was over a solemn gloom began to fill the shadowy vaults and aisles of the vast minster. Among the many monuments upon the wall I noticed as I passed out of the abbey the medallions of John and Charles Wesley and the bas-relief of John Wesley preaching on his father's grave.

I attended also the old Ludgate Church in the city, and found a congregation of only eight persons. I visited, too, the old Savoy Church, now partly under ground, where the celebrated Savoy Conference, for the revision of the Prayer-Book, was held.

In my walk I passed half-a-dozen palaces, each haunted with the memory of English Sovereigns—Buckingham Palace, the residence of the Queen; the town-houses of the Prince of Wales and Duke of Edinburgh; St. James' Palace, the residence of the English Kings from William III. to George IV.; Whitehall, from the window of which Charles I. stepped to the scaffold; and Somerset House, the home of three unhappy English Queens. But almost every street has memories of the past, which seem almost more real than the experiences of the present.

From Westminster Bridge, shown in the cut on page 27, is obtained one of the grandest views in Europe—the noble river front of the New Houses of Parliament on one side, and St. Thomas's Hospital and Lambeth Palace, with its memories of Cranmer and the Lollards, on the other. Along the river side, on either hand, are the splendid Victoria and Albert Embankments, one of which is shown in the initial cut of this chapter. Midway in this rises the famous Cleopatra's Needle, a memorial of the oldest civilization in the world erected in the heart of the newest. In the middle distance is Waterloo Bridge, and to the left the long façade of Somerset House.

CLEOPATRA'S NEEDLE, ON ORIGINAL SITE.

CHAPTER II.

France: Rouen—Paris.

ON the fourth of June I left London for my continental trip. Passing through the beautiful southern shires of England, I sailed from Newhaven for the French fishing-town of Dieppe. The chalk cliffs of Beachy Head soon disappeared and the French coast came into view. Dieppe is a very fitting introduction to continental life. Everything has a decidedly foreign flavour —the red-legged French soldiers; the nut-brown women with their high-peaked, snow-white Norman caps, knitting in the sun; the fish-wives with enormous and ill-smelling creels of fish upon their backs; the men wearing blue blouses and chattering a jargon of Norman-French. The ride to Rouen was a succession of beautiful pictures of quaint rural life, queer old chateaux with pepper-pot turrets; red-tiled or straw-thatched, low-walled granges, embowered amid orchards in full bloom; old moss-grown villages with their mouldering church, tiny mill, and rustic inn.

I spent my first night in France at Rouen, the ancient capital of Normandy, and the richest of French cities in mediæval architecture. In Paris almost everything that is old has disappeared before the modern improvements.

At Rouen, on the contrary almost everything and everybody, even the children, seemed at least five hundred years old. It was stepping back into the middle ages. The ancient timbered houses, with quaintly carved and high-pitched gables lean over the narrow crooked streets till they almost meet overhead. The Cathedral dates from 1207, and contains the tombs of Rollo of Normandy and of our English William Longue Epée, and the heart of Cœur de Lion. The shrine of the latter bears the inscription, "Hic jacet cor Ricardi, Regis Anglorum, cor leonis dicti."

It was in the dim twilight that I entered the church, and the deep shadows filling the vast and solemn nave and aisles, the tapers faintly burning before the various altars and shrines, the half-seen figures kneeling in the gloom all conspired to produce a strangely weird impression far more profound than that felt in the garish light of day.

The architectural gem of the city, however, is the Church of St. Ouen, one of the most beautiful gothic churches in existence. Its sculptured arch and niche and column; its great rose windows, stained with brightest hues; its carved effigies of saint and martyr, and of knights and kings and noble dames praying on their tombs; and the deep-toned organ peeling through the vaulted aisles, and the sweet singing of the choir-boys and chanting of the priests gave me my first vivid impression of the grandeur and strange fascination to its adherents of the old historic Romish ritual, which for hundreds of years cast its spell over mediæval Christendom.

One can walk completely around the roof of the church and thus get a near view of the grinning gargoyles through which the water is poured out. The monkish imagination seems to have run riot in carving quaint and grotesque devices—dragons, griffins, strange twi-formed creatures with the head of a goat or monkey or bird, and the body of a man, or *vice versa*, in every possible combination. One door is called the "Portail des Marmousets," from the little animals that gambol over its arches. Over the central door of many of these old churches are carved with admirable skill and infinite patience, elaborate groups representing scenes from the life of Christ and frequently the awful scene of the Last Judgment. At Notre Dame at Paris, for instance, Christ sits upon His throne, the Archangel sounds a trumpet, the dead burst from their tombs, and Satan is weighing their souls in a balance. Devils drive the lost to the left and torture them in flames, while angels lead the saved to the joys of Paradise. In the arch of a single door are no less than two hundred separate figures—one of them St. Denis, carrying his head in his hands—a symbol of the mode of his martyrdom.

In those early days art was religion, and the churches were a great stone Bible, often the only Bible the people had or could read. Over and over again is told the story of a man from his creation and fall to his final resurrection.

But most frequently and most fully is rehearsed the story of the life and sufferings of our Lord, and of the seven joys and seven sorrows of Mary. I was not prepared however, to find the presence of the comic element in this church decoration—the grinning and grimacing monkeys, the grotesque conflicts of saints and demons, in which the latter are sorely discomfited, and similar scenes.

I stood with painful interest upon the spot where well nigh five hundred years ago, by English hands, the heroic Joan of Arc was burned at the stake for the alleged crime of witchcraft. It is a page which one would gladly blot from his country's history. The patriot Maid of Orleans is a favourite subject of French art. I saw in Paris a beautiful statue representing her hearing the Divine voice which called her to conflict, to victory, and to martyrdom, for her country. The air of eager listening and the rapt inspiration of the noble and beautiful features was one of the grandest things I ever beheld.

A more agreeable reminiscence of the international relations of England and France is an elaborate series of stone reliefs representing the pomp and pageants of the Field of the Cloth of Gold. May no less friendly intercourse ever take place between the English and the gay, kind-hearted French race! I saw a striking instance of their cheerful gaiety during an evening stroll at Rouen. In an open square about thirty full-grown men and women, in their respective blue blouses and snowy Norman caps, but dusty with toil, were merrily playing in a ring, as I have seen school children in Canada, and singing a simple childish rhyme. They seemed as happy as a school let loose. I observed no rudeness or indecorum; but it looked very odd to see men and women at such child's play.

The Duke of Wellington was once asked how he spoke French. "With the greatest intrepidity, Madam," was his reply. In like manner I carried on my intercourse with these interesting people. Even when they spoke English I found that rather harder to understand than the French, so I made the most of my slender linguistic acquirements in that language. They never laughed at my mistakes or awkward phrases, although I had often to laugh at them myself. They are very quick and bright-witted, and I had slight difficulty in getting any information I wanted. I found the English very polite; but I must confess the French surpassed them. For instance, riding in an omnibus I happened to ask my next neighbour the way to some place. In a minute there was a council of war over my map, several persons, including one or two ladies, proffered advice, and it ended by one of the gentlemen getting out with me to show me the spot. And that is but a specimen of the treatment everywhere in France. One lady, indeed, assured me that they looked upon Canadians almost as fellow-countrymen. "We used to own all that country," she said. But even when my nationality was unknown the politeness was the same. At a fine museum in Paris, the Musée de

PLACE DE LA CONCORDE.

Cluny, to which admission is granted by a special order, but without a fee, I recorded my name as desiring an order, and soon received a large official document containing it. Before it arrived, however, happening to be in the neighbourhood, I asked admission, which was courteously granted, and every assistance given in studying the valuable collections.

I have said that I was disappointed at the brand-new appearance of the greater part of Paris. I was also struck with the monotony—a splendid monotony it is true—of its street architecture. Broad boulevards and streets radiate from numerous points, so, according to Baron Haussmann's design, I was informed, as to be commanded by cannon from these strategic points. On either side of these streets rise uniform blocks and wedges of houses, of cream-coloured stone,—five, six, or seven stories high, with iron balconies, and bright shop fronts. Many of the boulevards are lined with noble trees, giving a refreshing shade and coolness amid the glare and heat of the city. Many of them are also paved with concrete or asphalt, which has the double advantage of being noiseless and of furnishing poor material for the erection of barricades— the favourite amusement of the Parisians in times of political excitement. At night the streets are brilliant with light—electric lamps, glowing like mimic suns ; the cafés ablaze with gas, and occupying with their little round tables half of the broad side-walks; and the numerous shops flashing with jewellery or glowing with costly fabrics.

The public squares, of which there are many, are full of life and movement and rich in colour, adorned with noble trees, flashing fountains and snowy statuary, and filled with brilliant equipages and promenaders, with everywhere the ubiquitous gens d'armes. Of all the parks in the world I suppose the Champs Elysées is the grandest —not so much in natural beauty, for it shares the splendid monotony of the city, but in the stately architecture by which it is surrounded, the noble vista it presents, and the brilliant concourse by which it is thronged; and over all is thrown an intense historic interest by the tragic memories with which it is haunted. On its broad Place de la Concorde, the guillotine began its bloody work with the execution of Louis XVI. Then in swift succession followed the judicial murders of his ill-fated and lovely queen Marie Antoinette, his sister Madame Elizabeth, and Philippe Egalité, Duke of Orléans; and here, too, the archconspirator Robespierre with many of his companions in crime met a stern retribution. Nearly three thousand persons in all here became the victims of that tremendous social earthquake, which overthrew both throne and altar in the dust, and shook all Europe with its throes. And here, within the last eight years, were renewed, in the wild orgies of the Commune, the darkest tragedies of the Reign of Terror. The crumbling and crannied walls of the Tuileries, blackened and blasted with fire, the seat of the pomp and pride of the late Empire, look down upon the stately palace-garden, as striking a proof of the mutability of earthly greatness as the ruins of Cæsar's imperial palace, near which I pen these lines*. And even as I write come the tidings of the tragic death, by a Zulu assegai in an obscure African jungle, of the young prince, born in the purple in those now ruined halls, the prospective heir of all their splendour and imperial power.

I was surprised on the whole to see so little evidence of the most memorable siege of history. Except the ruins of the Tuileries, the Hôtel de Ville and a few other public buildings, there was little to remind one of the dreadful scenes of the Commune or the siege. The Colonne de Vendôme, hurled from its base in detestation of the Imperialism which it commemorates, again rears its majestic form in air; and soon, throughout the gay pleasure-city all trace of its "baptism of fire" shall have disappeared.

The Tuileries, however, even in their best estate would not compare with the stately architecture of the Louvre, the abode of a long line of sovereigns, and now the home of the immortal works of the mightier sovereigns of art. Its majestic façades with their sculptured and columned fronts, its noble statuary, its spacious courts, its vast galleries and its priceless treasures of art make it almost without a rival in the world. Here I must confess a heresy on the subject of art. I cannot feel the enthusiasm for the "old masters," which seems to be expected of all beholders. Ruskin says that nobody ever painted a tree correctly till Turner showed the way. I think that, at least in lands-

---

* This chapter was written in Rome.

cape, modern artists surpass those of any former age. In reverent sympathy with nature and faithful interpretation of her varied moods, I have seen nothing that, in my judgment, will compare with the modern galleries. Even the religious art of the great masters to me seems often conventional and insipid, and lacking soul and vitality. They possessed a mastery of form and colour, it is true ; but in this I think they are equalled by the moderns; and better than many of the famous pictures of the Louvre I liked the exhibition of works of living artists in the Palais de l'Industrie. The portraits seemed almost to speak, the water to flow, the flowers seemed not painted but modelled, the texture of armour, glass, ivory, and woven fabric was of startling realism. Hamlet's words to his mother, "Seems, madam ; nay, it *is*," kept continually coming to my mind.

In religious teaching they seemed also more direct and intense. A picture of our Lord and the Family at Bethany, instead of giving the conventional types of the art of the Renaissance, gave real portraits of living men and women —grave, earnest, intensely real, and speaking with strange power to the heart. In another, our Lord, with a countenance of ineffable and infinite love and pity, calls the afflicted unto Him, and varied types of wretchedness and sorrow clustered in sacred restfulness at His feet. In another, entitled "The Last Port of Refuge," the souls of shipwrecked voyagers are dimly seen struggling up through the whelming waves to the open gate of heaven, where Christ stands to welcome them home. And still another was more exquisitely suggestive than any of the scores of Renaissance "Flights into Egypt" that I have seen. The dark form of the Sphinx, as if propounding its awful riddle, fills the picture with gloom. Cradled in its arms, where He has been laid by Mary, lies the Holy Child, emitting a glory of Divine radiance, as if to show that He was the solution of the dark problem of the ages. In the foreground a thin column of smoke from Joseph's camp-fire climbs the sky, giving an intense conception of the vastness and loneliness of the desert. But mere words can give a very faint idea of the power and impressiveness of these pictures. Delaroche's famous "hémicycle" at the Palais des Beaux-Arts is one of the most impressive paintings I ever saw. It has seventy-five colossal figures, twenty-three feet high, representing the arts. The effect is majestic.

Several of the old French palaces are surrendered to purposes of trade. One of these, the Palais Royal, is entirely occupied by shops and cafés. It was built by Cardinal Richelieu, and was the palace of Anne of Austria, Louis XIV. and Philip of Orléans. Here were celebrated those disgraceful orgies which helped to bring on the Revolution. It is a vast court adorned with fountains, statuary, trees, and surrounded by the palace buildings. One of the cafés overlooking the garden was a favourite place for dining after a hard day's work in the adjacent Louvre. Here in the ancient halls of kings, regaled with music by the band of the Garde Républicaine—one of the best in the world—I could obtain an excellent dinner of soup, three courses and dessert, with wine or coffee—I took the coffee—in the company of priests, abbés, artists, and ladies, for the sum of fifty cents—and be waited on, too, by a magnificent gentleman in full dress.

The most interesting palace, however, in or near Paris, is the Palace of Versailles. I made the trip—it is twenty miles by rail—in the company of a French gentleman from Canada who crossed in the same ship. We rode in the "Imperial" or open upper story of the railway carriage, and thus enjoyed a fine view of the country. The omnibuses and street-cars have also these upper stories, which are much the best for sight-seeing. The palace cost the treasury of Louis XIV. the enormous sum of a thousand million francs, and at one time 36,000 men and 6,000 horses were employed in constructing its terraces. When the starving people sent a deputation demanding, "What shall we eat?" they received the mocking answer, "Eat grass." No wonder a revolution swept away the evil dynasty with a besom of destruction. The chief consolation in visiting these monuments of royal tyranny is the fact that they are no longer the palaces of kings, but the palaces of the people—the private apartments of once mighty sovereigns, and the boudoirs of queens, are open to the poorest in the land. How time brings its revenges!

We were shown the Legislative Chamber, in which the day before it had been decided to restore the seat of government to the City of Paris, which felt sorely aggrieved at the long deprivation it had endured. The palace is a quarter of a mile long and contains some of the grandest courts, galleries, and saloons in the world, adorned with priceless paintings—one of Vernet's battle-pieces is seventy-one feet long and sixteen feet high—Sèvres vases, malachite tables, marble mantels and the like, beyond computation. During the late war these stately apartments were turned into hospitals for the German wounded; and in the celebrated *Salle des Glaces*, by a strange irony of fate, the King of Prussia was proclaimed Emperor of United Germany. Here also is shown the bed-chamber of Louis XIV. where the Grand Monarque used to receive his courtiers as he rose from bed—hence our word *levée*—and the royal chamberlains had the honour of arraying his sacred majesty in his wig, robes, and shoes and stockings. Here also is shown the state-bed on which he died, and the window where the herald proclaimed, "Le Roi est mort! Vive le Roi!" Of greater interest, however, are the private apartments of the amiable and unfortunate Louis XVI. and of his highborn but low-laid consort, Marie Antoinette. Here is her boudoir, her writing- and work-table, her library—and on the doors are the identical locks, of excellent workmanship, wrought by the royal locksmith, her husband. From the window is seen the long and noble avenue, up which swarmed the riotous mob of enraged men and women clamouring for blood. On this marble stairway the gentlemen of the guard kept the mob at bay, faithful

CHURCH OF ST. DENIS.

unto death. The narrow passage through which the Queen attempted to escape is also pointed out. It makes the tragic story of those horrible days very real to see these mementoes of their horrors.

The vast and monotonous park, with its formal parterres, its long avenues of trees clipped into accurate cubes, its terraces and fountains with their Neptunes and Tritons and river-gods have a weary monotony that palls upon the mind. The Great and Little Trianons, built for royal mistresses, and the collection of unwieldy and heavily gilt state-carriages recall only memories of guilty pomp and pride.

Far more beautiful, because more natural, is the noble park of St. Cloud, with its avenues of stately trees, its bosky solitudes, its swelling hills and magnificent panorama of Paris and the winding Seine. From the windows of Versailles, it is said, was visible the distant Church of St. Denis, the mausoleum of a long line of French Kings. To shut out the unwelcome view, therefore, Louis XIV. erected the pleasure palace of St. Cloud, and filled it with every luxury that despotic power could command. The shells of the Prussians, however, spared not the pride of kings, and the blackened walls of the ruined palace are a monument of the vicissitudes of earthly greatness.

One of the most interesting places in Paris is the Hôtel de Cluny. Here the Roman Emperor Constantius Chlorus in the third century founded a palace, the vast baths of which are still in good preservation. Here Julian was proclaimed Emperor in 360, and here the early Frankish monarchs resided. On the site of the palace the Monks of Cluny in the 15th century built the present exquisite mediæval abbey which became again the residence of the sovereigns of France. It is now one of the most interesting museums of mediæval relics in the world. In the very heart of the crowded and busy city one may lounge in the quaint old monkish garden or explore the still older Roman baths, carrying one back to the very dawn of Gallic history.

I attended a vesper service at the venerable Cathedral of Notre Dame, which was very impressive. As the organ pealed through the vaulted aisles I thought of the many *Te Deums* for famous victories, coronations, marriage and funeral pomps of the sovereigns of France that had here been celebrated; and then of the orgies of the Reign of Terror, when a ballet-dancer was here enthroned as the Goddess of Reason; and of its more recent desecration, when the Communists made it a military depot, and when compelled to retreat set it on fire. The jeweled wealth of its sacristry is of priceless cost, and of rare historic interest.

Near by is that chamber of horrors, the Morgue, where six hundred unknown dead, chiefly suicides, are, during the year, placed for recognition. A morbidly curious throng were surging in and out, as I passed, to gaze on the dishonoured relics of mortality exposed on marble slabs within.

The dark secrets of that house, could they be told, would reveal deeper tragedies than poet ever feigned.

I visited with especial interest the celebrated cemetery of Père Lachaise—the last resting place of so many of the noblest dead of France. My feet turned first to the tomb of Abélard and Heloïse, whose tale of love and sorrow, after the lapse of seven long centuries, still touches the heart of the world with perennial power. Their effigies lie, with hands clasped in prayer, side by side, and the simple inscription reads " Les restes d'Heloïse et d'Abélard sont reunis dans ce tombeau." Dissevered in their lives, their dust mingles together with its kindred clay. Garlands of fresh and fragrant flowers, placed by loving hands upon their tomb, attested the living sympathy which is still felt for their sorrows. Here, too, is the narrow house of the money-king, Rothschild, and of those queens of tragedy, Rachel and Menken.

Among the other distinguished dead interred in this populous city of the dead are Fourier, Champollion, Abbé Seiyès, Pastor Monod, Eugene Scribe, Michelet, Talma, Cherubini, Chopin, Rossini, Béranger, La Fontaine, Molière, Gay-Lussac, Laplace, Arago, Madame de Genlis, Alfred de Musset and many another whose name and fame have filled the world.

The French exhibit much kindly sentiment in decorating the graves of their departed with wreaths of flowers and immortelles; and over many of these are constructed glass pent-houses for their protection. I noticed, too, that even rough fellows in their blouses reverently took off their hats when a funeral passed. On many tombs I observed the prayer for the dead: "Requiem æternam dona eis Domine, et lux perpetua luceat eos." In the mortuary chapel was a beautiful marble angel crowned with living flowers, bearing a Bible, open at the text so full of hope for all the sorrowing; "Beati mortui qui in Domino morientur." The cemetery was one of the last strongholds of the Commune, and amid the funereal cypress and marble monuments of the dead were waged one of the most desperate conflicts of the living. In the neighbouring prison of La Roquette, was perpetrated one of the most lurid crimes of that reign of terror. The venerable Monseigneur Darboy, Archbishop of Paris, with four other distinguished ecclesiastics, were, after a mock trial and gross outrage, ruthlessly shot in the court-yard of the prison. The robes of the murdered archbishop, stained with his blood, are shown at the sacristy of Notre Dame.

Near Père Lachaise, rise the heights of Les Buttes-Chaumont, the most picturesque park in Paris. It is situated in the Belleville faubourg, the very heart of the Commune despotism. To reach it, I had to pass through streets crowded with men and women of the labouring class, many of whom looked quite capable of repeating the dark deeds of those dreadful days. The park was a waste where the rubbish of the city was deposited till the civic government of the late Emperor converted it into a garden of fairy-like loveliness. Artificial lakes, cascades, and grottoes; cliff and crag mantled with foliage and climbing-plants, and gay with flowers of brightest hue; and a magnificent view from a Belvidere crowning a lofty height, make it the most attractive bit of scenery in the city. The large and fashionable Bois de Boulogne is tame and uninteresting in comparison. The latter was denuded of its trees during the siege, and those since planted have attained only a rather meagre growth. Its walks and bosky vistas, its lakes and cascades, and its magnificent parterres of flowers, and masses of rich shrubbery are very charming. But it is, I think, inferior in natural beauty to Fairmount at Philadelphia, and in artificial picturesqueness to Central Park, New York. My visit was made at sunset's pensive hour, when the world of fashion had retired from its pleasant drives, and its sylvan scenes were as silent and lonely as a desert. The water fowl splashed in their quiet ponds as fearlessly as though they were in some far-off forest solitude. In the long purple twilight and through the deepening dusk, I found my way back to the gay and brilliant city.

But my time and space would fail before I could enumerate half the attractions of this pleasure city. One of the most delightful of these is the Luxembourg Palace, with its noble galleries of sculpture and painting, its vast and elegant though rather formal garden, its pleasant promenade concerts, where Fair France appears in her most tasteful toilette—and very tasteful it is. Ladies of the wealthier class always wear bonnets or hats; women of the poorer class, domestic servants and the like, wear a very neat and snowy white muslin cap; those of an intermediate grade trip through the streets with their heads covered only by a somewhat elaborate arrangement of their hair.

The flower markets are also very bright and pleasant places, with the gay colours, the fragrance, and the exquisite beauty of their flowers. The Jardin des Plantes and Jardin d'Acclimatation, with their noble trees, fountains, flowers, and collections of strange animals, are very interesting and instructive resorts. At the latter it is very amusing to see the children enjoying their rides on the camel or elephant, or in the ostrich or zebra carriage.

The tomb of Napoleon I. beneath the vast dome of the Church des Invalides, is the noblest mausoleum I think, I ever saw. In the centre of a large circular crypt sunk in the marble floor lies the huge sarcophagus hewn out of a single block of Finland granite, weighing sixty-seven tons. Twelve colossal marble Victories, with wreath and palm, guard the dust of that stormy heart now still for ever, which shook all Europe with its throbs. A faint bluish light streams down from the lofty dome, and the sombre aspect of the crypt and its surroundings contribute greatly to the solemn grandeur of the scene.

The Panthéon and the Madeleine are more like pagan temples than like Christian churches; but in the Sainte Chapelle, gothic architecture has achieved one of its most splendid triumphs. Of sinister interest is the Church of

St. Germain l'Auxerrois; for from its tower the fatal tocsin tolled forth the funeral knell of the awful night of St. Bartholomew's dread massacre. At the Church of the Trinity I witnessed an imposing funeral ceremony —or "pompe" as the Parisians call it—sable palls and plumes with silver mountings, a lofty bier, burning tapers, incense, and sonorous chanting. And at Ste. Clotilde I witnessed a wedding in high life—the bride, veiled in white, and the bridegroom kneeling at the high altar; the priests, robed in golden tissue, repeating the marriage service, while a very fashionable company "assisted" by their presence.

I had not much opportunity of judging of the moral or religious condition of Paris. There may be vice, but it certainly does not flaunt itself on the highway. Nowhere have I seen public order or decorum better observed. On Sunday many of the stores, it is true, were open; but many of them also were closed. I was surprised to find French Protestantism so strong. Some of the largest churches of the city belong to the old Calvinistic communion, which shares with Romanism the support of the State. A grand evangelical work is going on through the agency of Mr. McAll, but I had no opportunity of judging of its modes.

One painful evidence of a deadly moral cancer eating out the heart of the nation came under my notice. The walls were placarded with large posters, soliciting subscriptions to a new social journal, established to counterwork a threatened agitation in favour of divorce. It was a cry to her fellow-women wrung from a woman's heart. "In the name of maternity," it read, " in the name of the family, down with divorce—à bas le divorce !" "Do you forget," it went on, " that we have all the evils ? Will you not protest against this crime against humanity ?" Beneath the fair and gay exterior of Parisian life there must be many aching hearts and many joyless homes. This question was evidently attracting much attention, for I saw other placards announcing public lectures in defence of this agitation. If the French are wise they will do nothing to weaken the already too feeble restraints of conjugal obligation. The family is the foundation of the State. If the family bonds be loosened, the State will fall to ruin. It was so with ancient Rome ; it will be so with modern France.

My last view of this beautiful city, the night before I left, was a bird's eye view from the grand balloon which ascends from the Place des Tuileries. It is tethered to the earth by a strong cable which is coiled upon a huge drum, turned by two engines of three hundred horse-power. Its diameter is thirty-six yards, and its contents of gas 25,000 cubic yards. It ascends about 1,500 feet, and takes up fifty persons at a time. In mounting and descending there is an absolute unconsciousness of motion ; but when grappled by the anchors on returning, the huge thing sways and strains at its fetters like a thing of life. As one ascends the horizon seems to rise and the city to sink till the latter is spread out like a map beneath him—every street and square and house and tree clearly shown. The people and carriages look like emmets crawling on the ground. It looked like a toy city, or like the models of the French ports shown in the Musée de Marine in the Louvre. The noble vista of the Champs Elysées, the far-winding Seine, the grand environment of the city and glory of the setting sun made up a picture of natural beauty and historic interest not soon to be forgotten. A few days after my ascent this great balloon collapsed in a gale of wind, and has not since been used.

CHAPTER III.

Italy : Mont Cenis—Turin—Genoa—Pisa.

Thou art the garden of the world, the home
Of all Art yields, and Nature can decree;
E'en in thy desert, what is like to thee?
Thy very weeds are beautiful, thy waste
More rich than other climes' fertility,
Thy wreck a glory, and thy ruin graced
With an immaculate charm which cannot be effaced.
—*Childe Harold.*

IT is a railway ride of five hundred miles from Paris to Turin, the first city at which I stopped in Italy.*
The journey through South-eastern France is rather monotonous, till we reach the valley of the Rhone, and soon after the foot-hills of the Cottian Alps. Long processions of tall Lombardy poplars march in close files, like plumed grenadiers, on either side of the road, and picturesque villages nestle amid their orchards and their vines. Many a city of old renown also lifts its embattled towers above the far-extending plain—Melun, Fontainebleau, Sens, Dijon, Chalons, and others of lesser note.

---

* On the top of an omnibus in Paris I made the acquaintance of a young gentleman from New York State, who became my companion in travel during a month's wandering in Italy. We shared, accordingly, all the adventures herein described, till I crossed the Alps into Switzerland.

Soon after crossing the swift and turbid Rhone, the train begins to climb the broad slopes of the foot-hills. It was with a great leap of the heart that I first beheld

MOUNTAIN TORRENT.

the snowy range of the Alps of Savoy, with their sharp serrated outline, cut like a cameo against the deep blue sky. Higher and higher wound the train by many a zigzag, giving broader, grander views over a sea of mountains at every turn. The pinnacled crags reveal in their tortured strata the energy of the primeval forces, by which they were heaved high in air. The mountain villages cling like eagles' nests to the face of the cliffs; and down the mountain sides leap foaming torrents, "like tears of gladness o'er a giant's face." At length the train plunges into the heart of the mountain, four thousand feet beneath its summit,—through the Mont Cenis Tunnel. The tunnel is nearly eight miles long, and four thousand men were employed for ten years in its construction. Emerging from midnight darkness to the glare of snow-clad mountains, the train glides rapidly down the wild valley of the Dora, giving views of a dizzy gorge up which winds, in many folds, like a huge serpent, the old post road over the mountain pass. At Susa, an ancient town, is an old Roman triumphal arch, dating from the year 8 A.D. Descending the beautiful chestnut-covered slopes, and traversing a broad and fertile plain, we reach at length the ancient capital of Piedmont, the fair city of Turin.

My first impressions of Italian peasant life, as caught from the windows of a railway carriage, were of its extreme poverty. I saw hundreds of poor peasants returning from market, brown as berries, riding in their paltry little carts, or on their meagre donkeys, but mostly toiling on foot along the hot and dusty highway, driving a few goats or gaunt and hungry-looking swine—both men and women coarsened with field labour, unintelligent, and in appearance anything but the light-hearted, picturesque race they are so often portrayed by poet or painter. The Italians of the better class who shared our railway carriage, possessed more of the vivacity and sprightliness attributed to their race. I was much amused at the impassioned gesticulation and intonation of a young lady and a military officer, who seemed to converse as much by gesture and tone of voice as by articulate expression. Our military friend was very polite, and took evident pleasure in answering my questions, and pointing out the points of interest on the road, and on leaving the carriage, raised his hat, as I found was the general custom, to each person in the compartment.

Turin is a stately city of 200,000 inhabitants. From 1859 to 1865, it was the capital of United Italy and the residence of the King. It was somewhat of a surprise to find that the royal palace, although inferior in extent to that of Versailles, was much more sumptuous in its internal decoration. The royal armoury is especially magnificent.

Turin, although a town upon its site was destroyed by Hannibal, B.C. 218, is essentially a modern city, abounding in handsome squares, and adorned with splendid street architecture. A peculiar feature is the open arcades which run beneath the buildings, upon which the elegant shops open. The foot-passenger is thus protected from sun and rain, and from the reckless driving of Italian Jehus. The only striking bit of mediæval architecture is the grim Palazzo Madama, a stern fortress of the 13th century, dominating the heart of the city. The Chapel of the Holy Napkin—which is said to contain the linen in which our Lord's body was wrapped—is a circular chamber of dark brown marble, approached by thirty-seven marble steps, and lighted with Rembrandt-like effect from a lofty dome. At Turin I obtained my first view of full-blown Mariolatry. It was at the Church of La Consolata, a huge structure, which contains a miracle-working image of the Madonna. The vast church, with every approach to it, was crowded with worshippers, and mass was being celebrated at several altars at once. The street without was thronged like a fair, with booths for the sale of sacred pictures, medals, tapers, rosaries; and boys and women were hawking printed accounts of the latest miracle of the Saint. In the corridors of the church were hundreds of votive offerings and pictures, commemorating her wonder-working power. The pictures were, for the most part, wretched daubs, representing miraculous escapes from accidents and violent deaths of every conceivable character. The whole scene was coarse, mercenary, and degrading in the last degree.

In the afternoon I walked out to visit the ancient Capuchin monastery—*Il Monte*. It is situated on a lofty hill, commanding a magnificent view of the city, of the " wandering Po," and of the snowy-peaked Alps in the background. The rule of the Order is very austere. Their garb is a coarse brown tunic, fastened with a girdle. Their only head-covering is an ample hood, and on their naked feet they wear coarse sandals. The cells, which open on gloomy cloisters, are narrow vaults, scarce larger than a grave, and here the monks are buried alive—for their lives of poverty and indolence are little better than a living death. One venerable looking old fellow kindly drew from a deep well, with an old-fashioned wheel, water to quench my thirst.

A ride of a hundred miles, for the most part through grand mountain scenery, brings one to the ancient city of Genoa. On the way we pass the famous field of Marengo, where, in 1800, was fought during twelve long hours, the battle which changed the destinies of the whole of Europe. With its noble terraces of frescoed palaces rising tier above tier from the sea, Genoa sits like a queen on the slopes of the lovely Gulf, and well deserves the proud name of *La Superba*. No city in Italy contains so many old ducal palaces. These are, for the most part built in a hollow square, with magnificent marble stairways leading to the stately halls and apartments of the upper stories. The outer walls bear elaborate frescoes, which still preserve much of their original brightness. The lower windows are heavily barred with iron, which gives the streets a narrow, gloomy and prison-like appearance. At the entry to the great houses stands the *concierge*, magnificent in gold-laced livery, silk stockings and gold-headed staff of office. Many of the palaces, with their priceless art treasures, are freely thrown open to the inspection of tourists; and though now exhibiting "a faded splendour wan," they recall its golden prime, when Genoa vied with Venice for the mastery of the Mediterranean. Some of the most interesting memories of Genoa are connected with that intrepid genius who first unveiled the western world to European eyes. A noble marble monument of the great discoverer, with reliefs of the principal scenes of his life, graces one of its squares. In the Municipal Palace I saw the famous bust of Columbus, about which Mark Twain so bothered his unfortunate guide, also the ill written autograph letters, which any American boy could surpass. I noticed that the signature was a sort of play upon his name—XPOFERENS.

Genoa has a thoroughly foreign aspect—the narrow streets, some are not more than five feet wide; the trains of laden mules, with jingling bells on their necks; the gloomy arcades under many of the buildings; the black-lace veils, worn as the only head-dress of ladies in the streets; and other peculiarities remind us that we are in Italy. It was the *festa* of St. John the Baptist, and the churches were gay with floral decorations. The cathedral of San Lorenzo, especially, was festooned with wreaths, and at night illuminated with countless lamps. I stood in the square and listened to the sweet-toned clangour of the joyous *festa* bells. In this same old church is preserved, with great veneration, the so-called "Holy Grail," or vessel out of which our Lord partook, it is said, the Last Supper with His disciples.

The most sumptuous church in Genoa is that of S. Annunziata,—an ugly brick structure without, but within a perfect blaze of gold and marble, lapis lazuli and precious stones. The city is wonderfully irregular in surface. The Ponte Carignano is a bridge leaping across a densely-peopled valley, a hundred feet deep—some of the houses are nine stories high—while the still higher grounds are crowned with villas and gardens. From these an enchanting view is obtained of the far-shimmering surface of the

BIRD'S-EYE VIEW OF GENOA.*

blue Mediterranean, the majestic sweep of the coast-line, and the noble and fortress-crowned heights that girdle the city. As an illustration of Italian courtesy, I may mention that I made the casual acquaintance, in the public gardens, of Signor Di Rossi, a leading merchant of the city, who showed me much attention, gave me valuable information and invited me to share the hospitality of his own house.

* The accompanying small bird's-eye view of the city will give an idea of its splendid harbour and engirdling chain of forts on the surrounding hills.

The ride from Genoa to Pisa, about a hundred miles, is one of the most magnificent in Italy. The railway skirts the wild and romantic sea coast, with its bold and rocky promontories. In that short distance it traverses no less than eighty tunnels—an indication of the rugged character of the country. On one side stretches the deep blue surface of the Mediterranean whose surf dashes in snowy foam upon the rocky coast, and on the other the vine-and-olive-clad slopes of the Appenines, dotted with villas, orange

PISA—BIRD'S EYE VIEW.

and lemon plantations, with clumps of cypress, palms, and stone pines, citrons, oleanders and myrtles. We swept round the noble gulf of Spezzia, to which the memory of Shelley who was drowned in its waters and his body burned on its shore, lent a pathetic interest.

Pisa presents probably the most wonderful group of buildings in the world—the Cathedral, Leaning Tower, Baptistery, and Campo Santo, the general relations of which are indicated in the small bird's eye view. The Cathedral is a vast structure, dating, except its restorations, from the eleventh century. Its alternate bands of black and white marble, with its magnificent façade of columned arcades, gives it a unique and striking appearance. The effect of the interior is of unusual solemnity and awe. From the vast and shadowy dome looks down, in act of benediction, a mosaic effigy of Christ, by Cimabue, in the austere Byzantine style, of date A.D. 1302. The gilded roof is supported by sixty-eight ancient Greek and Roman monolithic marble or porphyry columns, captured by the Pisans in war. No two of these columns are quite alike in height or thickness; but a sort of symmetry is given by adding capitals and bases of different heights. The effect of the whole is far from unpleasing. In the nave hangs the large bronze lamp, whose swaying to and fro is said to have suggested to Galileo the idea of the pendulum. I visited, in an obscure back street, the house in which the great astronomer was born.

The Baptistery is a circular marble building, a hundred feet in diameter, surrounded by columned arcades, and surmounted by a lofty dome. The pulpit and large octagonal font are marvels of marble fretwork—like exquisite lace hardened into stone. That which, to me at last, gave its chief interest to the building, was its exquisite echo. My guide sang over and over again a series of notes, and the softened sounds fell back from the lofty dome, faint and far, yet clear and distinct, and with an unearthly sweetness, like elfin notes in fairy land.

More famous than any other building of the group is the

Leaning Tower—a structure of remarkable beauty. It consists of eight stories of marble colonades, rising one hundred and seventy-nine feet high, and leaning thirteen feet out of the perpendicular. It causes a strange sensation of fancied insecurity to look down from the overhanging edge of the airy structure. One involuntarily begins to pick out the place where he is going to fall, for to fall seems for the moment inevitable. Yet for five hundred years and more, this lovely "leaning miracle" has reared its form of beauty to the wondering gaze of successive generations.

The Campo Santo is a large quadrangle surrounded by spacious arcades, with gothic tracery of exquisite beauty. The enclosure contains fifty-three shiploads of earth brought from Mount Calvary, in order that the dead might repose in holy ground. The walls are covered with frescoes by Orcagna and other early Tuscan artists. Among the more striking of these are representations of the Triumph of Death and the Last Judgment. In the former a group of gay and gallant horsemen come suddenly upon three open coffins, from which even the horses shrink with shuddering horror. In the latter the crude and dreadful representations of the regions of eternal gloom, which Dante afterwards set forth in undying verse, are portrayed with a repulsive vividness in fading fresco. The Italians seem fond of multiplying such morbid mementoes of death and the under world. For five long centuries these realistic paintings have been reading their ghastly lessons of mortality to successive generations of mankind.

At the very door of the cathedral on that bright and sunny morning, I was confronted by another strange *memento mori*, a hideous figure, dressed in a long robe of black, with a black hood over his head, through the ghastly eye-holes of which his dark eyes looked out on the world without. With a hollow voice he asked alms for the burial of the dead—for to that sad office the brethren of the *Misericordia* devote their lives. A striking contrast to this dismal apparition was a brilliant procession of ecclesiastics in scarlet and purple and gold, proceeding from the church to the Baptistery; but it was but another illustration of the manner in which Rome employs outward pomp and pageantry to impress the imagination of her devotees.

With peculiar interest I visited the site of the famous Hunger Tower, immortalized by Dante in one of the most tragic episodes of the *Inferno*. For the alleged crime of treason Count Ugolino and his sons were condemned to be starved to death in this gruesome prison, 1288. The closing scene is thus vividly described. The ghost of Ugolino addresses the Tuscan poet in the world of gloom.

> " Both hands for very anguish did I gnaw,
>   They thinking that I tore them with desire
>   Of food, rose sudden from their dungeon straw,
> And spoke : ' Less grief it were, of us, O sire ;
>   If thou would'st eat—These limbs, thou, by our birth,
>   Did'st clothe. Despoil them now if need require ! '

>   Not to increase their pangs of grief and dearth,
>   I calmed me. Two days more all mute we stood:
>   Wherefore didst thou not open, pitiless earth!
>   Now when our fourth sad morning was renewed,
>   Gaddo fell at my feet, outstretched and cold,
>   Crying, 'Wilt thou not, father, give me food?'
>   There did he die; and as thine eyes behold
>   Me now, so saw I three, fall one by one,
>   On the fifth day and sixth; where in that hold,
>   I, now grown blind, over each lifeless son,
>   Stretched forth mine arms. Three days I called their names—
>   Then Fast achieved what Grief had not yet done."

From Pisa to Rome, by way of the sea coast, is a journey of over two hundred miles. The route is a rather monotonous and uninteresting one, leading through the low and marshy Maremme—a region almost abandoned by its inhabitants during the summer, on account of the much dreaded malaria. Those who remain, by their hollow eyes and cadaverous features, bear witness to the insalubrity of the climate. Here I first saw the long-horned, mouse-coloured buffalo of the Roman marshes. The gaunt and hungry-looking Italian swine looked more like greyhounds than like their obese and rounded congeners of a Canadian farm-yard. The lithe lizards gliding in the sun, the noisy cicada, sung by Sappho two thousand years ago, and the crimson poppies flaunting in the meadows, all give evidence of our southern latitude. Civita Vecchia, and Ostia, the ancient port of Rome, with a melancholy mediæval fortress, are at length reached, and traversing a dreary tract of the Campagna, with the Alban and Sabine Mountains in the background, right and left,

I arrived late at night at the city of Rome. It was rather a disenchantment of my dream of romance to behold a splendid new railway station, and be hailed by a mob of vociferous cabmen, and driven through a gas-lighted street to an elegant hotel with electric bells, and all the other appliances of the latest civilization. But the wondrous spell of the ancient city soon reasserted itself.

OLD FORT AT OSTIA.

CHAPTER IV.

Rome: The Forum—Colosseum—St. Peter's—Catacombs—Appian Way—Santa Scala—Pantheon—St. Clement—The Vatican—Up the Tiber.

> The Niobe of nations! there she stands
> Childless and crownless in her voiceless woe;
> An empty urn within her withered hands,
> Whose holy dust was scattered long ago. . . .
>
> The Goth, the Christian, Time, War, Flood, and Fire,
> Have dealt upon the seven-hilled city's pride;
> She saw her glories star by star expire,
> And up the steep barbarian monarchs ride.
> Where the car climbed the Capitol; far and wide
> Temple and tower went down, nor left a site. . . .
>
> Alas! the lofty city, and alas!
> The trebly hundred triumphs! and the day
> When Brutus made the dagger's edge surpass
> The conqueror's sword in bearing fame away!
> Alas! for Tully's voice, and Virgil's lay,
> And Livy's pictured page!—but these shall be
> Her resurrection; all beside—decay.
> —*Childe Harold.*

ROME at last! The goal of a thousand hopes—"the city of the soul"—"the Mecca of the mind"—"lone mother of dead Empires"—the city of the Cæsars and the Popes.

Nothing so struck me in my first drive through Rome—through the Forum to the Colosseum and the Palatine Hill—as the appalling desolation of those once proud abodes of imperial splendour. The scene of some of the most heroic achievements of the Republic and Empire is now a half buried chaos of broken arch and column. Here stood the rostrum where Tully fulmined against Cataline, and where, after death, his eloquent tongue was pierced through and through by the bodkin of a revengeful woman. Here the Roman father slew his child to save her from dishonour. Here, "at the base of Pompey's statue," the well-beloved Brutus stabbed the foremost man of all

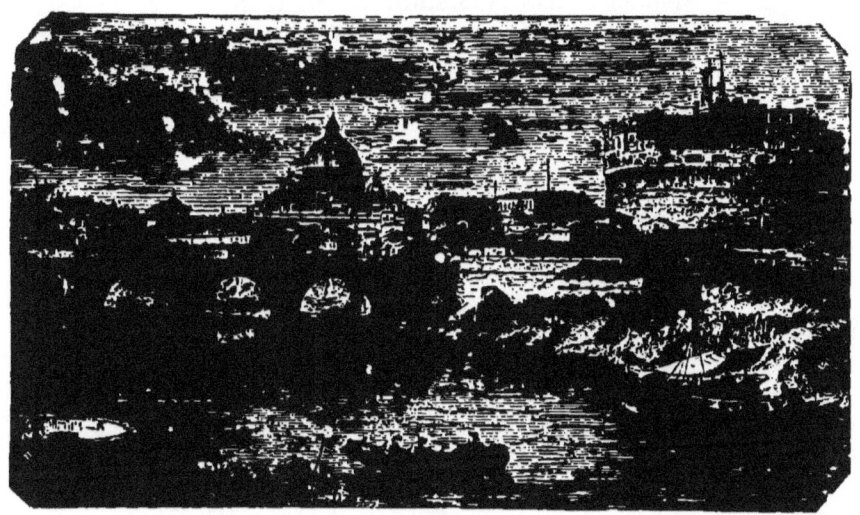

ST. PETER'S AND THE CASTLE OF ST. ANGELO.

this world. Here is the *Via Sacra*, through which passed the triumphal processions to the now ruined temples of the gods. But for a thousand years these ruins have been the quarries and the lime-kilns for the monasteries and churches of the modern city, till little is left save the shadow of their former greatness.

More utterly desolate than aught else were the pleasure palaces of the proud emperors of the world—the Golden

House of Nero, the palaces of Tiberius, Caligula, the Flavii,—monuments of the colossal vice which called down the wrath of Heaven on the guilty piles. All are now mere mounds of splendid desolation, amid whose broken arches I saw fair English girls sketching the crumbling halls where ruled and revelled the lords of the world.

> Cypress and ivy, wind and wallflower grown
> Matted and massed together, hillocks heap'd
> On what were chambers, arch crush'd, column strewn
> In fragments, choked-up vaults, and frescoes steep'd
> In subterranean damps, where the owl peep'd,
> Deeming it midnight.

INTERIOR OF THE COLOSSEUM.

Near by rise the cliff-like walls of the Colosseum, stern monument of Rome's Christless creed. Tier above tier rise the circling seats, whence twice eighty thousand cruel eyes gloated upon the dying martyr's pangs, "butchered to make a Roman holiday." Ten thousand Jewish captives were employed in its construction, and at its inauguration five thousand wild beasts were slain in bloody con-conflict with human antagonists. The dens in which the lions were confined, the gates through which the leopards leaped upon their victims may still be seen; and before us stretches the broad arena where even Rome's proud dames, unsexed and slain in gladiatorial conflict, lay trampled in the sand.

EXTERIOR OF THE COLOSSEUM.

As I clambered over those time-defying walls, and plucked from their crannied niches the bluebell and anemone, the soldiers of King Humbert were drilling in the meadow near its base, and the sharp words of command came softened by the distance. Save these, no sound of life was audible in this once humming hive of human passion and activity. The accompanying cuts give interior and exterior views of this world-famous ruin.

> A ruin—yet what ruin! from its mass
> Walls, palaces, half-cities have been rear'd;
> Yet oft the enormous skeleton we pass,
> And marvel where the spoil could have appear'd.
> Hath it indeed been plundered or but clear'd?

Near the walls of the Colosseum rises one of the most interesting monuments of ancient Rome—the Arch of

THE ARENA OF THE COLOSSEUM.

Titus, erected to commemorate the destruction of Jerusalem, A.D. 70. On the crumbling frieze is carved a relief of the triumphal procession bearing the spoils of the Temple, with the table of shew-bread, the seven-branched candlestick, and a group of captive Jews. To this day, it is said, the Jews of Rome refuse to pass beneath this monument of their national degradation. A drive through the Ghetto, or Jews' quarter, reveals the squalor and degradation in which these long-suffering and bitterly persecuted people still dwell. Whenever the carriage stopped, they swarmed out of the crowded shops in which they hive, and almost insisted in rigging me out from top to toe, in a suit of clothing most probably second hand. I visited one of the synagogues, on which, instead of their homes, they seem to lavish their wealth. A dark-eyed daughter of Israel did the honours, but kept a keen eye meanwhile for the expected fee.

Nothing, perhaps, gives a more vivid conception of the boundless wealth and pomp and luxury of the Roman emperors than the vast public Baths of which the very ruins are stupendous. The most notable of these are the Baths of Caracalla, covering several acres of ground. They contained not only hot, cold, and tepid chambers, large enough to accommodate 1,600 bathers at once, but also vast *palestræ* or gymnasia, a racecourse, and the like. Solid towers of masonry crowned with trees and matted foliage rise high in air; vast chambers once cased with marbles or mosaic, with hypocausts for hot and caleducts in the walls for cold air, bear witness to the Sybaritic luxury of the later days of the Empire. From the summit of one of these massy towers I enjoyed a glorious sunset view of the mouldering ruins which rose above the sea of verdure all around, and of the far-spreading and desolate Campagna.

The most notable of the churches of Rome is, of course, St. Peter's. I shall not attempt to describe what defies description. Its vastness awes and almost overwhelms the beholder. Its mighty dome swells in a sky-like vault overhead, and its splendour of detail deepens the impression made by its majestic vistas. The interior effect is incomparably finer than that from without. The vast sweep of the corridors and the elevation of the portico in front of the church quite dwarf the dome which the genius of Angelo hung high in air. But the very harmony of proportion of the interior prevents that striking impression made by other lesser piles.

> Enter: the grandeur overwhelms thee not;
> And why? it is not lessened, but thy mind,
> Expanded by the genius of the spot,
> Has grown colossal.

It is only when you observe that the cherubs on the holy water vessels near the entrance are larger than the largest men; when you walk down the long vista of the nave, over six hundred feet; when you learn that its area is 26,163 square yards, or more than twice that of St. Paul's at London, that the dome rises four hundred feet above your head, that its supporting pillars are 230 feet in circumference, and that the letters in the frieze are over six feet high, that some conception of the real dimensions of this mighty temple enters the mind. It covers half a dozen acres, has been enriched during three hundred years by the donations of two score of popes, who have lavished upon it $60,000,000. The mere cost of its repair is $30,000 a year.

No mere enumeration of the wealth of bronze and vari-coloured marbles, mosaics, paintings and sculpture can give an adequate idea of its costly splendour. The view, from the summit of the dome, of the gardens of the Vatican, of the winding Tiber, the modern city, the ruins of old Rome, the far-extending walls, the wide sweep of the Campagna, and in the purple distance the far Alban and Sabine hills, is one that well repays the fatigue of the ascent.

It was my fortune to witness the celebration of the feast of St. Peter and St. Paul in this very centre of Romish ritual and ecclesiastical pageantry. The subterranean crypts, containing the shrine of St. Peter, a spot so holy that no woman may enter save once a year, were thrown open and illuminated with hundreds of lamps and decorated with a profusion of flowers. Thousands of persons filled the space beneath the dome—priests, barefooted friars of orders white, black, and gray; nuns, military officers, soldiers, civilians, peasants in gala dress, and ladies—all standing, for not a single seat is provided for the comfort of worshippers in this grandest temple in Christendom. High mass was celebrated at the high altar by a very exalted personage, assisted by a whole college of priests in embroidered robes of scarlet and purple, and of gold and silver tissue. The acolytes swung the jewelled censers to and fro, the aromatic incense filled the air, officers with swords of state stood on guard, and the service for the day was chanted in the sonorous Latin tongue. Two choirs of well-trained voices, accompanied by two organs and instrumental orchestra, sang the majestic music of the mass. As the grand chorus rose and swelled and filled the sky-like dome, although my judgment could not but condemn the semi-pagan pageantry, I felt the spell of that mighty sorcery. which, through the ages, has beguiled the hearts of men. I missed, however, in the harmony the sweet tones of the female voice, for in the holy precincts of St. Peter's no woman's tongue may join in the worship of her Redeemer.

The bronze statue of St. Peter in the nave, originally, it is said, a pagan statue of Jove, was sumptuously robed in vestments of purple and gold,—the imperial robes, it is averred, of the Emperor Charlemagne—a piece of frippery that utterly destroyed any native dignity the statue may have possessed.

It was a very notable day in my experience that I drove out to the Abbey of the Three Fountains, the Catacombs, and the Appian Way. On the route I stopped to visit the Protestant cemetery, where sleep the remains of many pilgrims from a foreign land, for whose return their loved ones wait in vain. Overshadowed by a melancholy cypress, I found the grave of the erring genius Shelley.

On his tombstone are the simple words "cor cordium"—only his heart is buried there. His body was burned in the Bay of Spezzia, where it was washed ashore. I plucked a rose from his grave, heaved a sigh to his memory, and turned away. Close by is the grave of the gentler spirit, Keats, with its touching inscription,—"Here lies one whose name was writ in water."

The Church of St. Paul's without the Walls is a restoration of an early Basilica built by Constantine. According to tradition, it covers the crypt in which the body of St. Paul was buried. It is now a vast and sumptuous structure, supported on eighty monolithic columns, and paved and walled with costliest marbles—in striking contrast to the lowliness of the humble tent-maker whose name it bears. Of still greater interest is the Church of the Three Fountains, on the alleged scene of the Apostle's martyrdom. According to the legend, the martyr's head made three leaps on the ground after his decapitation, and at each spot where it touched the earth a fountain gushed forth. These are now walled with marble, and covered by a stately church. A Trappist monk recounts the story, and offers the faithful water from the fountain, which is supposed to possess great spiritual efficacy. My guide showed me the cells of the monks—bare, bleak apartments. The brotherhood long occupied the position as a sort of forlorn hope, so unhealthy was the site on account of the malaria; but its sanitary condition has been greatly improved by planting the eucalyptus or

Australian gum tree. Some which I saw had attained a large growth and diffused an aromatic odour through the air.

A drive across the Campagna soon brings one to the Church of St. Sebastian—the only entrance to the Catacombs which remained open during the middle ages. In an adjacent crypt is shown the very vault in which tradition affirms that the bodies of St. Peter and Paul lay for forty years, till stolen away. Unbolting a side door of the church, a serge-clad monk, giving us each a taper, led the way down a long steep stairway to the dark and gloomy corridors of the Catacombs. Through the winding labyrinth we advanced, our dim lights shedding a feeble glimmer as we passed, upon the open graves that yawned weirdly on either side. Deep shadows crouched around, and the unfleshed skeletons lay upon their stony beds to which they had been consigned by loving hands in the early centuries so long ago. Much more interesting, however, on account of its greater extent and better preservation, is the adjacent Catacomb of Calixtus, of which I made a more thorough inspection. Here are large and lofty chambers, containing the tomb of St. Cecilia, virgin and martyr, and of several of the persecuted bishops of the early Church. The fading frescoes, pious inscriptions, and sacred symbols on the walls all bring vividly before us, as nothing else on earth can do, the faith and courage and moral nobleness of the primitive Church of the Catacombs.

These Christian cemeteries are situated chiefly near the great roads leading from the city, and, for the most part, within a circle of three miles from the walls. From this circumstance they have been compared to the "encampment of a Christian host besieging Pagan Rome, and driving inward its mines and trenches with an assurance of final victory." The openings of the Catacombs are scattered over the Campagna, whose mournful desolation

ENTRANCE TO THE CATACOMB OF ST. PRISCILLA.

surrounds the city; often among the mouldering mausolea that lie, like stranded wrecks, above the rolling sea of verdure of the tomb-abounding plain. On every side are tombs—tombs above and tombs below—the graves of contending races, the sepulchres of vanished generations: "*Piena di sepolture è la Campagna.*" From a careful survey and estimate it has been computed that the aggregate length of all the passages is 587 geographical miles, equal to the entire extent of Italy from Etna's fires to Alpine snows; and they contain between three and four million tombs.

How marvellous that beneath the remains of a proud pagan civilization exist the early monuments of that power before which the myths of paganism faded away as the spectres of darkness before the rising sun, and the religion and institutions of Rome were entirely changed. Beneath the ruined palaces and temples, the crumbling tombs and dismantled villas, of the august mistress of the world, we find the most interesting relics of early Christianity on the face of the earth. In traversing these tangled labyrinths of graves we are brought face to face with the primitive ages; we are present at the worship of the infant Church; we observe its rites; we study its institutions; we witness the deep emotions of the first believers as they commit their dead, often their martyred dead, to their last long resting-place; we decipher the touching record of their sorrow, of the holy hopes by which they are sustained, of "their faith triumphant o'er their fears," and of their assurance of the resurrection of the dead and of the life everlasting. We read in the testimony of the Catacombs the confession of faith of the early Christians, sometimes accompanied by the records of their persecution, the symbols of their martyrdom, and even the very instruments of their torture. For in these halls of silence and gloom slumbers the dust of many of the martyrs and confessors, who sealed their testimony with their blood during the sanguinary ages of persecution; of many of the early bishops and pastors of the Church, who shepherded the flock of Christ amid the dangers of those troublous times ; of many who heard the word of life from teachers who lived in or near the apostolic age, perhaps from the lips of the Apostles themselves. Indeed, if we would accept ancient tradition, we would even believe that the bodies of St. Peter and St. Paul were laid to rest in those hallowed crypts—a true *terra sancta*, inferior in sacred interest only to that rock-hewn sepulchre consecrated evermore by the body of our Lord. These reflections lend to the study of the Catacombs an interest of the highest and intensest character.

The entrance to the abandoned Catacomb is sometimes a low-browed aperture like a fox's burrow, almost concealed by long and tangled grass, and overshadowed by the melancholy cypress or gray-leaved ilex. Sometimes an ancient arch can be discerned, as at the Catacomb of St. Priscilla, or the remains of the chamber for the celebration of the festivals of the martyrs. In all cases there is a stairway, often long and steep, crumbling with time and worn with the feet of pious generations. The following illustration shows the entrance to the Catacomb of Prætextatus on the Appian Way, trodden in the primitive ages by the early martyrs and confessors, or perhaps by the armed soldiery of the oppressors, hunting to earth the persecuted flock of Christ. Here, too, in mediæval times, the martial clang of the armed knights may have awaked unwonted echoes among the hollow arches; or the gliding footstep of the sandaled monk scarce disturbed the silence as he passed. In later times pilgrims from every land have visited, with pious reverence or idle curiosity, this early shrine of the Christian faith.

The Catacombs are excavated in the volcanic rock which abounds in the neighbourhood of Rome. It is a granulated, grayish rock, of a coarse, loose texture, easily cut with a knife, and bearing still the marks of the mattocks with which it was

ENTRANCE TO A CATACOMB.

dug. In the firmer volcanic rock of Naples the excavations are larger and loftier than those of Rome; but the latter although they have less of apparent majesty, have more of funereal mystery. The Catacombs consist essentially of two parts—corridors and chambers, or *cubicula*. The former are long, narrow and intricate passages, forming a complete underground net-work. They are for the most part straight, and intersect one another at approximate right angles. The main corridors vary from three to five

GALLERY WITH TOMBS.

feet in width, but the lateral passages are much narrower, often affording room for but one person to pass. They will average about eight feet in height, though in some places as low as five or six. The ceiling is generally vaulted, though sometimes flat; and the floor, though for the most part level, has occasionally a slight incline. The walls are generally of the naked *tufa*, though sometimes plastered; and where they have given way are in places strengthened with masonry. At the corners of these passages there are frequently niches, in which lamps were placed, without which, indeed, they must have been an impenetrable labyrinth. Cardinal Wiseman recounts a touching legend of a young girl who was employed as a guide to the places of worship in the Catacombs, because, on account of her blindness, their sombre avenues were as familiar to her accustomed feet as the streets of Rome to others.

Both sides of the corridors are thickly lined with *loculi* or graves, which have somewhat the appearance of berths in a ship, or of the shelves in a grocer's shop; but the contents are the bones and ashes of the dead, and for labels we have their epitaphs. The cut on the preceding page will illustrate the general character of these galleries and *loculi*.

These graves were once all hermetically sealed by slabs of marble, or tiles of *terra cotta*. The former were generally of one piece which fitted into a groove or mortice cut into the rock at the grave's mouth and were securely cemented to their places, as, indeed, was absolutely necessary, from the open character of the galleries in which the graves were placed. Most of these slabs and tiles have disappeared, and many of the graves have long been rifled of their contents. In others may still be seen the mouldering skeleton of what was once man in his strength, woman in her beauty, or a child in its innocence and glee. If these bones be touched they will generally crumble into a white, flaky powder. The engraving shows one in which this " dry dust of death " still retains the outline of a human skeleton. Verily, *"pulvis et umbra sumus."*

VALERIA SLEEPS IN PEACE.

The other constituents of the Catacombs, besides the corridors mentioned, are the *cubicula*, as they are called. These are chambers from eight or ten to as much as twenty feet square, generally in pairs on either side of the passage, and for the most part lined with graves. They were probably family vaults, though they were sometimes used for worship or for refuge in time of persecution.

These chambers were lighted by shafts leading up to the open air, through which the brilliant Italian sunshine to-day lights up the pictured figures on the walls as it must have illumined the fair brow of the Christian maiden, the silvery hair of the venerable pastor, or the calm face of the holy dead, in those long bygone early centuries.

But frequently "beneath this depth there is a lower deep" or even three or four tiers of galleries, to which

CHAMBER IN THE CATACOMB OF ST. AGNES, WITH SEATS FOR CATECHISTS AND CATECHUMENS.

access is gained by stairways cut in the rock. The awful silence and almost palpable darkness of these deepest dungeons is absolutely appalling. They are fitly described by the epithet applied by Dante to the realms of eternal gloom: *loco d'ogni luce muto*—a spot mute of all light

Here death reigns supreme. Not even so much as a lizard or a bat has penetrated these obscure recesses. Nought but skulls and skeletons, dust and ashes, are on every side. The air is impure and deadly, and difficult to breathe. "The cursed dew of the dungeon's damp" distils from the walls, and a sense of oppression, like the

SECTION OF DOUBLE CHAMBER, CORRIDOR AND LIGHT AND AIR SHAFT.

patriarch's "horror of great darkness," broods over the scene. Many of these chambers are beautifully painted with symbolical or Biblical figures. Indeed the whole story of the Bible from the Fall of Man in the Garden to his redemption by Christ is represented in these sacred paintings. In the cut on page 92 it will be observed that the Good Shepherd occupies the position of prominence and dignity in the compartment over the arched tomb balanced by Daniel in the lion's den and the three Hebrews in the furnace. On the left hand is a shelf for lamps, magnified in Romish imagination into a Credence Table for supporting the elements of the Eucharist. In the ceiling are praying figures and lambs.

PAINTED CHAMBER IN THE CATACOMB OF ST. AGNES.

The New Testament cycle, as it is called, depicting the principal events in the life of our Lord, and the miracles which He wrought is very complete, especially in the sculptures of the sarcophagi or stone coffins, of which many examples are preserved in the Lateran Museum. In the fine example shown in the cut, which is of the 4th or 5th century, we have first Simon the Cyrenian bearing the cross, then Christ crowned not with thorns, but with flowers, as if to symbolize His triumph; then Christ guarded by a Roman soldier; and in the last compartment He witnesses a good confession before Pontius Pilate.

SARCOPHHAGUS IN THE LATERAN MUSEUM.

In the Catacombs have also been found large quantities of lamps, vases, gems, rings, seals, toilet articles, and other objects of much interest—even children's jointed dolls and toys, placed by loving hands in their tiny graves long, long centuries ago. The inscriptions of the Catacombs also throw great light on the doctrines and institutions of the Primitive Church, and on the domestic and social relations and conjugal and filial affections of the early Christians. The present writer has elsewhere treated this subject with great fulness of detail and copious pictorial illustrations.*

---

* *The Catacombs of Rome and their Testimony relative to Primitive Christianity*, by the Rev. W. H. WITHROW, M.A. New York: Phillips & Hunt; London: Hodder & Stoughton, 3rd ed. Cr. 8vo., 560 pages, 134 engravings. Price $2.50.

Great was the contrast between the cold, damp crypts of the Catacombs and the hot glare of the Italian sunshine as with my companion in travel I emerged from their gloomy depths and rode along the Appian Way. But greater still was the contrast between the lowly tombs of the early Christians and the massy monuments of pagan pride that lined that street of tombs, now mere crumbling mounds of ruins, majestic even in decay. Most striking of all is the stately mausoleum of Cæcilia Metella, wife of the triumvir Crassus.

> There is a stern round tower of other days,
> Firm as a fortress with its fence of stone,
> Such as an army's baffled strength delays,
> Standing with half its battlements alone,
> And with two thousand years of ivy grown,
> The garland of eternity, where wave
> The green leaves over all by time o'erthrown:
> What was this tower of strength? within its cave,
> What treasure lay so locked, so hid?—A woman's grave.

I entered and explored several of these proud patrician tombs, but found naught but crumbling arch and column and shattered marble effigies of their former tenants.

But only the wealthy could be entombed in those stately *mausolea*, or be wrapped in those "marble cerements." For the mass of the population *columbaria* were provided, in whose narrow niches, like the compartments of a dove-cote—the *terra cotta* urns containing their ashes were placed, sometimes to the number of six thousand in a single *columbarium*. They also contained sometimes the urns of the great.

I visited several of these; a description of one will suffice. Steep steps lead down into a square vault, supported by a central pier which, like the walls, contains a number of niches. Each niche contains two or more cinerary urns, with covers. Removing several of these I found within the ashes and charred bones of the dependants of great Roman houses, whose bodies had undergone

TOMBS ON THE APPIAN WAY.

cremation. The brief epitaphs of the deceased were often inscribed above the niche. These structures take their names from their resemblance to a dove-cote—*columbarium*.

A striking contrast to the pomp of the tombs on the Appian Way are these *columbaria* in which for the most part the ashes of the slaves are deposited.

Over the lava pavement of this Queen of Roads, as the Romans proudly called it,* along which I drove for miles, once thundered the legions that conquered the world; and by this very way St. Paul and his companions entered the great Imperial City. Now, the gardens and villas which studded the Campagna are a desolation, and only ruins rise, like stranded wrecks, above the tomb-abounding plain. The most conspicuous and beneficent monuments of the power of ancient Rome are the vast aqueducts which bestride, with their long series of arches the undulating Campagna. Most of these are now broken and crumbling ruins, but some of them, restored in modern times, still supply the city with streams of the cool and limpid water from the far-off Alban hills. Here I may remark that no city I have seen has such an abundant supply of pure water as Rome. It leaps and flashes in the great fountains of the public squares, and ripples and gurgles in its mossy channels in almost every courtyard and quadrangle. In several of these I observed ancient sarcophagi, which once perhaps held the body of a prince, converted into a horse-trough.

One of the most ancient structures of Rome is the Mammertine Prison. It consists of two chambers, one below the other. The lower was originally accessible only through a hole in the ceiling. In this dismal dungeon Jugurtha, the British king Vercingetorix, and other conquered enemies of Rome perished. Here also tradition

---

* "*Regina Viarum.*"—*Stat Syl.*

affirms St. Peter was imprisoned, in confirmation whereof is shown the deep depression in the solid stone said to have been made by the head of the Apostle when his jailor knocked it against the wall, and the fountain averred to have sprung up miraculously that he might baptize the remorseful man. If you doubt the fact, the *custode* points in triumph to these occular evidences still extant. It being the anniversary of the Saint on which I visited this ancient prison, a constant stream of devotees passed through, to whom a priest in much-soiled vestments was giving drafts of water from the sacred fountain.

Of still greater sanctity are the so-called *Scala Santa* or Holy Stairs. These consist of twenty-eight marble steps, said to have been those of Pilate's house, which were ascended by our Lord. They were brought from Jerusalem, so runs the legend, by the Empress Helena, A.D. 326. No one may ascend them except on his knees. It was while Luther was painfully toiling up their long incline, just like a bare-footed monk whom I saw repeating, with many prayers, the same act, devoutly kissing each step, that there flashed through his mind the emancipating message, "The just shall live by faith." "*Non est in toto sanctior orbe locus,*" says a marble legend,— "There is on earth no holier spot than this." I came upon another relic of Luther in the Augustinian monastery in which he resided during his sojourn in Rome. Here I witnessed a Roman funeral, rendered as ghastly as possible by the sable velvet pall embroidered with skulls and cross-bones and skeletons. A procession of barefooted friars bore the body on a bier to the church, where,

THE PANTHEON, ROME.

surrounded by burning tapers, it kept its solemn state while darkness filled the shadowy vault.

One of the most impressive churches of Rome is that still best known by its Pagan name of "The Pantheon." It is the only building of ancient Rome which still retains its roof and walls intact. It is almost as perfect to-day as when it was erected over nineteen hundred years ago. Its external appearance is well shown in the cut. The odious little campaniles which destroy the majestic effect of the façade are the addition of Bernini, 1640, after whom they are named "ass's ears." As one enters the door, and the great dome—the largest in the world—spreads its vault above his head, he feels the sublimity of the grand old pile. The effect is still further enhanced by the broad opening, twenty-eight feet across, in the centre of the vault, through which pours down a flood of bright Italian sun-light on the shrines and altars and worshippers beneath. Here where the incense arose of old at the altars of the Pagan gods it still ascends at the shrines of the papal saints, amid surroundings of gorgeous pageantry surpassing even that of the priests and augurs of ancient Rome. A small plain slab in the wall marks the tomb of Raphäel, and a more sumptuous monument that of King Victor Emanuel.

> Simple, erect, severe, austere, sublime—
> Shrine of all saints and temple of all gods,
> From Jove to Jesus—spared and blessed by time,
> Looking tranquility, while falls or nods
> Arch, empire, each thing round thee, and man plods
> His way through thorns to ashes— glorious dome !
> Shalt thou not last? Time's scythe and tyrant's rods
> Shiver upon thee—sanctuary and home
> Of art and piety—Pantheon ! pride of Rome.

One other church in Rome I must mention on account of the unique and extraordinary character of its burial crypts. This is the Church of the Capuchins. Its vaults are filled with sacred soil, from Jerusalem, in which the monks were buried. After several years' interment the skeletons were exhumed and arranged in architectural devices—columns, niches, and arches—a figure of Justice with her scales, a clock-face, and the like, all in human bones. In several of the niches stood the unfleshed skeletons, wearing the coarse serge gown and hood the living monk had worn, with his name, Brother Bartholomeo, or Brother Jiacomo, written on his skull—a ghastly mockery of life. In all, the remains of 6,000 monks are contained in these vaults. The Government has forbidden the continuance of this revolting custom.

At the Church of St. Clement—the oldest in Rome—I met with the only instance I encountered in Italy of discourtesy from an ecclesiastic; they are, generally, exceedingly polite. The monk in charge, I am sorry to say, was so much under the influence of wine that he was quite incapable of carrying the taper and exhibiting the relics—a task which he had to delegate to a boy. Beneath the upper church have recently been discovered, and in part excavated, two earlier churches—one reaching back to the third century. The frescoes and mosaics on the walls are many of them quite like those of the Catacombs, a proof of their early date. The various collections of sarcophagi, inscriptions, lamps, vases, and other objects from those repositories of the early Christian dead in the various museums were studied with profound interest.

I was fortunate in obtaining a few specimens of these antiquities, both Christian and pagan, as *souvenirs* of ancient Rome.

I went one afternoon with a friend to see the Mausoleum of Augustus, where the great Emperor with many of his successors were buried. We found a huge circular building open to the sky, in whose substructions the mortuary tombs of the ancient lords of the world may still be seen; and here in later days the body of Rienzi, "the last of the Tribunes" was buried. But—what a sarcastic comment on human greatness!—we found the vast arena used as an open air summer theatre, and a mock emperor, with snowy toga and gilded wreath was enacting some story of the heroic days of Rome. Sometimes, I was informed, the ancient mausoleum is used as a circus, and harlequin plays his pranks upon an emperor's tomb.

Few things in Rome bring up more vividly the recollections of the storied past than the walk along the banks of the Tiber, the *Flavus Tiberis* of our school-boy days. Through the city it steals its way between lordly palaces or beneath the crowded and towering piles of Trastivere and the Ghetto—its tawny current turbid with the sand of the Campagna which it sweeps down to the sea.

Of the many bridges by which it is bestrode, the most interesting is that of St. Angelo, the Ælian Bridge of ancient Rome. (See initial cut of this chapter, page 73.) On either side are majestic figures of angels, so that, as Clement IX. expressed it, "an avenue of the heavenly host should welcome the pilgrim to the shrine of the great Apostle." Here as St. Gregory, during a fatal pestilence, passed over at the head of a penitential procession, chanting solemn litanies, he saw, or feigned that he saw, the avenging angel alight on the mausoleum of Hadrian and sheath his sword in token that the plague was stayed. And there the majestic figure of St. Michael stands in bronze to-day, as if the tutelary guardian of Rome. On this very bridge, too, took place the fierce hand to hand conflict during the sack of Rome by the ferocious mercenaries of the Constable of Bourbon, while the Tiber beneath ran red with blood.

The island of the Tiber with its picturesque twin bridges is rich in ancient memories. But of special interest to me was the site of the Milvian Bridge, where in his conflict with Maxentius for the empire of the world, Constantine saw, or thought he saw, the sign of the cross in the midday heavens, and adopted the sign of salvation as his standard of battle. Of this scene there is a striking picture in the Vatican. Here, too, the seven-branched candlestick from the temple at Jerusalem was thrown into the Tiber, where it probably still remains, and may yet be recovered. Although admonished that I should remain indoors in the evening on account of the malaria, I could not resist the temptation to visit this memory-haunted spot, and the famed Pincian Hill and the Villa Borghese at " twilight's enchanted hour."

No public resorts furnish so good an opportunity for the study of Roman life and character as the gardens of the Pincian Hill and those of the Villa Borghese. The former is on the site of the famous gardens of Lucullus, where the Empress Messalina afterwards celebrated her orgies. It is now the fashionable evening drive of Rome, where the gay and pleasure-loving aristocracy pay and receive visits in their open carriages. The long arcades are adorned with busts and statues; a curious clypsydra or water-clock marks the hours, and a moving multitude of promenaders give life and variety to the scene. The sunset view from the terrace is magnificent—St. Peter's dome, the round castle of St. Angelo, and many a stately campanile are defined like a silhouette against the glowing western sky. A long range of the engirdling wall of the city, rising in places sixty or seventy feet, is also brought into view. (See frontispiece.)

DOME OF ST. PETER'S.

From one point of view in the bosky glades of the garden the dome of St. Peter's may be seen as if surrounded by a leafy frame.

The gardens of the Villa Borghese are without the walls. They have a strangely antique appearance. In the grounds is a ruined temple, its pillared portico half broken down and the statue of an unworshipped goddess standing on her deserted shrine. Marble seats, fountains, and statues—chipped, moss-grown, and time-stained—are seen beneath

FALLS OF TIVOLI.

the vistas of venerable trees. The stately villa itself, the property of one of the noblest families of Rome, contains a superb art gallery and museum. I saw several times the King and Queen of Italy driving through the gardens and streets without escort, and graciously returning the loyal greetings that they received from all ranks of the people.

I was somewhat surprised at the absence of the picturesque national costume. I saw, however, some very good examples in a family of artists' models, who took the evening air at an antique fountain near my hotel. The family consisted of a venerable-looking old peasant woman, her son, and two daughters. I found the young man, who spoke French very well, quite intelligent and communicative. They came, he said, from Tivoli, and made their living by sitting for their portraits in the picturesque

ORVIETO.

costume of the country. The daughters had an air of modest refinement one would hardly expect in the peasant class. Their portraits would make admirable Madonnas of the type which so abounds in Italian religious art.

The subject of fine art in Rome is too large to treat, however cursorily, in these brief notes. As I lingered for hours in the corridors of the Vatican and Museum of the Capitol, entranced with the treasures rescued from the *débris* of the Old Roman World, and, wondered, in mute amazement, how great was the glory of its mighty prime, I felt that ancient sculpture had never been equalled by the work of the modern chisel. The achievements of Canova, Thorwaldsen, Gibson, and other masters, however, almost rival in my humble judgment the finest works of antiquity. With painting it is otherwise. I cannot feel the enthusiasm that many express concerning the great Italian masters. Even the celebrated "Last Judgment" of Michael Angelo in the Sistine Chapel, failed to impress me as other than a grand *tour de force,* whose chief object seemed to be the display of the master's skill in the foreshortened representation of the human figure in every possible attitude of contortion. These dimly-lighted pictures, blackened with the smoke of centuries are, however, an unfavourable exhibition of his powers. I liked much better the works of Raphäel in the Stanze and Loggie, which bear his name; although my untutored taste cannot subscribe to the dictum which pronounces them "unquestionably the noblest works of modern art in existence." I have seen many pictures that impressed me more.

The Vatican itself, in which these much-prized art treasures are housed, is the most extensive and magnificent palace in the world. It is said to contain eleven thousand halls, chapels, saloons, and private apartments, besides extensive courts and gardens. Here the Papal power is supreme. The successor of the humble fisherman of Galilee is attended by a guard of armed soldiers, accoutred in a singularly bizarre-looking uniform of yellow and red, like one of earth's proudest monarchs. Yet

TODI.

we read of "the prisoner of the Vatican," and Peter's pence are collected from the poor throughout Catholic Christendom for the maintenance of this unapostolic state.

Conditions of time and space forbid further account of the innumerable objects of antiquarian interest in the City of the Seven Hills, "that was eternal named." New Rome, under the vigorous administration of its constitutional government, is fast asserting its place and influence as the political centre of United Italy. But its chief and imperishable interest to the pilgrims from many lands who visit its storied scenes, consists of the memories of its mighty past, and while time endures these memories shall never lose their power.

One of the most charming excursions from Rome is that to the ancient town of Tivoli, with its furze-clad slopes, its sparkling waterfalls and its vast Villa of Hadrian, where the lord of the world revelled in a pleasure-place which, with its gardens, grounds, temples, theatres and baths filled a circuit of ten miles. (See page 104.)

More lovely than even the falls of Tivoli are those of Terni shown in our engraving. The impetuous Velius hurls its water in three successive leaps down a rugged ravine, clad with richest verdure. The contrast between the snowy foam and the vivid foliage ever glistening in the spray is intense, and poets' song and painters' skill alike fail to give an adequate conception of this most beautiful of Italian waterfalls.

Following up the banks of the Tiber, we reach the ancient town of Orte, commanding from its castle height a magnificent view of the far-winding stream. A peculiarity of this region is the number of small thick-walled fortress towns, each perched upon the summit of an island of tufa rising above the sea of verdure of the surrounding country. Along the steep road leading to these eagle-like eyries toil beneath the burning sun the peasant men and women and their patient donkeys, looking exceedingly picturesque and uncomfortable. A good example of these relics of the old feudal times is the Civita Bagnorea shown on page 111.

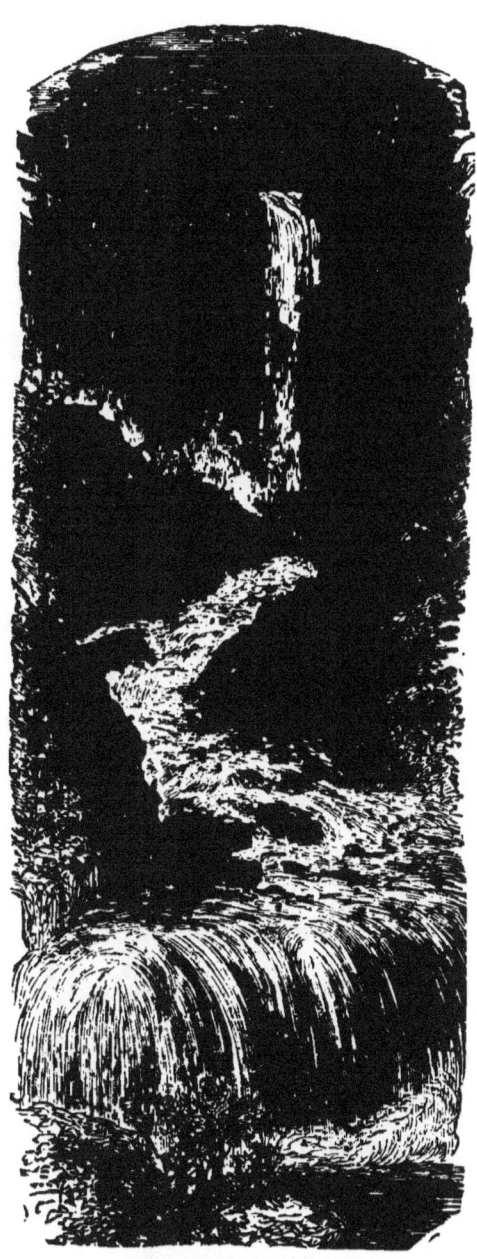

FALLS OF TERNI.

THE TIBER FROM ORTE.

Orvieto is another similar hill-fortress, a stronghold of the Guelphs, and graced with a cathedral of peculiar sumptuousness and splendour. (See page 105.)

On the steeply sloping banks of the Tiber is Todi, so steep that through many of its streets carriages may not pass. Here was born the author of the immortal hymn *Stabat Mater Dolorosa*, wedded to immortal music by the genius of Rossini.

Not far from Todi is the littlet own of Assisi, with the famous convent and church of St. Francis. The story of the life and labours of the "Seraphic Doctor" who is reported to have enjoyed in life the beatific vision of the Lord

CIVITA BAGNOREA.

he served with such entire devotion and to have retained in his body the marks of His passion lend an intenser in-

TEMPLE OF THE CLITUMNUS.

terest to the stately architecture and sumptuous adorning of the church and convent erected over his bones. (See page 114.)

Near Assisi on the banks of the crystal Clitumnus is the beautiful temple of the deity of the stream, so sweetly besung by Byron's classic muse, the picturesque surroundings and historic associations of which make it a favourite subject for the study of both artist and scholar.

THE SOURCE OF THE TIBER.

Following still further the course of the storied Tiber, the traveller reaches its birthplace among the rugged Appenines. Beneath the shadow of a vast beech forest, the crystal stream, so often dyed with blood of contending races, gambols on its way through a daisy-dappled sod of richest green, laughing and leaping from ledge to ledge like an innocent child at play.

CONVENT AND CHURCH OF ST. FRANCIS, ASSISI.

CHAPTER V.

NAPLES—PUTEOLI—BAIÆ—CAPRI—VESUVIUS—POMPEII.

"Vedi Napoli e poi mori."—"See Naples and then die."
—*Neapolitan Proverb.*

FROM Rome to Naples is a railway ride of a hundred and sixty miles. The road for a considerable part of the way leads along the slopes of the Appenines, their splintered and pinnacled crags rising in verdureless desolation in the fierce blaze of an almost tropical sun. I was surprised at the sparseness of the foliage; that of the olive tree, which chiefly abounds, being of a thin and meagre quality, and of a dull grey colour. I saw nothing to compare with the rich fresh foliage of our Canadian forests, except where natural or artificial irrigation obtains. There, indeed, the foliage and flowers of the fig, orange, and lemon groves, and of the oleander and magnolia, were of richest luxuriance and exquisite fragrance. The grape-vines are dwarfed-looking growths, more like our garden peas than what I expected a vineyard to be like. Where they are festooned from tree to tree in the orchards, they are, however, of much finer growth. The blood-red poppies in the fields look like cups of wine borne by Mænads in a Bacchic dance. Among the places of interest passed *en route* are Aquino, the birth-place of the satirist Juvenal, and of the

"Angelic Doctor," Thomas Aquinas; the celebrated castle-like monastery of Monte Casino, founded by St. Benedict, A. D. 529, with one of the most precious libraries in the world, crowning a lofty height; and Capua, once the second city in Italy, famed in Roman story. It had, in ancient times, 300,000 inhabitants, but has now shrunk to a miserable town. In its vast amphitheatre, next in size to the Colosseum, broke out the dangerous "Gladiators' War," under Spartacus, whose stirring speech is dear to every school-boy's heart. The modern villages we pass look poor and mean; and the peasantry anything but the picturesque objects we see in artists' sketches. The women were toiling in the fields and quarries, and attending the railway crossings, and gave slight indications of the classic beauty for which this region was once famous. At the railway stations nut-brown girls, with hair and eyes black as night, cried, with musical voices, their *aqua gelata*, or iced water, and fruits so grateful to the hot and thirsty traveller.

It was with keen interest that I first caught sight of the distant cone of Mount Vesuvius, with its lofty column of smoke and steam,—a pillar of cloud by day, of fire by night. My first impressions of Naples were anything but favourable. After escaping from the hands of importunate "commissionaires," who attempted to force their services upon me in spite of my protests, I was driven through miles of narrow streets, flanked by lofty and monotonous houses, and crowded with pedestrians, overladen donkeys, clamorous venders of fruit, vegetables, ice-water, etc., and tinkers, cobblers, and artizans of every class, working out of doors,—the population is about half a million. The magnificent prospect from the balcony of my hotel, however, far up the slope of the amphitheatre on which the city lies, more than fulfilled my highest anticipations. There, in the soft sunset light, glanced and shimmered the blue waters of the lovely bay—its shore sweeping like a huge sickle in majestic curve to the base of far off Vesuvius, the white walled houses gleaming fair, in a continuous street, beyond the rippling sea.

Naples received its name—Neapolis, "the new city"—nearly three thousand years ago—what a strange misnomer it seems!—to distinguish it from Palæopolis, "the old city," founded by Greek colonists at a still earlier date Yet here, on the site of one of the oldest civilizations in the world, from my hotel windows I saw a man watering the streets by means of two barrels with the bungs out, on a rude cart drawn by an ox and a horse.

The city itself contains little of special interest. Its history, like its volcanic soil, has been disturbed by many social convulsions, which have left little of antiquarian value or architectural beauty to reward the attention. Its five forts are vast, some of them strikingly picturesque structures. It has two curious mediæval gates, and numerous churches, most of them in a debased Renaissance style of architecture. The Church of St. Januarius is the largest and most sumptuous. Here takes place, thrice a year, the alleged miracle of liquefaction of the martyr's blood. Nowhere did I witness such abject Mariolatry as here. I observed one tawdry image of the Virgin, decked out in a figured silk dress, a silver crown on her clustering curls, rings on her fingers, and a bouquet in her hand, like a fine lady dressed for a ball. One woman I saw raise the robe of the Virgin to her lips and reverently kiss it; another, I saw lying prostrate and motionless on the stone floor before the altar; and everywhere I beheld such abject superstition as I never witnessed before.

I had been told that, in Naples, I should see the lazaroni lying around like lizards in the sun, basking in luxurious idleness. But I did not. On the contrary, everybody seemed as busy as could be. Indeed, so poor is the community that they have to work or starve. The squalor of the lanes and alleys, in which the poor swarm like bees, is painful to witness. One street is called the Street of Seven Sorrows—an allusion to the woes of the Virgin. I thought it significant of the sevenfold sorrows, the poverty, ignorance and superstition and other miseries, of her devotees. Very few of the people can read: in a public arcade, I saw several writers at their desks, to one of whom a woman was dictating a letter. They seem also very impulsive and quick-tempered, and possess very little self-control. They beat their donkeys unmercifully; they gesticulate violently, and seem disposed to quarrel about merest trifles. I noticed one handsome black-eyed woman make a rush at her little girl who had displeased her in something, and with a panther-like fierceness raise her arm to her teeth and bite it. I thought it the most vicious-looking thing I ever saw.

I shall have a higher respect for the whole race of donkeys as long as I live, on account of the patient toil of the donkeys of Naples. Such loads as they carry! such huge panniers of fruits, vegetables, snow from the distant mountains—just as described by Horace eighteen hundred years ago,—and wine and water jars, and every conceivable burden! Often you can hardly see the donkey for the load he bears. But a great offset to their virtues is the frightful noise of their nocturnal braying. Of all the lugubrious sounds that ever murdered sleep and made night hideous, commend me to the melancholy long-drawn braying of the Neapolitan donkey.

The harness of the horses is the most extraordinary thing of the sort I ever saw. On the animal's back is a kind of saddle, on which towers, a foot or more in height, a brass-covered, brightly burnished structure, terminating in a little vane or a cluster of bells which swing and ring at every step. The drivers, true to the genius of their craft the world over, are an extortionate set of rascals; but after you once drive a bargain with them they will serve you faithfully—at least such was my experience.

If Naples itself has few attractions, its immediate surroundings present many objects of surpassing interest One of the most delightful excursions in the neighbour hood is that to Pozzuoli—the Puteoli where St. Paul "tarried seven days" on his way to Rome—and Baja, the ancient Baiæ of Horace's epistle. The road leads first through the Grotta di Posilipo—a tunnel through a sandstone rock nearly half a mile long, and in places a hundred feet high. It dates from the time of Augustus and is ascribed by the peasants to the arts of the great magician, Virgil. Emerging from the gaslit grotto into the glorious Italian sunlight, one enters a region once crowded with stately Roman palaces and villas, long since reduced to ruins by the tremendous volcanic convulsions of which it has been the theatre. But Nature clothes with perennial beauty this lovely strand; and the golden sunshine falls, and the sapphire sea expands, and the summer foliage mantles every peak and cape and crag. I visited the celebrated *Grotta del Cane,* in which carbonic acid gas accumulates so as instantly to extinguish a lighted torch thrust into it. It is said that a pistol cannot be fired beneath its surface, as the powder will not ignite. I waded in some distance and stooped for a moment beneath the surface of the gas, but experienced a strange suffocating sensation. The guide thrust into the gas one of the numerous dogs who earns his living by dying daily; but the poor animal looked up so wistfully that I ordered his release, and he bounded eagerly away. The Solfatara—an extinct crater—and sulphurous exhalations from the rocks, are evidences of volcanic action. In places the soil was so hot that I could not hold my hand near it.

Pozzuoli, once the most important commercial city in

Italy, is now a mere shadow of its former greatness. In St. Paul's day it was the chief depot for the corn ships and trade in spices, silks, ivory, and oriental luxuries from Egypt and the remoter East. Here he "found brethren," probably Jewish converts from Alexandria or Jerusalem. Here was early established a Christian church, and in the third century, Januarius, its bishop, was, by the orders of Diocletian, exposed to wild beasts in its vast amphitheatre. This is one of the most perfect in Italy. The dens of the lions and leopards, the cells of the gladiators, and the subterranean passages and conduits can be distinctly seen. Even more interesting is the ruined temple of Serapis. The oscillations of level are shown by the watermarks and borings of marine worms on the surface of the ancient columns of the temple, which are shown in the accompanying engraving. The importunities of the beggars and would-be guides of Pozzuoli would be amusing if not so annoying. One picturesque-looking rascal ran beside the carriage, on a hot day, for nearly a mile. I could only get rid of him by buying the torch he was determined to sell.

This whole region is rife with memories of Virgil and his immortal poem. I drove around the gloomy Lake Avernus, the scene, according to the poet, of the descent of Æneas into the netherworld. It lay like "the dark tarn of Auber, in the mystic, mid-region of Weir." Over its haunted surface, local tradition asserts, no bird will fly. With my travelling companion, who was a classical enthusiast, I visited the so-called Sibyl's Grotto, where Æneas consulted that mythic personage. Entering an opening in the hillside, we penetrated by torchlight a long, dark, winding passage. Coming to a steep incline my

TEMPLE OF SERAPIS.

guide, a grisly old fellow, with a decidedly bandit look, stooped down and said, "Montez." I mounted on his back accordingly, and he plunged into a stream of inky blackness—the River Styx he called it—and waded into a little cell, which he described as the Sibyl's Chamber. By the red glare of the torch light our grisly guide, who looked grim enough for Cerberus himself, pointed out the Sibyl's bed, her bath, her chair, and the very hole in the wall through which she uttered her oracles! Who could doubt the story with such an evidence before him? In this uncanny place our guides demanded their fee, but we insisted on their carrying us back to daylight before paying them.

On our way to the ruins of ancient Cumæ we passed through another long and lofty tunnel, constructed by Agrippa, and lighted at infrequent intervals by large shafts from above. Our stock of matches gave out, so we could not light our torch. Our guides had therefore to grope their way through the darkness from one light hole to another which only illumined a very limited area. The bright Italian sunshine, as we emerged from that sepulchral gloom, was especially grateful. Cumæ was founded B.C. 1050, and was the place where Greek civilization first found entrance to Italy. We were shown its foliage-mantled amphitheatre and lofty Acropolis. Here dwelt the Cumæan Sibyl, hence came the mysterious Sibyline books, and from hence Greek letters and the arts were dffused throughout Etruscan Italy.

"Nothing in the world," says Horace, "can be compared with the lovely bay of Baiæ." Even in its ruinous estate this once gay Roman pleasure scene deserves all the praise which can be given it. The whole region abounds with the ruins of temples, and of the palaces and villas of the ancient masters of the world. Here Julius Cæsar, Augustus, Tiberius, Nero, Lucullus, and many a wealthy Roman had their pleasure-palaces and gardens. In one of these Nero planned, and in the Lucrine Lake near by

BAY OF BAJA.

was attempted, the murder of his mother, Agrippina. A guide who had picked up a little English, strangely twisted into Italian idioms, conducted us through the temples of Diana, Venus and Mercury; the latter, a large, dome-shaped structure with a fine echo. The most remarkable ruin is the Piscina Mirabilis, a vaulted cistern with lofty arches supported by forty-eight huge columns. It is a vast reservoir, fed by the Julian Aqueduct from far-distant springs, and intended for watering the Roman fleet in the harbour of Misenum far below. Of this fleet the elder Pliny, who perished in the irruption of Vesuvius in A.D. 79, was commander. I chipped off some of the lime de-

CAPE MISENUM.

posit from the walls, which showed that it had been in use for a long period. The flat-roofed white stone houses have a singular oriental look. I climbed over stone threshing floors, on elevated places, and saw the cattle treading out the corn. It was then winnowed by tossing it into the air, that the wind might blow the chaff away. Stone oil and wine presses accented the Eastern aspect of the scene. The interiors of the houses were crowded and comfortless, and uncleanly. The food was coarse, and cooked in earthenware vessels at a rude fire-place. The holiday costume of the peasants—red upper garment and gold embroidery—betrayed their Greek origin. They offered for our refreshment black bread and cheese, fruit and wine. The view from the house-top was superb—the rocky Cape Misenum, the lovely Bay of Baja, in the offing the volcanic islands of the Procida and Ischia, and at our feet a gloomy lake in an old crater called *Mare Morto*, the Sea of Death.

The ride back to Naples in the golden afternoon light was glorious. The blue waves broke in snowy spray upon the silver strand; bronzed fishermen, with eager gestures and much noise, were hauling their nets, rich with finny spoil, ashore; and muleteers were urging their slow convoys along the dusty highway. The road climbs the broad shoulder of a hill, gaining ever wider views, till all at once the glorious Bay of Naples, with its painted villas, its gardens of richest foliage, its rocky cliffs and sheltered coves, and the magical sunset sheen on its blue waves, bursts upon the sight. It is a memory of delight that no words can reproduce. I stopped the carriage over and over again to gaze and gaze upon the charming scene, and could scarcely tear myself away.

One feels with Rogers:—

> " This region, surely, was not of the earth.
> Was it not dropped from Heaven ? Not a grove,

> Citron or pine or cedar, not a grot
> Sea-worn and mantled with the gadding vine,
> But breathes enchantment. Not a cliff, but flings
> On the clear wave some image of delight."

Among the evil memories of this lovely coast is that of the Villa of Vedius Pollio, with the fish ponds where he used to feed his lampreys with the flesh of his slaves. The Grotto of Sejanus, Tomb of Virgil, and, more remote, the Villa of Cicero, are also places of interest.

Another delightful excursion is that to Sorrento and the island of Capri. As one embarks on the steamer, half-naked boys disporting in the water cry out, "Monnaie, signor, monnaie." When coins are thrown them, they dive like dolphins and bring them up in their teeth. Sorrento, the birth-place of Tasso, sits like a queen on a throne of rock, embowered amid groves of orange, olive, mulberry, pomegranates, figs, and aloes—a very garden of delight. A few miles out in the gulf lies the beautiful island of Capri. If I had not seen it, I could not have believed it possible that water could be so intensely blue as that of this lovely bay. In the sunshine it was a light, and in a shadow a deep, ultra marine; but as clear as crystal. I could see the star fish on the bottom in from five to ten fathoms of water, and the dolphins, disporting in the waves, were visible at a much greater distance. These favourites of Apollo can outstrip the swiftest steamer, so rapidly do they swim. To them the principle shrine of Apollo owed its name, also the French Province of Dauphiné, which gave the title to the heir to the throne of France. They could not be eaten during Lent without sin, because they are not really fish but mammals.

Capri consists of two craggy peaks, so precipitous that at only two points can a landing be effected. Covered with foliage, it gleams like an emerald set in sapphire. Here the Emperor Tiberius, when sated and sickened with ruling the world, retired to indulge in the most infamous vices, and truculent cruelty. The ruins of his villa still crown the summit of the island,—a part of it is now used as a cow-byre. The gem of the island, however, is the celebrated Blue Grotto. It is entered from the sea by a low arch scarce three feet high. The visitor must lie down in the bottom of the boat. Within, it expands to a large vaulted chamber. The effect of the blue refraction of the light is dazzling, and the body of the boatman who swims about in the water gleams like silver. I climbed the cliff by a steep and rugged path, dined at an inn where the orange blossoms filled the air with fragrance, and descending on the other side to a delightfully picturesque harbour, sailed round the island in a boat manned by three stout-armed fishermen. We penetrated the White Grotto, where the waves looked like curdled milk, the Green Grotto, and the Stalactite Grotto; and sailed beneath a magnificent natural arch, and under volcanic cliffs rising precipitously a thousand feet in air.

The grandest excursion from Naples, however, is that to Mount Vesuvius. In order to avoid the heat, I left

Naples with a friend, by carriage, shortly after midnight, and rode through the silent streets of the beautiful city—the tall white houses gleaming like marble in the glorious moonlight. At many of the corners lamps were burning before a shrine of the Virgin.

Like the red eye of Cyclops burned the dull fire of the mountain. But all day long the mysterious column of white smoke ascends—"solemn and slow as erst from Ararat" the smoke of the patriarch's sacrifice.

After an hour's drive we reached Resina, a village at the foot of the mountain. Our *veturino* knocked loudly at a door, and we were almost instantly surrounded by a swarm of guides, all anxious to prey upon their victims. I suppose they sleep in their clothes and turn out at a moment's notice. Making a bargain with the chief we were soon mounted, with the aid of much officious assistance, on good stout horses. Through the stone-paved streets of the little town we clattered, and soon began to climb the mountain, between luxuriant vineyards and fig and almond orchards growing upon the fertile volcanic soil. Our train was soon increased by four hangers-on, besides the guide. They well deserved this name, in its most literal sense, for they would catch hold of our horses' tails, and so for part of the way we helped them instead of their helping us. At length the road became so steep that horses could no longer climb, and we were forced to dismount.

Now the use of the guides whom our horses had dragged

up became apparent. It was their turn to drag us up. One stout fellow tied a leather strap to a stick and gave me the stick, which I held with both hands while he took the other end of the strap over his shoulder, and another guide pushed me from behind. Between the two, by scrambling in zig-zags up the mountain's side—the most fatiguing climb I ever had in my life,—I at last reached the top and stood on the edge of the crater. The weird grandeur of the sight well repaid the toil of the ascent.

CRATER OF MOUNT VESUVIUS.

A crumbling ledge of rock ran round the summit, sloping suddenly down to a large irregular depression which was covered, and floored as it were, with black lava, which had cooled and hardened, retaining the form in which it had boiled up and flowed forth. This floor was studded with a number of smaller cones from which gas and steam were escaping with a violent hissing noise. Among them was one very much larger than the others—the active crater—from which issued the most frightful bellowings. About every two minutes came a violent explosion, and a large quantity of stones and scoria were thrown high in the air, and fell back into the fiery throat of this tremendous furnace. The general appearance of the scene is shown in the accompanying small engraving.

"Do you wish to go down into the crater?" asked our guides.

"Of course we do, that is what we came for," was the answer. Then they haggled for an extra three francs apiece. At length we scrambled down the steep and crumbling wall amid almost suffocating sulphurous fumes, and clambered over the tortured and uneven lava floor. Through numerous cracks and crevices steam and gas were escaping; the rocks were stained yellow, red, and purple with the sulphur incrustations, and I could feel the heat through the thick soles of my boots. In many of the crevices the rock was seen to be red hot, and when I thrust in my staff it suddenly caught fire. Soon one of the guides gave a loud cry, and called us to see the molten lava which we found boiling up through the black floor, and flowing along in a thick, viscid stream, like tar, only of a fiery colour. The heat was great, but I could approach so near as to take some of it on the end of my staff, and press into it some copper coins which I had in my pocket, having first been shown how by the guides. When the lava cooled these were firmly imbedded, and I brought them away as souvenirs of the occasion.

My guide climbed a small cone and broke off the top with his staff. Instantly, with a violent noise, a jet of steam escaped, throwing fragments of rock into the air. As may be imagined, I hurried down as fast as possible. I should have liked very much to have looked down into the active crater; but it was quite unsafe, so frequent were the showers of falling stones; yet the guides offered to take us up for 300 francs. I suspect, however, it was mere bravado on their part. From the summit we had a magnificent view of the distant city and beautiful bay with the wide sweep of its sickle-shaped shore. After luncheon on the mountain top, part of which consisted of eggs cooked by the natural heat of this great furnace, we descended much more rapidly than we went up. All we had to do was to lift our feet well out of the cinders and down we went with tremendous strides.

By means of the inclined railway up the cone tourists may now ascend in a few minutes what cost us weary hours.

We remounted our horses and rode down through vast slopes covered with the black lava of recent eruptions, which in places had flowed far over the plain, destroying numerous houses and vineyards in its progress. In the eruptions of 1872 many lives were lost; in that of 1794, four hundred perished; and by one earlier still, three thousand. In the recent great eruption, ashes and scoria were hurled eight thousand feet in the air and carried by the wind a distance of one hundred and forty miles.

It was a bright sunny afternoon that I drove, with my companion in travel, from Mount Vesuvius to Pompeii. It is about a ten miles' drive through what is almost one continuous city—a humming hive of industry scarce surpassed in Naples itself. A prominent employment is the making of maccaroni and vermicelli, in the manufacture of which multitudes of half naked men and boys were employed. The long loops and festoons of this favourite food were hanging in the sun to dry and almost bake, so intense was the heat. Pompeii, it will be remembered, was buried beneath twenty feet of volcanic ashes and pumice stone, just eighteen hundred years ago. About the middle of the last century it was re-discovered, and ever since its excavation has been prosecuted with varying energy. A large part has now been disinterred, and the result is a revelation of the conditions of old Roman life, such as is exhibited nowhere else.

You may follow its minutest details. You may accompany the rich patrician to the public forum and the court; to the amphitheatre and share his seat, and look down with him into the arena where the gladiators fight; to the temple and behold the altars still stained with the smoke of sacrifice, and see, what he could not, the secret opening behind the image of the god, through which the priest spoke his oracles. You may go to the public baths and see the hypocausts for fire, the aqueducts and caleducts for hot water and cold air, the cabinets for his clothing, and niches for his soaps, strigils and unguents. You may enter the privacy of his home and behold the images of his ancestors, and the lares and penates of his fire-side. You may criticise the frescoes on his walls, the furnishings of his house, and his mode of entertaining his friends. You may enter his kitchen and examine the domestic economy of the family. You may even penetrate the privacy of his wife's apartment, and behold the interesting mysteries—dear to the female heart—of her toilet table, the rouge pots, cosmetics, and mirrors, the jewellery and other articles of personal adornment. You may examine the surgeon's instrument case, its lancets and scalpels, and probes, and cupping-glasses—three hundred instruments in all. You may visit the baker's shop and see the kneading-troughs, the ovens, even the loaves of bread stamped with the baker's name. You may study the different avocations and modes of work of the fuller, dyer, miller, barber, colour-man, grocer, perfumer, and wine-merchant, and may examine the commodities which they sold, and note the stains of the wine-cup on the marble counters, and the amphoræ on the floor.

The houses, of course, are roofless, the woodwork having been ignited by the red-hot ashes and scoria. But their internal arrangements, their paintings, and their contents are perfectly preserved. It produces a strange sensation to walk down the narrow streets of this long-buried city—they vary from fourteen to twenty-four feet wide—to observe the ruts made by the cart-wheels eighteen centuries ago, and to see the stepping-stones across the streets, bearing the marks of horses' hoofs. On either side are small shops, just like those of Naples to-day, for the sale of bread, meat, oil, wine, drugs, and other articles. The signs of the shop-keepers can, in places, be seen. A barber shop, a soap factory, a tannery, a fuller's shop, a bakery with eighty loaves of bread in the oven, and several mills have also been found. At the street corners are stone fountains worn smooth by lengthened use, to which the maidens used to trip so lightly.

The dwelling-houses have a vestibule opening on the street, sometimes with the word "Salve," "Welcome," or a figure of a dog in mosaic on the floor with the words, "Cave canem," "Beware of the dog." Within is an open court surrounded by bedrooms, kitchen, *triclinium* or dining-room, etc. The walls and columns are beautifully painted in bright colours, chiefly red and yellow, and adorned with elegant frescoes of scenes in the mythic history of the pagan gods and godesses, landscapes, etc. In public places may be read election placards and wall-scribblings of idle soldiers and school-boys. Opposite one shop I observed the warning in Latin, "This is no place for lounging, idler depart." The public forum, the basilica, or court of justice, with its cells for prisoners; the temples of the gods, with their shrines and images, their altars stained with incense smoke and the chambers of the priests; the theatres with their stage, corridors, and rows of marble seats—one will hold five thousand, another twenty thousand persons; the public baths with marble basins for hot and cold water, etc.; the street of tombs lined with the monuments of the dead; and the ancient city walls and gates, may all be seen almost as they were when the wrath of Heaven descended upon the guilty city.

About two thousand persons, in all, are supposed to have perished in the ruins. In the house of Diomedes, in the wine-vaults, whither they had fled for refuge—now a capacious crypt—the bodies of seventeen women and children were found crowded together. At the garden gate was discovered the skeleton of the proprietor, with the key in his hand, and near him a slave with money and jewels. In the gladiators' barracks were found sixty-three skeletons, three of them in prison with iron stocks on their feet. In the museum are observed several casts made by pouring plaster into the consolidated matrix of ashes which had formed around the living body—long since returned to dust—of the ill-fated inhabitants in the attitude of flight, and in the very death-struggle. Among these are a young girl with a ring on her finger, a man lying on his side with remarkably well preserved features, and others. The very texture and embroidery of the dress, and the smooth, round contour of the young girl's arm, may be distinctly seen. At the entry to the guard-house was found the skeleton of a Roman sentinel—a man of giant mould, with his firm-laced sandals, his iron greaves, his sword, his shield, and grasping still his bronze-tipped spear—a monument of

Roman valour and fidelity—keeping his post even unto death. A priest of Isis was overtaken by the mephitic gases while endeavouring to break through the wall of the temple. Even the remains of the dumb animals have a pathetic interest—the horses in the stable of Albinus, the mule in the bakery, the dog in his kennel, and the dove upon her nest. The sight of this dead city, called forth from its grave of centuries, made that old Roman life more vivid and real to me than all the classic reading I had ever done.

The poet Rogers thus vividly describes the impression produced by a visit to the buried city :—

> "—But lo, engraven on a threshold-stone,
> That word of courtesy, so sacred once,
> HAIL! At a master's greeting we may enter.
> And lo, a fairy-palace! everywhere,
> As through the courts and chambers we advance,
> Floors of mosaic, walls of arabesque,
> And columns clustering in Patrician splendour.
> But hark, a footstep? May we not intrude?
> And now, methinks, I hear a gentle laugh,
> And gentle voices mingling as in converse!
> —And now a harp-string as struck carelessly,
> And now—along the corridor it comes—
> I cannot err, a filling as of baths!
> —Ah, no, 'tis but a mockery of the sense,
> Idle and vain! We are but where we were;
> Still wandering in the City of the Dead!"

In the National Museum at Naples are preserved a very large collection of the paintings and mosaics and other objects found at Pompeii. The frescoes are wonderfully fresh-looking, and the drawing is full of character and expression, although many of the subjects betray a depravation of morals, shocking every sentiment of propriety. A curious collection of articles of food and other objects found at Pompeii is also shown. Among these are specimens of oil, wine, meat, fish, eggs, loaves of bread with the baker's name stamped on them, almonds, dates, peas, onions, sandals, a purse with coins, etc. A very large collection of bronzes, objects of art, household utensils and

STREET IN POMPEII.

the like, gives a vivid conception of the life and habits of the inhabitants of the buried city. The following is a list of articles I jotted down as I walked through the rooms: Statuettes and images of the gods; candalabra and lamps of very ornate character; musical instruments, flutes, cymbals, plectra, etc.; surgical instruments in cases, many varieties, also cases of medicines; toilet articles, combs, mirrors, beautiful bracelets, brooches, amulets, rings, seals, gold ornaments and jewellery; spoons, buckles, spears, weapons of all sorts; cake cutters, and moulds for cakes in the form of pigs, rabbits, hearts, etc.; tongs, fire-irons, griddles, pots, pans, funnels, steel-yards, scales, large and small with weights, marked I., II., III., V., X., etc.; measures, chains, nails, tacks, screws, door-knockers, hinges, locks and keys for doors, spades, mattocks, hay-forks, sickles, pruning-knives, axes, shears, hammers, adzes, planes, iron beds and baths, vases of every size and shape, lead pipes and brass water-taps. Many of these are almost identical in shape with those used by the Italian peasantry of the present day.

Of special interest, however, to me was the gallery of portrait statues and busts. They were not ideal figures, but faithful copies from life, full of character and expression—magistrates or consuls, grave matrons, beautiful children, pure-faced vestal virgins, merry school boys and arch-looking Roman girls. It was the best presentation of ancient life and character I have seen. At Rome, also, I was greatly impressed by a domestic group. It was the portrait busts of a husband and wife of middle age, and of grave, almost austere, expression. The man held his wife's hand in his, while her arm was thrown confidingly over his shoulder. This was so admired by the historian Niebuhr, as a symbol of early Roman virtue, that he ordered a copy of it to be placed upon his own tomb.

Amid all the natural beauty of this lovely land, there is one thought that continually haunts one like a nightmare. It is the consciousness of the depressed and degraded condition of the people, and especially of the hard lot of woman. On her, unfitted by nature for such toil, some of the heaviest burdens fall. While the cities swarm with idle priests and sturdy mendicant friars, and uniformed soldiers swagger around the railway stations, I saw women toiling, like beasts of burden in the field, and performing the hardest and most menial drudgery. I saw one old woman carrying up large stones on her head out of a quarry. I saw another harnessed to a cart, and my travelling companion saw a woman and a cow harnessed together to a plough. I sometimes tried to alleviate a little their burdens, but what was my poor help against this mass of human misery! As I witnessed their sufferings, I often felt tears of pity start unbidden to my eyes.

Yet this is the land where Christianity won some of its earliest triumphs, and where the lips of an Apostle preached the New Evangel to the dying Roman world. And here, in this heart of Catholic Christendom, the self-named Vicar of Christ for centuries has had almost unbounded sway—and these be the results. It seems to me that no greater accusation can be brought against the Papacy than the ignorance and superstition and social degradation of the essentially noble race which it has had beneath its fostering care. The only hope for the moral and social elevation of these people is the pure Gospel of Christ. This is the lever of more than Archimedian power which can lift them to a higher plane of being.

And this divine agency is exerting its energising influence as never before, since the days of the Church of the Catacombs. English and American Methodism and other forms of Evangelical religion are, from many centres, leavening the surrounding mass. In this land, long groaning under pagan, and then under Papal persecution, the Gospel has now free untrammelled course. Under the shadow of the Vatican is the propaganda of the Bible Society, and on one of the best streets in Rome rises the handsome façade of a Methodist church. To use the figure of Bunyan, Giants Pope and Pagan may both munch with their toothless gums, but they cannot come at the pilgrims to harm them.

ROMAN RUINS IN SOUTHERN ITALY.

CHAPTER VI.

FLORENCE AND BOLOGNA.

I LEFT Naples at ten o'clock at night for Florence, a ride of three hundred and sixty miles. The glorious moonlight flooded the landscape with a silvery sheen, whose beauty almost forbade the thought of slumber. Stopping a few hours at Rome, I visited the new Government Buildings—a splendid pile, of recent construction—and the vast Baths of Diocletian, now converted into a church, containing a tomb of Salvator Rosa; an eye infirmary, and extensive barracks. It was a curious thing to see the letters, S. P. Q. R., the initials of the stately phrase *Senatus, Populusque, Romani*, under which the legions marched to conquest, painted on the water carts of the modern city. Leaving Rome, the train follows the yellow Tiber, passing near the Milvian Bridge, where Constantine seeing—or feigning that he saw—the sign of the Cross in the sky, conquered the persecuting Maxentius, and became sole ruler of the empire. As we proceed we obtain fine views of the "snowy Soracte" of Horace, of Lake Thrasymine, on whose banks Hannibal won a sanguinary victory over the Roman legions more than two thousand years ago,* and of Arezzo, the

---

* Far other scene is Thrasymine now ;
Her lake a sheet of silver and her plain

birthplace of Mæcenas, and, thirteen centuries later, of Petrarch.

Save Rome, no place in Italy, scarce any in the world, possesses such numerous attractions—historic, literary, and artistic—as Florence. The heroic memories of its struggles for liberty, the wonderful achievements of its sons in architecture, sculpture, painting, poetry, and science, invest it forever with profoundest interest.

Nestling in a lovely valley of the Appenines, its situation is singularly beautiful. Embalmed forever in Milton's undying verse are the names of leafy Vallombrosa, Val d'Arno, and fair Feisole, where the "Tuscan artist with his optic tube"—"the starry Galileo with his woes," explored the skies. A patriot writer thus rhaphsodizes over the beauties of "Firenze, la bella:"—"Like a waterlily rising on the mirror of a lake, so rests on this lovely ground the still more lovely Florence, with its everlasting works, and its inexhaustible riches. Each street contains a world of art; the walls of the city are the calyx, containing the fairest flowers of the human mind."

> "The Arno wins us to the fair white walls,
>   Where the Etrurian Athens claims and keeps
>   Rent by no ravage save the gentle plough ;
>   Her aged trees rise thick as once the slain
>   Lay where their roots are ; but a brook hath ta'en—
>   A rill of scanty stream and bed—
>   A name of blood from that day's sanguine rain :
>   And Sanguinette tells ye where the dead
>   Made the earth wet and turned the unwilling waters red.
>   —*Childe Harold.*

> A softer feeling for her fairy halls
> Girt by her theatre of hills; she reaps
> Her corn and wine and oil, and Plenty leaps
> To laughing life, with her redundant horn.
> And buried Learning rose, redeemed to a new morn."

In the portico of the Uffizi palace are the statues of celebrated Tuscans, most of them the sons or denizens of Florence. No city in the world, I think, can exhibit such a galaxy of illustrious names. Among others are the statues of Cosmo de Medici, Lorenzo il Magnifico, Orcagna, Giotto, Da Vinci, Michael Angelo, Dante, Petrarch, Boccacio, Macchiavelli, Galileo, and Benvenuto Cellini. Besides these, Savonarola, Bruneleschi, Ghiberti, Fra Angelico, Raphäel, and many another illustrious in letters and in art are forever associated with the memory of Florence.

Let us take a walk through this old historic city. We start from the Piazza della Signoria, once the forum of the Republic, and the scene of its memorable events. On the site of that great bronze fountain, erected three hundred years ago, on which disport Neptune and his tritons, Savonarola and two other monks, precursors of the Reformation, were burned at the stake, May 23rd, 1498. There, for near four hundred years, has stood in sun and shower, Michael Angelo's celebrated statue of David. That prison-like palace, with its slender tower rising like a mast three hundred feet in air, was the ancient seat of government. Let us climb its marble stairs. We enter stately chambers, carved and frescoed by great masters, once the home of the senate and councils of the Republic. In the topmost story are the private apartments of the princely Medici, sumptuous with dark, carved antique furniture, frescoes, and tapestries, but small and mean in size. From these prison-like windows looked forth on the lovely landscape the fair faces and dark eyes of the proud dames of the mediæval court; and in one of these very chambers Cosmo de Medici, with his own hand, slew his son Garzia for the murder of his brother Giovanni.

Descending to the Piazza, we face the Loggia dei Lanzi, a large open portico, of date 1376, fronting the square, and filled with masterpieces of sculpture in bronze and marble by Cellini and other Tuscan masters, which for three hundred years and more have entranced the gaze of successive generations.

Along a crowded street we proceed to the great Duomo. On the way we pass the Church of "St. Michael in the Garden,"—a church below, a corn exchange above—so called from a plot of grass in front, which was paved with stone six hundred years ago. How strange that the memory of that little plot of grass should be preserved in the name through all these centuries of chance and change! Further on we pass the house, with iron gratings and small bull's eye glass, in which Dante, "*il divino poeta*," as the inscription reads, was born, A.D. 1265.

There, at the end of this street, rises one of the most remarkable groups of buildings in the world—the Duomo, Giotto's Tower, and the Baptistery. The first was begun in 1294. It is a noble specimen of Italian gothic of black and white marble, fretted with exquisite carving and tracery. From its great carved pulpit, like a king upon his throne, Savonarola swayed the sceptre of his eloquence over the awe-struck souls of the people of Florence. Its mighty dome, added in 1420-34, surpasses in size even that of St. Peter's at Rome, and is the more daring, as the earlier achievement. Its interior is covered with gigantic mosaics of the Inferno, Purgatory, and Paradise; hideous figures of satyr-headed devils are torturing the lost in the flames with pitchforks—a dreadful and repulsive sight. The guide whispered against the wall, and I distinctly heard what he said on the opposite side of the dome. From the lantern, nearly four hundred feet in air, a magnificent view of the city at our feet, the far-winding Arno, and the engirdling hills, is enjoyed. In the square below is a statue of Brunelleschi, the architect of the dome, gazing upward with a look of triumph at his realized design. Here, too, is preserved a stone seat on which Dante used to sit and gaze with admiration on the scene, on summer evenings, six hundred years ago.

The Campanile, or Giotto's Tower, is an exquisite structure, rising, more and more ornate as it climbs, to a height of three hundred feet, enriched with carvings of the seven cardinal virtues, the seven works of mercy, the seven Beatitudes, and the seven Sacraments. Notwithstanding its beauty, it has yet a look of incompleteness, the spire of the original design having never been finished.

> " In the old Tuscan town stands Giotto's tower,
> The City of Florence blossoming in stone,—
> A vision, a delight, and a desire,—
> The builder's perfect and centennial flower,
> That in the night of ages bloomed alone,
> But wanting still the glory of the spire."

Opposite the Duomo is the still older Baptistery, venerable with the time-stains of seven, or perhaps eight, hundred years. Here are the famous bronze doors of Ghiberti, on which he expended the labours of forty years, worthy, said Michael Angelo, to be the gates of Paradise. They represent, in high relief—the figures stand out almost free—scenes from Scripture history, and are marvels of artistic skill. The vast and shadowy dome is covered with mosaics, in the austere and solemn style of the thirteenth century. On a gold ground are seen the majestic figures of the sacred choir of angels and archangels, principalities and powers, apostles and martyrs. Beneath are the awful scenes of the Last Judgment, the raptures of the saved, and the torments of the lost. I sat and pondered long upon those solemn designs, which for centuries have uttered their silent warning and exhortation to the generations of worshippers who knelt below.

Not far from the Duomo is the Church of Santa Croce, the Pantheon or Westminster Abbey of Italy. It is a building of simple dignity, five hundred feet in length, begun in 1294. Its chief attractions are the frescoes of

Giotto and the tombs of Michael Angelo, Macchiavelli, Galileo, the Medici, Alfieri, and many another famous son of Italy.

> "In Santa Croce's holy precincts lie
> Ashes which make them holier, dust which is
> Even in itself an immortality
> Though there were nothing save the past, and this,
> The particle of those sublimities,
> Which have relapsed to chaos:—here repose
> Angelo's, Alfieri's bones, and his,
> The starry Galileo with his woes;
> Here Macchiavelli's earth returned to whence it rose."

In front of the church is the splendid monument of Dante, inaugurated on the six hundreth anniversary of his birth. In the adjacent cloisters I saw an ancient statue of God the Father, an offensive attempt to represent to sense the Eternal and Invisible.

The chief glory of Florence is the unrivalled art collection in the galleries of the Uffizi and Pitti Palaces. Through these long corridors and stately chambers one wanders, sated with delight in the study of the art treasures on every side. There "the goddess loves in stone;" here the Virgin breathes on canvass; and heroes and martyrs and saints live forever—immortalized by the genius of Raphäel, Fra Angelico, Fra Lippi, Titian, Guido, and their fellows in the mighty brotherhood of art. These palaces are on opposite sides of the Arno, but are connected by a long covered gallery, lined with pictures, over the Ponte Vecchio, which it takes fifteen minutes to traverse. As I stood upon the ancient bridge and watched the sun set over the Arno, I thought how often from that very spot Dante, Angelo, and Raphäel must have watched his setting long centuries ago.

Adjoining the royal Pitti Palace are the famous Boboli Gardens laid out by Cosmo I. It required but little effort of the imagination to repeople its pleached alleys and noble vistas, adorned with many a marble statue and diamond-flashing fountain,—fit scenes for Boccaccio's tales of love,—with the gay forms of the cavaliers and ladies fair of Florence in her golden prime.

One of the most interesting visits which I made in Florence was to the once famous, now suppressed, Monastery of San Marco. It gave me the best insight that I got in Europe of the mediæval monastic life. Here were the cloisters in which the cowled brotherhood were wont to walk and con their breviary; the large bare refectory, with its pulpit for the reader, who edified the brethren while they "sat at meat," and the pious paintings on the wall; the scriptorium, with its treasures of vellum manuscripts and music; and the prison-like cells of the monks. One of these possessed a peculiar fascination. It was the bare, bleak cell of the martyr-monk Savonarola, the place of whose funeral pyre I had just seen in the great square. I sat in his chair; I saw his eagle-visaged portrait, his robes, his rosary, his crucifix, his Bible—richly annotated in his own fine, clear hand—and his MS. sermons which so shook the Papacy; and I seemed brought nearer to that heroic soul who kindled, four hundred years ago, a light in Italy that has not yet gone out.

Here, too, are the cell and many of the pictures of the saintly painter, Fra Angelico. The pure and holy faces of his angels, from which he derives his name, give an insight into his inner nature; for only in a saintly soul could such sacred fancies dwell. A Last Judgment, by this artist, greatly impressed me with its realistic power. Christ is throned aloft in a glory of angels. An archangel blows the trump of doom. The graves open, and the sheeted dead come forth. To the right, a rapturous throng of the saved sweep through asphodel meadows to the gates of Paradise, welcomed by shining seraph forms. To the left, devils drive the lost to caves of horror and despair, where "their tongues for very anguish they do gnaw," as described with such dreadful vividness by the burning pen of Dante.

Not among the "giants" of the time, but one of its tenderest and most loving spirits, is the "Angelic Brother" whose lovely frescoes of saints and angels and Madonnas still adorn these cells and corridors. He could not preach, but he could paint such beatific visions as fill our eyes with tears to-day. He "never touched his brush till he had steeped his inmost soul in prayer." Overcome with emotion, the tears often streamed down his face as he painted the seven sorrows of Mary, or the raptures of the saved. He would take no money for his work: it was its own exceeding great reward. When offered the archbishopric of Florence he humbly declined, and recommended for that dignity a brother monk. He died at Rome while sitting at his easel—caught away to behold with open face the beatific vision on which his inner sight so long had dwelt. The holy faces of his angels still haunt our memory with a spell of power.

Here, also, are the cells in which Cosmo I., a-weary of the world, retired to die, and that in which Pope Eugene slept four centuries ago. In the laboratory of the monastery are still prepared the drugs and medicines for which it was famous when all chemical knowledge was confined to the monkish brotherhood.

In the Church of San Lorenzo are the tombs of the Medician princes, on which have been lavished £1,000,000. Here are the masterpieces of Angelo, his Night and Day, which age after age keep their solemn watch in the chamber of the dead.

With the fortress-like Palazzo del Podesta, erected A.D. 1250, many tragic memories are linked. I stood in the chamber, originally a chapel, but for centuries a gloomy prison, in which the victims of tyranny languished and died; and saw the spot in the courtyard below where one of the greatest of the doges of Florence fell beneath the headsman's axe. It is now converted into a national museum, filled with treasures of art and historic relics. I was greatly impressed with a bronze figure of Mercury, "new lighted on a heaven-kissing hill!" Its äeriel grace and lightness were exquisite. Very different was the effect of a wonderfully realistic representation of the appalling scenes of the plague as described in Boccaccio's "Decameron." In looking at it, one could almost smell the foulness of the charnel house. Here also are the very telescopes and instruments of Galileo, and the crutches that supported the tottering steps of Michael Angelo, in his eighty-ninth year.

Among the more recent memories of this fair city is the fact that here Mrs. Browning, the greatest woman poet of all time, lived, and wrote, and died. I inquired at several book-stores and at the hotel for her house, but no one seemed to have ever heard of her. Mine host offered to look for her name in the directory.

I left with regret this lovely city, and took rail for Bologna, a ride of eighty miles. The route is one of the grandest in Italy, crossing the Appenines through a deep and romantic ravine, and passing through no less than forty-four tunnels. Bologna is one of the most quaint and mediæval looking cities of Italy. It has shared little of the modern progress of ideas of New Italy, and is the centre of a mouldy, reactionary ecclesiasticism; and here, appropriately, the Council of Trent held several of its sessions. It seems to have stood still for centuries while the rest of the world has been moving on. It has no less than one hundred and thirty churches, and twenty monasteries, and dates back before the Punic wars. Its University, which I visited, is one of the oldest in the world, founded in 1119. In 1262 it had ten thousand students;

it has now only four hundred. It was here that galvanism was discovered by Prof. Galvani, in 1789. It has had several distinguished lady professors, one of whom, Novella d'Andræa, is said to have been so beautiful that she lectured behind a curtain to prevent the distraction of the susceptible minds of the students. The narrow streets, the covered arcades on either side, the numerous old fortress-like palaces, the venerable churches with their lofty campaniles—all give a peculiar aspect to the city. In the choir of St. Petronio, a large dilapidated-looking church, begun in 1390, but never finished, Charles V. was crowned in 1530. Two leaning towers, quite close together, rise to a height respectively of one hundred and thirty-two, and two hundred and seventy-four feet. The latter, especially, as I sat at its base, seemed to soar aloft like a mast, and looked as if it would topple over on the huxter stalls beneath. Yet for seven centuries and a-half they have both hung poised, as it were, in air. Near by is St. Stephano, a group of seven connected churches, the oldest founded in the fifth century on the site of the temple of Isis. They are very odd, on different levels, and of mixed pagan and Christian styles of architecture. In one is a column which tradition affirms measures exactly the stature of our Lord. In the art gallery is Raphäel's celebrated St. Cecilia listening to the heavenly music in an ecstatic trance; but it failed to impress me very profoundly. As I lingered in an ancient square, a squadron of cavalry, with their long, plumed lances, galloped by—a strange contrast of the present with the past.

In going from Bologna to Venice we pass the decayed old city of Ferrara, with its mouldering palaces, its deserted streets, and its memories of Tasso, Ariosto, the princely house of Este, and the infamous Lucretia Borgia. At Padua, once next to Rome in wealth, the church of St. Antonio is larger than that of St. Mark's, at Venice. Indeed, the whole of Northern Italy is studded with cities of historic renown—Parma, Modena, Ravenna, Mantua, Pavia, Cremona, Verona—which it was tantalizing to be so near and yet not have time to see.

It is curious what different motives tourists have in travelling. I met three Roman Catholic priests, while on my way to Venice, who chose to forego the art treasures and immortal memories of Florence that they might make a long and expensive journey to the " Holy House of the Virgin," at Loretto. This Holy House is a small brick building, averred to have been brought by angels through the air, from Nazareth, first to Dalmatia, in 1291, and afterwards to Loretto. It is covered by a magnificent church, and surrounded by a gorgeous marble screen. The priests with whom I journeyed described with great enthusiasm its appearance. I ventured to question the reality of the alleged miracle, when one of them gravely assured me that there was quite as good ground for believing its genuinness as for believing in that of the Colosseum of Rome. But if anyone were to assure me that the Colosseum had been carried by angels a thousand miles through the air, I should take the liberty to question it. But it was useless to argue against such blind credulity as that of my travelling companions. They reminded me of the robust, unreasoning faith of one of the early Fathers, who said, "*Credo quia impossibile*—I believe, because it is impossible." The other great object of their pious pilgrimage was the Grotto of our Lady of Lourdes, away off in the Pyrenees, in all the fabulous stories about whom they seemed to have the most unquestioning faith.

CHAPTER VII.

Venice—Milan.

> There is a glorious City in the sea.
> The sea is in the broad, the narrow streets,
> Ebbing and flowing; and the salt sea-weed
> Clings to the marble of the palaces.
> No track of men, no footsteps to and fro,
> Lead to her gates. The path lies o'er the sea,
> Invisible; and from the land we went,
> As to a floating city—steering in,
> And gliding up her streets as in a dream,
> So smoothly, silently.
> —*Rogers.*

AS we glide along the iron way, eagerly scanning the horizon, a dark blue line of towers and churches, seeming to float upon the waves, comes gradually into view; and with a leap of the heart we greet "the longed-for, the most fair, the best beloved City of the Sea."

> "She looks a sea-Cybele fresh from ocean,
> Rising from her tiara of proud towers
> At airy distance with majestic motion,
> A ruler of the waters and their powers. . . . .
>
> I saw from out the wave her structures rise
> As at the stroke of the enchanter's wand:
> A thousand years their cloudy wings expand
> Around me, and a dying glory smiles
> O'er the far times, when many a subject land
> Looked to the wingèd Lion's marble piles
> Where Venice sat in state, throned on her hundred isles."

We quickly cross from the mainland, by a bridge over two miles long, to the far-famed Queen of the Adriatic.

In the fourth century a band of fishermen, flying from the ravages of Atilla, the Scourge of God, built their homes like waterfowl amid the waves. Bold, skilful, adventurous, they extended their commerce and conquests over the entire Levant; and soon, like an exhalation from the deep, rose the fair City of the Sea. During the Crusades the city rose to opulence by the trade thereby developed. In 1204 she became mistress of Constantinople and "held the gorgeous East in fee." The names of her merchant princes were familiar as household words in the bazaars of Damascus and Ispahan. Her marble palaces were gorgeous with the wealth of Ormuz and of Inde. Her daughters were clothed with the silks of Iran and the shawls of Cashmere. Their boudoirs were fragrant with the perfumes of Arabia Felix, and tuneful with the notes of the bulbul from the gardens of Schiraz; and her walls were glowing with the breathing canvas of Titian and Giorgione.

> "Her daughters had their dowers
> From spoils of nations, and the exhaustless East
> Poured in her lap all gems in sparkling showers.
> In purple was she robed, and of her feast
> Monarchs partook, and deemed their dignity increased."

In her golden prime Venice had forty thousand sailors, and her fleet carried the banner of St. Mark defiantly over every sea. At length the son of her ancient rival, Genoa, discovered a New World beyond the western wave, and snatched forever from Venice the keys of the commerce of the seas. Cadiz, Bristol, London, Amsterdam, became the new centres of trade; and the discrowned Queen of the Adriatic saw her glories fade away.

> "City of palaces, Venice, once enthroned
> Secure, a queen mid fence of flashing waters,
> Whom East and West with rival homage owned
> A wealthy mother with fair trooping daughters.
> What art thou now ? Thy walls are grey and old :
> In thy lone hall the spider weaves his woof,
> A leprous crust creeps o'er the house of gold.*
> And the cold rain drips through the pictured roof."

It is very odd on reaching Venice, instead of being driven to one's hotel in a noisy fiacre or rumbling omnibus, to be borne over the water streets, as smoothly as in a dream, in a luxurious gondola.† In the strange stillness there was a suggestion of mystery, as though the silent gliding figures that we passed were not living men of the present, but the ghosts of the dim generations of the shadowy past.

After dinner I sallied out for a sunset row upon the Grand Canal. I had only to step to the door and hold up my finger, when a gondolier, with a stroke of his oar, brought his bark to my feet. The charm of that first ride along that memory-haunted water way, whose beauties are portrayed in every gallery in Europe, will never be

---

* The celebrated *Ca d'Oro*, on the grand canal, so called on account of the richness of the decoration.

† An American lady is credited with the remark that she did not see Venice to advantage, because the streets were all flooded when she was there.

forgotten. I was alone—as one should be to let fancy conjure up the past. Onward I glided silently—

> " By many a dome
> Mosque-like and many a stately portico,
> The statues ranged along an azure sky;
> By many a pile of more than Eastern pride,
> Of old the residence of merchant kings.
> The fronts of some, though Time had shattered them,
> Still glowing with the richest hues of art,
> As though the wealth within them had run o'er."

Others were of a faded splendour wan, and seemed, Narcissus-like, to brood over their reflection in the wave. Here are the old historic palaces, whose very names are potent spells—the Palazzi Manzoni, Contarini, Foscari, Dandolo, Loredan, once the abodes of kings and doges and nobles. Here swept the bannered mediæval pageants as the doges sailed in gilded galley to the annual marriage of the Adriatic. There is the house, says tradition, of the hapless Desdemona. Now we glide beneath the Rialto, with its memories of Shylock, the Jew, and the Merchant of Venice. And

> " Now a Jessica
> Sings to her lute, her signal as she sits
> At her half-open lattice."

I directed the gondolier to stop at Gli Scalzi, a sumptuous church of the barefooted friars, and attended the singing of the Angelus. The scene was very impressive. The sweet-voiced organ filled the shadowy vaults with music. The tapers gleamed on the high altar, reflected by the porphyry and marble columns. A throng of worshippers knelt upon the floor and softly chanted the responses to the choir. And at that sunset hour the fishermen on the lagunes, the sailor on the sea, the peasant on the shore, the maiden at her book, the mother by her babe, pause as they list the vesper-bell and whisper the angel's salutation to the blessed among women.

As the sun went down I sailed out into the broad lagune, over the glowing waves which seemed like the sea of glass mingled with fire. The sunset fires burned out to ashen grey. The light faded from the sky; the towers and campaniles gleamed rosy red, then paled to spectral white; and the shadows crept over sea and land. The gondolier lit the lamp at the little vessel's prow, and rowed me back to my hotel through a labyrinth of narrow canals threading the Ghetto, or Jews' quarter, and the crowded dwellings of the poor. The twinkling lights from the lattices quivered on the waves, and the boatman devoutly crossed himself where the lamp burned before the rude shrine of the Madonna. As we traversed the narrow canals, the cries of the gondoliers to pass to the right or left—*preme,* or *stali*—were heard amid the darkness, and great skill was exhibited in avoiding collision. During the night, in the strange stillness of that silent city, without sound of horse or carriage, the distant strains of music, as some belated gondolier sang a snatch, perchance from Tasso or Ariosto, penetrated even the drowsy land of sleep, till I scarce knew whether my strange experience were real or but the figment of a dream.

The great centre and focus of Venetian life is the Piazza of St. Mark. It is a large stone-paved square, surrounded by the marble palaces of the ancient Republic. The only place in Venice large enough for a public promenade, it is crowded in the evening by a well-dressed throng of diverse nationalities, many of them in picturesque foreign costumes, listening to the military band, sipping coffee at the cafés, or lounging under the arcades. Among the throng may be seen jet-black Tunisians with their snowy robes; Turks with their fez and embroidered vests; Albanians, Greeks and Armenians; English, French, German, Russian, Austrian, and American tourists. The women of Venice have very regular features and fine classic profiles, a circumstance which I attribute to the large infusion of Greek blood arising from the intimate relations for centuries of the Republic with Greece and the Levant. They wear a graceful mantilla over their heads, in quite an oriental manner; and a dark bodice, scarlet kerchief, and frequently a yellow skirt and blue apron—a bright symphony of colour that would delight an artist's eye.

A curious illustration is here given of the permanence of European institutions and customs. An extraordinary number of pigeons will be seen nestling in the nooks and crannies of the surrounding buildings, perched on the façade of St. Mark, billing and cooing, and tamely hopping about almost under the feet of the promenaders. At two o'clock every day a large bell is rung, and instantly the whirr of wings is heard, and hundreds of snowy pigeons are seen flocking from all directions to an opening near the roof of the municipal palace, where they are fed by public dole. This beautiful custom, recalling the expression of Scripture, "flying as doves to their windows," has been observed during six stormy and changeful centuries. According to tradition, the old doge, Dandolo, in the thirteenth century, sent the tidings of the conquest of Candia by carrier pigeons to Venice, and by a decree of the Republic their descendants were ordered forever to be maintained at the expense of the State.

The glory of this stately square, however, is the grand historic church of St. Mark. All words of description must be tame and commonplace after Ruskin's glowing pen-picture of this glorious pile:—" A multitude of pillars and white domes, clustered into a long, low pyramid of coloured light; a treasure heap it seems, partly of gold, and partly of opal and mother-of-pearl, hollowed beneath into five great vaulted porches, ceiled with fair mosaic, and beset with sculptures of alabaster, clear as amber and delicate as ivory. And round the walls of the porches there are set pillars of variegated stones, jasper and porphyry and deep-green serpentine, spotted with flakes of snow, and marbles that half refuse and half yield to the sunshine, Cleopatra-like, their bluest veins to kiss,—the shadow, as it steals back from them, revealing line after line of azure undulation, as a receding tide leaves the waved sand; their capitals, rich with interwoven tracery, rooted knots of herbage, and drifting leaves of ancanthus and vine, and mystical signs all beginning and ending in the Cross; and above them in the broad archivolts a continuous chain of language and life—angels and the signs of heaven, and the labours of men, each in its appointed season upon the earth; and above these another range of glittering pinnacles, mixed with white arches edged with scarlet flowers—a confusion of delight amid which the breasts of the Greek horses are seen blazing in their breadth of golden strength, and the St. Mark's Lion lifted on a blue field covered with stars; until at last, as if in ecstasy, the crests of the arches break into a marble foam, and toss themselves far into the blue sky, in flashes and wreaths of sculptured spray, as if the breakers on the Lido shore had been frost bound before they fell, and the seanymphs had inlaid them with coral and amethyst."*

Above the great portal ramp the Greek bronze horses brought by Constantine to Byzantium, by Dandolo to Venice, by Napoleon to Paris, and restored to their present position by the Emperor Francis.

"They strike the ground resounding with their feet,
And from their nostrils breathe etherial flame."

As we cross the portico we step upon a porphyry slab, on which, seven centuries ago, the Emperor Barbarossa

---

* The Vandal-like proposal has recently been made to "restore" this matchless façade in modern workmanship. Such a vigorous protest, however, is raised against the scheme, that it will hardly be carried into execution.

knelt and received upon his neck the foot of Pope Alexander III., who chanted the while the versicle, "Thou shalt tread upon the lion and the adder, the young lion and the dragon shalt thou trample under foot." "To Saint Peter I kneel, not to thee," said the Emperor, stung with the humiliation. "To *me* and to Saint Peter," replied the haughty Pontiff, pressing once more his foot upon his vassal's neck. The proud monarch was then obliged to hold the stirrup of the priest as he mounted his ass, not "meek and lowly," like his master, but more haughty than earth's mightiest monarchs.

In that same porch the Doge, Dandolo, "near his hundredth year, and blind—his eyes put out—stood with his armour on," ere with five hundred gallant ships he sailed away, in his hand the gonfalon of Venice, which was soon to float in victory over the mosques and minarets of proud Byzantium. Here

> "In an after time, beside the doge,
> Sat one yet greater, one whose verse shall live
> When the wave rolls o'er Venice—
> The tuneful Petrarch crowned with laurel."

Let us enter the church. A vast and shadowy vault opens before us. The mosaic pavement heaves and falls in marble waves upon the floor. "The roof sheeted with gold, and the polished wall covered with alabaster," reflect the light of the altar lamps, "and the glories around the heads of the saints flash upon us as we pass them and sink into the gloom." The austere mosaics, some dating back to the tenth century, made the old church during long ages a great illuminated Bible—its burden the abiding truth, "Christ is risen!" "Christ shall come!" "Not in the wantonness of wealth," writes Ruskin, "were those marbles hewn into transparent strength, and those arches arrayed in the colours of the iris. There is a message written in the dyes of them that once was written in blood; and a sound in the echoes of their vaults that one day shall fill the vault of heaven—' He shall return to do judgment and justice.'" The old church was to the unlettered people a visible "image of the Bride, all glorious within, her raiment of wrought gold."

I lingered for hours, spell-bound, studying the antique frescoes of patriarchs, prophets, kings, apostles, martyrs, angels and dragons, forms beautiful and terrible, the whole story of the Old and New Testament, the life and miracles of Christ, and the final glories and terrors of the Apocalypse; and listening the while to the chanting of the priests and the solemn cadence of the organ and choir. On the high altar are reliefs of the eleventh century, containing nearly three hundred figures; and alabaster columns, according to tradition, from the temple of Solomon, through which the light of a taper shines; and underneath are the so-called tomb and relics of St. Mark. I stood in the ancient pulpit, descended into the dim weird crypts, and climbed to the corridor that goes around the building within and without, and felt to the full the the spell of this old historic church.

In the piazza rises, to the height of over three hundred feet, the isolated square campanile of St. Mark, from which I enjoyed a magnificent sunset view of the city, the lagunes, the curving shore of the Adriatic, and the distant Tyrolese and Julian Alps. A tourist, with an artist's eye, and poet's pen, thus describes the beauty of the scene. "The burning sunset turns all the sky to opal, all the churches to pearl, all the sea to crimson and gold. The distant mountains glow like lines of lapis lazuli washed with gold; the islands are bowers of greenery, springing from the bosom of the purple waves. Great painted saffron and crimson sails come out from the distance, looking in the sunlight like the wings of some gigantic tropical bird; flowers and glittering ornaments hang at the mast head; everywhere you hear music and song, the splash of swift oars, the hum of human voices; everywhere you drink in the charm, the subtle intoxication, the glory of this beloved queen among the nations." For six centuries and more the grey old tower, which Galileo used to climb, has looked down upon the square, the scene of so many stately pageants. It has witnessed the doges borne in their chairs of state, and borne upon their biers; triumphal fêtes and funeral processions; the madness of the masquerade and carnival; and the tragedy of the scaffold and the headsman's axe.

Near the church is the far-famed Palace of the Doges, with its stately banquet chambers and council halls. Ascending the grand stairway on which the doges were crowned, where the venerable Faliero in his eightieth year was executed, and down which rolled his gory head, and the Scala d'Oro, which only the nobles inscribed in the Golden Book were permitted to tread, we enter the great galeries filled with paintings of the triumphs of Venice, her splendour, pomp, and pride, and portraits of seventy-six doges. Here is the largest painting in the world, the "Paradise" of Tintoretto, crowded with hundreds of figures. The halls of the Senate, the Council of Ten, and of the Inquisitors of the Republic, with their historic frescoes, their antique furniture and fine caryatides supporting the marble mantels, and their memories of glory and of tyranny, all exert a strange fascination over the mind. In the splendid library I saw a copy of the first printed edition of Homer, and rare old specimens of the famous Aldine classics.

Crossing the gloomy Bridge of Sighs, I entered the still more gloomy prison of the doges, haunted with the spectres of their murdered victims. There are two tiers of dungeons—one below the level of the canal, whose sullen waves could be heard by the prisoner lapping against the walls of his cell. The guide showed the instruments of torture, the hideous apparatus of murder, the channels made for the flowing blood, the secret opening by which bodies of the victims were conveyed to the canal, and the cell in which the Doge Marino Faliero was confined. In the latter, he told me, although I doubt the story, that Byron once spent forty-eight hours, that he might gain inspiration for his gloomy tragedy upon the subject. The guide took away his taper for a time, that I might realize the condition of the unhappy prisoner. The darkness was intense, and could almost be felt. A very few minutes was long enough for me.

The ancient arsenal is an interesting relic of the golden prime of Venice. It once employed 16,000 men, and Dante compares the Stygian smoke of the Inferno to that from its seething caldrons of tar. In its magazine are the remains of the *Bucentaur*, the golden galley with three hundred rowers, from which the doge, arrayed in more than oriental pomp, used annually to wed the Adriatic by throwing into it a ring, with the words, "*Desponsumus te, mare, in signum veri perpetuique dominii*".—"We wed thee, O Sea, in token of our true and perpetual sovereignty."

> "The spouseless Adriatic mourns her lord;
> And, annual marriage now no more renewed,
> The *Bucentaur* lies rotting unrestored,
> Neglected garment of her widowhood."

The swords of the Foscari, the armour of the doges, the iron helmet of Attila, the "oriflammes that fluttered in the hot breath of battle in the days of the crusades," and other relics of the past, are also shown. At the gate is seen an antique lion from the plain of Marathon.

Many of the other churches of Venice, as well as St. Mark's, are of great interest, especially those containing the sumptuous tombs of the doges and the monuments of

Titian and Canova. In one epitaph I read the significant words, "The terror of the Greeks lies here." I visited also the great hospital of St. Mark, with six hundred patients well cared for in the magnificent apartments of a mediæval palace.

The people whom I saw in the churches seemed very devout and very superstitious. I saw one woman rub and kiss the calico dress of an image of the Virgin with seven swords in her heart, as if in hope of deriving spiritual efficacy therefrom. I saw another exposing her sick child to the influence of a relic held in the hands of a priest, just as she would hold it to a fire to warm it. On the Rialto, once the commercial exchange, " where merchants most do congregate," now lined on either side with small huxter shops, I bought, as a souvenir, a black-faced Byzantine image of the Virgin. I had previously bought at Naples, for the modest sum of a penny, a couple of scapulars—a much-prized charm against sickness and danger. I visited two of the private palaces on the Grand Canal, whose owners were summering in Switzerland or at some German spa. Everything was as the family left it, even to the carved chessmen set out upon the board. The antique furniture, rich tapestry, and stamped leather arras, the paintings and statuary, seemed relics of the golden time when the merchant kings of Venice were lords of all the seas.

Two of the most interesting industries of Venice are the mosaic factory on the Grand Canal, and the glass works on the Island of Murano. The mosaic is made of glass cubes, of which, I was told, 10,000 different shades were employed to imitate the colours of the paintings to be copied. The result, however, was less beautiful than at the stone mosaic factory which I visited at Florence. The Venetian glass work is of wonderful delicacy and beauty; and the flowers, portraits and other designs, which are spun by the yard and which appear on the surface of the cross section, are of almost incomprehensible ingenuity and skill.

As I was rowed out to Murano, I passed on a lonely island, the cemetery of Venice. How dreary must their funerals be—the sable bark like that which bore Elaine, " the lily maid of Astolat," gliding with muffled oars across the sullen waves.

The gondola, in its best estate, is a sombre funereal-looking bark, draped in solemn black, its steel-beaked prow curving like a swan's neck from the wave. Its points are thus epitomized by Byron :—

> "'Tis a long covered boat that's common here,
>   Carved at the prow, built lightly but compactly,
> Rowed by two rowers, each called a gondolier;
>   It glides along the water looking blackly,
>   Just like a coffin clapped in a canoe
> Where none can make out what you say or do."

There are, of course, no wells in Venice, except an Artesian boring; but in each parish is a stone cistern, which is filled every night by a water boat from the mainland. The iron cover over this is unlocked every morning by the priest of the neighbouring church; and one of the most picturesque sights of the city is to see the girls and women tripping to the wells, with two brass vessels supported by a yoke upon their shoulders, for the daily supply of water.

Gliding along a lateral canal in my gondola one day, I saw on a wall the words "Methodist Chapel." I soon after found it out. It was a private house in a very narrow street. I introduced myself, and was very warmly greeted by the worthy pastor, the Rev. Henry Borelly, and his wife. They were both Italian, but spoke French fluently. They represent the Methodist Episcopal Church of the United States. They showed me the chapel, a very comfortable room which would hold two hundred persons; but they spoke of the great discouragements and difficulties under which they laboured, and asked for the prayers of the Methodists of America on their behalf. After a very agreeable interview, Mr. Borelly courteously accompanied me back to my hotel, and gave me at parting a hearty God speed and "*bon voyage.*"

On the last evening before I left Venice, I sailed in a glowing sunset to the Lido shore. In the golden radiance, the marble city seemed transfigured to chrysophrase and alabaster, reflected in the glassy wave. The purple curtains of the night closed round the scene, and only the long line of twinkling lights revealed where the Sea Queen lay. It was with a keen regret that I tore myself away; for no spot in Italy, I think, exercises such a potent fascination over mind and heart. " There can be no farewell to scenes like these."

From Venice to Milan is a railway ride of one hundred and seventy-five miles. The principal town on the route is Verona, a decayed and poverty-stricken place, with a population of 60,000. Its chief sights are its vast amphitheatre, which could hold 100,000 persons; the tomb of the Scaligers, the house of the Capulets, and the tomb of Shakespeare's Juliet. Proceeding from Verona, we have a good survey of the Lago de Garda, on whose banks was fought the fierce battle of Solferino, 1859.

Milan, the capital of Lombardy, is one of the most ancient and most interesting towns in Italy, dating from the sixth century B.C. Since the fourth century A.D., it has surpassed, both in extent and importance, Rome itself. It became an imperial residence, and the Church of Milan was long the rival of that of Rome. It has now 300,000 inhabitants, and is the most progressive city of the peninsula, the representative of New Italy, with its energy, its aspirations, its civil and religious liberty.

Of course the great attraction of Milan is its celebrated cathedral, and to it I first of all made my way. There it stood in the great square with its hundred glistening pinnacles and two thousand marble statues, like some exquisite creation of frostwork, which one might almost expect to see melt and disappear. The Milanese call it the eighth wonder of the world. Next to St. Peter's at Rome and the Cathedral at Seville, it is the largest church in Europe.

As I entered the vast and shadowy interior, the transition from the hot glare of the stone-paved piazza without to the cool and "dim religious light" cast by the "storied windows richly dight" was most refreshing. At first one can but dimly see the sweeping lines of the arches meeting one hundred and fifty feet above his head, and the cave-like vault of the chancel, with its sapphire-and-ruby-coloured traceried windows. High above the altar hung in air a life-sized image of our Lord upon a golden cross. Full upon the face of Christ fell a beam of light from the great rose window in the western façade, bringing it into brilliant contrast with the dark background. Rembrandt never executed anything so beautiful—nay, so sublime—as that glorified face of the Divine Sufferer, irradiating the darkness and scattering the gloom. It was a symbol and a prophecy, I thought, of the time when the glorious manifestation of our Lord, undimmed by the clouds of human ignorance and superstition, should scatter the darkness and shine forth in all His true Divinity. It was the most impressive interior I saw in Europe; and when the chanting of the choir and music of the organ sounded through the long drawn aisles and fretted vaults, the effect was indescribably sublime.

Under the altar is the shrine and tomb of the good bishop St. Charles Borromeo; and for the sum of five francs those who are curious in such matters may see his mummy-like remains, blazing with jewellery, in ghastly mockery of death. Of noble rank and immense wealth, he devoted himself to the temporal and spiritual welfare of his diocese; and when the secular magistrates fled from the presence of the plague, he fell a martyr to his zeal in ministering to the dying and burying the dead. He is regarded as the first founder of Sunday-schools, and every Sunday, in one of the chapels of the cathedral, the children are instructed and catechised to the present.day. His tomb is visited as a sacred shrine, and his monument in hollow bronze, a hundred and twelve feet high, crowns a neighbouring height.

From the roof of the cathedral is obtained one of the finest views of the whole range of the Alps to be anywhere had, their sharp serrated outline clearly cut against the sky. The roof is studded with a perfect grove of pinnacles, flying buttresses and statues, all beautifully finished, notwithstanding their inaccessible positions, " for the gods see everywhere." The solid marble is fretted into a lace-like tracery or filagree in stone. This part, the guides call " the flower garden," and it truly seems as if the marble had blossomed into beauty at the artist's touch.

The most interesting church in Milan, on account of its historic associations, is that of San Ambrogio, founded on the site of a temple of Bacchus by St. Ambrose in the fourth century. The old Lombard architecture is very quaint and sometimes very rude, especially the ancient stone pulpit and the episcopal throne. The mosaics, dating from the ninth century, have a very stiff and infantile expression, like the inartistic drawing of a child. In the nave on a column is a brazen serpent, averred to be that raised by Moses in the wilderness, although I was of opinion that that had been broken to pieces by King Hezekiah, (see II. Kings xviii. 4). The rude bronze doors of the church are, more plausibly, said to be those which St. Ambrose closed against the Emperor Theodosius on account of the cruel massacre of Thessalonica. The Emperor remonstrated that even David had been guilty of bloodshed. " You have imitated David in his crime," replied the undaunted Ambrose, "imitate him also in his repentance;" and for eight months the lord of the world did penance on this very spot. Through this portal also passed Augustine, to be baptized by St. Ambrose in the presence of his mother, Monica.

It was a great festa the day I was there. The church was full, and a crowd of ecclesiastics took part in the service, chanting the same Ambrosian hymns which for fifteen centuries have been sung upon this spot. Few things which I saw so linked the present with the past as did this.

In the refectory of the suppressed monastery of Santa Maria della Grazia, now a cavalry barrack, I saw the original " Last Supper " of Leonardo da Vinci, one of the most celebrated paintings in the world, so familiar by copies in almost every house. It is painted in oils upon the wall, and is much injured by time. Yet it is full of sublime expression. There is a beauty, a grandeur, a majesty enthroned in the face of our Lord, that is reproduced in none of the copies, although not less than a score of these, of rare excellence, were in the room. It is one of the grandest paintings I ever saw. In a neighbouring square is a noble statue of Da Vinci, and near it a magnificent gallery, or sort of crystal palace, lined on either side with elegant shops, and crowned at the intersection of its arms by a glass dome one hundred and eighty feet high. Structures of this kind are very common in Europe, but this is the finest of them all.

I visited also the celebrated Ospedale Maggiore, one of the largest hospitals in existence, having accommodation, I was told, for 2,400 patients. Its façade, like that of several other Milanese buildings, was entirely covered with bright red terra-cotta mouldings, tracery, etc., and adorned with a great number of busts. A large arena for races and the like, constructed by Napoleon I., in imitation of the ancient amphitheatres, will afford seats for 30,000 persons. It is a curious illustration of the Cæsarism of the modern Colossus, who would bestride the world in imitation of the ancient despots of mankind.

CHAPTER VIII.

THE ITALIAN LAKES—ST. GOTTHARD PASS—MEMORIES OF TELL—
LAKE OF THE FOUR CANTONS—THE RIGHI—LUCERNE.

THE Italian lakes, Como, Lugano, and Maggiore, have challenged the admiration of poet and painter from the days of Virgil to the present time. Less sublime in their environment than those of Switzerland, they are far more beautiful. The surrounding foliage, also, is much richer; the orange and myrtle take the place of the spruce and the pine. The sky is of a sunnier blue, and the air of a balmier breath, and the water of a deeper and more transparent hue.

Lake Como is only an hour's ride from Milan, through a fertile and hilly country. *En route* we pass the ancient town of Monza, where is preserved the iron crown with which Constantine, Charlemagne, Charles V., and Napoleon, besides two score of Lombard kings, have been crowned. Como, which lies amid an amphitheatre of hills, was the birthplace of the elder and younger Pliny. The mountains rise in verdurous slopes, clothed to their summits with chestnuts and olives, to the height of 7,000 feet. At their base nestle the gay villas of the Milanese aristocracy, embowered amid lemon and myrtle groves. Lovely bays, continued into winding valleys, run up between the jutting capes and towering mountains. The richest effects of glowing light and creeping shadows, like the play of smiles on a lovely face, give expression to the landscape. Like a swift shuttle, the steamer darts across

HIGH STREET, SWISS VILLAGE.

the narrow lake from village to village. The glowing sunlight, the warm tints of the frescoed villas, the snowy campaniles, and the gay costumes, mobile features, and animated gestures of the peasantry, gave a wondrous life and colour to the scene.

On a high and jutting promontory is Bellagio, the culminating point of beauty on the lake. After dinner at the Hotel *Grande Bretagne*, whose windows command one of the loveliest views I ever beheld, I set forth with a companion for a sunset sail on fair Como. Softly crept the purple shadows over wave and shore. Gliding beneath the lofty cliffs, our boatman woke the echoes with his song. Snowy sails glided by like sheeted ghosts in the deepening twilight. At nine o'clock the Benediction rang from the village campaniles—one after another taking up the strain—now near, now far, the liquid notes floating over the waves like the music of the spheres. As we listened in silence, with suspended oar, to the solemn voices calling to us through the darkness—

> We heard the sounds of sorrow and delight,
> The manifold soft chimes
> That fill the haunted chambers of the night
> Like some old poet's rhymes.

Next day we crossed by private carriage, with jangling bells and quaint harness on our horses, from Lake Como to Lakes Lugano and Maggiore—a delightful drive, up hill and down, through romantic scenery and picturesque villages. At the top of one long, steep slope, commanding a map-like view of the winding Como far beneath, our driver stopped beneath an iron-grated window of an ancient church. Behind the grating were about a hundred skulls, and just opposite, a receptacle for money, with a petition for alms for the repose of the souls of the former owners of those skulls. It was the most extraordinary

ITALIAN-SWISS VILLAGE.

appeal *ad misericordiam* that I ever saw. Two or three times during the day we crossed the frontier between Italy and Switzerland, with its inevitable guard-house and knot of soldiers.

A charming sail on Lake Maggiore, with magnificent views of the distant snow-clad Alps, brought us in the evening to Isola Bella—" the beautiful island." In the seventeenth century, a famous Count Borromeo converted this barren crag into a garden of delight. It rises in ten terraces a hundred feet above the lake; and is stocked with luxuriant orange and lemon trees, cypresses, laurels, magnolias, magnificent oleanders, and fragrant camphor

ARMS OF ITALY AT BOUNDARY LINE.

trees. Fountains, grottoes, and statuary adorn this lovely spot. We found the chateau and gardens closed; but by dint of perseverance we effected an entrance, and, by a judicious fee, obtained permission to explore the beauties of the scene. Near by is the many-turreted chateau of Baveno, where Queen Victoria was an honoured guest during her recent visit to Italy.

In the after-glow of a golden sunset, we were rowed by a pirate-looking boatman to Stresa, where I parted with my companion in travel, he crossing the Alps by the Simplon route, and I by the St. Gotthard Pass.

On a lofty hill near the lake, overlooking the country which he loved so well, is a colossal statue of St. Charles Borromeo, one hundred and twelve feet high, his hand stretched out in perpetual benediction upon its hamlets and villages.

Traversing the entire length of Lake Maggiore, between towering mountains on either side, I took the train for Biasca, the present terminus of the railway. The road follows the winding valley of the Ticino. The scenery is a blending of Alpine grandeur, with soft Italian beauty. Villas, churches, and ancient castles crown the neighbouring heights. Snowy cascades gleam through the dense foliage and leap headlong from the cliffs. Huge fallen rocks bestrew the valley, as though the Titans had here piled Pelion on Ossa, striving to storm the skies.

From the dining-table of the hotel at Biasca, I looked up and up to a cliff towering hundreds of feet above my head, making at night a deeper blackness in the air, from which leaped with a single bound a snowy waterfall. Before sunset I set out for my first Alpine climb. A steep winding path ascended the hill to a pilgrimage chapel. Along the wayside were a number of shrines adorned with glaring frescoes, and rudely carved pathetic dead Christs, with an offering of withered flowers before them. I gathered some beautiful anemones, which swung their censers in the mountain air, and drank deep delight from the sublimity of the prospect. Coming down I lost the path, when a peasant woman, mowing in the fields, kindly dropped her scythe and tripped down the steep slope to point out the narrow winding way. It led me down to a little group of houses, rudely built of stone, and covered with heavy stone slabs instead of shingles. Indeed, stone seems more plentiful than wood; it is used for fences, bridges, supports for vine trellis, etc. One of the peasants, at my request, showed me his house. It was very comfortless, with bare floors and rude home-made furniture. He showed me also his stock of wooden shoes and his silkworms' eggs, for he eked out a living by winding silk. A very old Romanesque church crowned a neighbouring height, with a giant St. Christopher frescoed on the wall; beside it was the quiet God's acre, in which for long centuries—

"The peaceful fathers of the hamlet sleep."

Early next morning I climbed to my seat on the top of the lumbering *diligence* in which I was to cross the Alps. The *diligence* is a huge vehicle with broad-tired wheels, set about six feet apart to prevent upsetting, and formidable with brakes, and drags, and chains, suggestive of mountain perils. It is like a stage coach, with another coach cut in two and placed part in front and part aloft behind. The luggage is stored on a strong deck on top. I was fortunate in securing a place outside, *en banquette* as it is called, but I gave it up to two fellow-tourists condemned to the *interieur*, and sat with the guard upon the luggage. We rattled through the squalid, stone paved, ill-smelling town, and through many like it, climbing ever higher and higher. The Ticino, whose banks the road follows, tears its way down in foaming cataracts of the wildest character through a mountain cleft. There is not even room for the road, which is carried through tunnels, or on arches over the boiling flood. On either side the milky torrents stream down the mountain side, "like tears of gladness o'er a giant's face." I noticed far up a distant slope a huge cross, like a sign of consecration, formed of snow drifts.

At Airolo, where we stopped for lunch, a peasant fair was in progress, and the costumes of both men and women were very picturesque. Some of the women wear a most extraordinary tiara of silver, almost like a nimbus, on their heads. Here is the southern end of the St. Gotthard Tunnel, some nine miles long which pierces the mountain, and has this year been opened. From this point we climb to the summit of the pass by some ve irty zigzags, dragged up by seven stout horses, which c.fr advance no faster than a slow walk. Ever wider horizons open on every side. The vines and chestnuts, the mulberries and olives are left far below. The trees of my native land, the pines and spruces, assert their reign.

They climb in serried ranks; and on lone inaccessible heights stand majestic and sublime, grappling firm foot-

IN THE HIGH ALPS.

hold on the everlasting rocks, and bidding defiance to the winds of heaven. These in turn become dwarfed and disappear, and only the beautiful Alpine rose clothes the rocks, like humble virtue breathing its beauty amid a cold and unfriendly environment. Vast upland meadows and mountain pastures are covered with these beautiful flowers. At last even these give way to the icy desolation of eternal winter. We passed through snow-drifts over thirty feet deep, and from the top of the *diligence* I could gather snowballs; and once the road led through a tunnel in the snow. Only the chamois and the mountain eagle dwell amid these lone solitudes.

The change from the burning plains of Lombardy to these Alpine solitudes—from lands of sun to lands of snow—was very striking. I thank God for the revelation of His might and majesty in those everlasting mountains. They give a new sense of vastness, of power, of sublimity to the soul. After busy months spent in crowded cities— the work of men—it is a moral tonic to be brought face to face with the grandest works of God. Yet even to this sanctuary of nature the warring passions of man have found their way. In 1799, the Russian General, Suwarrow, led an army through these bleak defiles, and on a huge rock near the summit is engraven the legend, SUWARROW VICTOR. Several stone defences against avalanches, and refuges for storm-stayed travellers, also occur.

At the summit of the pass, 7,000 feet above the sea, is a large and gloomy Italian inn, and near it a *hospice*, erected by the Canton, containing fifteen beds for poor travellers, who are received gratuitously. I made my way up the dark stairway, in an exploring mood, and came to the conclusion that they must be very poor travellers who take refuge in these dismal cells. In a large room I found a telegraph office and signal station, and was told that in that bleak outpost the sentinels of civilization kept their

IN ST. GOTTHARD PASS.

lonely watch the long winter through. At this great height are several small lakes, fed from the snow-clad mountains which tower all around. Passing the summit, our huge vehicle rattles down a desolate valley in a very alarming manner, threatening, as it turns the sharp angles, to topple over the low wall into the abyss below. But strong arms are at the brakes, and after ten miles' descent we dash into the little Alpine village of Andermatt.

I wished to see before dark the celebrated "Devil's Bridge" across the Reuss, so I hurried on without waiting for dinner. The bridge is a single stone arch, which leaps across a brawling torrent at a giddy height above the water. The scenery is of the wildest and grandest character. On either side rise in tremendous cliffs the everlasting battlements of rock. Against these walls of adamant the tortured river hurls itself, and plunges into an abyss a hundred feet deep. A scene of more appalling desolation it is scarce possible to conceive. Yet a sterner aspect has been given by the wrath of man. Here, amid these sublimities of nature, was fought a terrible battle between the French and Russians in 1799. The river ran red with blood, and hundreds of soldiers were hurled into the abyss and drowned, or dashed to pieces. As I stood and watched the raging torrent in the twilight, made the darker by the shadows of the steep mountain cliffs, I seemed to see the poor fellows struggling with their fate in the dreadful gorge.

The legend of the building of the *Teufelsbrucke* is thus recorded in Longfellow's "Golden Legend:"—

> This bridge is called the Devil's Bridge.
> With a single arch from ridge to ridge
> It leaps across the terrible chasm
> Yawning beneath it black and deep,
> As if in some convulsive spasm

> The summits of the hills had cracked,
> And made a road for the cataract
> That raves and rages down the steep.
> Never any bridge but this
> Could stand across the wild abyss;
> All the rest of wood or stone,
> By the Devil's hand were overthrown.
> He toppled crags from the precipice;
> And whatsoever was built by day,
> In the night was swept away;
> None could stand but this alone.
> Abbot Giraldus, of Einsiedel,
> For pilgrims on their way to Rome,
> Built this at last, with a single arch,
> Under which, in its endless march,
> Runs the river white with foam,
> Like a thread through the eye of a needle.
> And the Devil promised to let it stand,
> Under compact and condition
> That the first living thing which crossed
> Should be surrendered into his hand
> And be beyond redemption lost.
> At length, the bridge being all completed,
> The Abbot, standing at its head,
> Threw across it a loaf of bread,
> Which a hungry dog sprang after;
> And the rocks re-echoed with peals of laughter
> To see the Devil thus defeated.

I returned about nine o'clock to the quaint old Swiss hotel, the "Drei Könige" or "Three Kings," and enjoyed a good dinner after a hard day's work. I was shown up the winding stair to my room, in which was an old-fashioned high bedstead with a feather bed on top by way of comforter. And very glad I was to crawl under it, for the air was very cold.

The morning broke bright and clear. From the quaint

IN THE SCHÖLLENEN PASS.

little windows of the hotel I looked out upon a rapid stream rushing swiftly below, and down the village street. The houses had all broad overhanging roofs, with carved gables and timbers, and had altogether a very comfortable and hospitable look.

The ride from Andermatt to Flüellen, on Lake Lucerne, was, I think, the finest I ever had in my life. The snow-clad mountains, the dark green forests, the deep valleys, the foaming torrents and waterfalls, the bright sunshine, made up a picture of sublimity and beauty which I thank God for permitting me to behold. In one narrow defile —the Schöllenen—precipices rise a thousand feet in the air, and the snowy Reuss raves along its channel far below. In four leagues the river descends 2,500 feet. The road winds along the edge of the chasm, or boldly leaps across in a single arch. Far up the mountain sides can be seen the mountain cattle and goats, on slopes so steep that you wonder they do not slide down. The loftier summits glisten with their crown of snow, or are swathed in a mantle of cloud. Human moles are everywhere busy delving and tunnelling for the St. Gotthard Railway. The firing of blasts, sometimes so near that I feared they would startle our horses, woke the echoes of the mountains. Waggons loaded with timber, wheelbarrows, spades, pick-axes, and railway plant, almost blocked the narrow road.

The whole region is rife with legends of William Tell. On our way we passed through the little village of Alt-dorf, where he is said to have shot the apple off his son's head. Critics try to make us believe that this never happened, because a similar story is told in the Hindoo mythology. But I am not going to give up my faith in Tell. I was shown the village in which he was born, and his statue, with a crossbow in his hand, erected on the very spot where he is said to have fired the arrow. A hundred and fifty paces distant is a fountain, on the place where his son is said to have stood with the apple on his head. After all this, how can I help believing the grand old story? I crossed the noisy Saachen, in which, when an old man, he was drowned while trying to save the life of a little child—a death worthy of his heroic fame.

At Flüellen, the grandeur of the Lake of the Four Forest Cantons—*Vierwaldstätter-See*—or, as it is also called, the Lake of Uri, bursts upon the view. The mountains rise abruptly from the lake, from eight to ten thousand feet. I walked some miles along the Axenstrasse— a road hewn in the mountain side, high above the lake, and beneath tremendous overhanging cliffs of tortured strata, which in places are pierced by tunnels—and lingered for hours enchanted with the blended beauty and sublimity of the views. With quickened pulse of expectation, I descended the cliff to the site of the far-famed Tell's Chapel, so familiar in pictures. But what was my disappointment to find not one stone left on another! That great modern destroyer of the romantic, a railway, was being constructed along the lake margin, and the time-honoured chapel, said to be five hundred years old, had been removed. A workman showed me the plans of a brand new one which was to be erected near the spot; which I felt to be almost sacrilege.

Embarking at Flüellen, I sailed down the memory-haunted lake, passing the field of Rütli, where, five hundred years ago, the midnight oath was taken by the men of Uri, which was the first bond of the Swiss Confederacy; and further on the monument of Schiller, the bard of Tell. The lake lies like a huge St. Andrew's cross among the mountains, which rise abruptly from its deep, dark waves—

> That sacred lake, withdrawn among the hills,
> Its depth of waters flanked as with a wall,
> Built by the giant race before the flood,
> Each cliff and headland and green promontory
> Graven with the records of the past;
> Where not a cross or chapel but inspires
> Holy delight, lifting our thoughts to God
> From godlike men.

The whole region is a sanctuary of liberty. Memories of Sempach and Morgarten and Rütli; of Winkelried and Fürst and Tell; of purest patriotism and heroic valour, forever hallow this lovely land.

I stopped at Vitznau to ascend the Righi, 5,906 feet above the sea. A railway leads from the picturesque village to the summit. The engine climbs up by means of a cog-wheel, which catches into teeth on the track. In one place it crosses a skeleton iron bridge. As we climb higher and higher, the view widens, till, as we round a shoulder of the mountain, there bursts upon the sight a wondrous panorama of mountain, lakes, and meadows, studded with chalets, villages and hamlets, and distant towns. As the sun went down, a yellow haze, like gold dust, filled the air and glorified the entire landscape. The view in fine weather sweeps a circle of 300 miles, and commands an unrivalled prospect of the whole Bernese Oberland. But just as we reached the summit, we plunged into a dense mist, and groped our way to a huge hotel which loomed vaguely through the fog. Here, a mile high among the clouds, a hundred and sixty guests—English, French, German, Russian, and American, and of every grade of rank—sat down to a sumptuous *table d'hôte* in the highest hotel in Europe, and one of the finest. A perfect Babel of languages was heard, and in the bed-rooms the following unique announcement was posted :—" Considering the great affluence [influx] of visitors from all nations to this house, we beg [you] to take goode care and to lock well the door during the night." It was bitter cold, and the wind howled and moaned without, but in the elegant *salons* the music, mirth, and gaiety seemed a strange contrast to the bleakness of the situation.

At four o'clock in the morning, the unearthly sound of an Alpine horn rang through the corridors, and a motley group of shivering mortals turned out to witness the glories of the sun-rise. The strangely-muffled forms that paced the summit of the mountain, bore slight resemblance to the elegantly dressed ladies and gallant carpet knights of the evening before. Tantalizing glimpses of the glorious panorama were caught through rifts in the swirling clouds; but sullen and grim they swathed us round, and sullen and grim we crept back to bed. Dr. Cheever, who was favoured with a fine view of this revelation of glory, says: "It was as if an angel had flown round the horizon of mountain ranges and lighted up each of their pyramidal peaks in succession, like a row of gigantic cressets, burning with rosy fires. A devout soul might also have felt, seeing these fires kindled on the altars of God, as if it heard the voice of the Seraphim crying, 'Holy, holy, holy is the Lord of hosts, the whole earth is full of His glory.'"

I had the good fortune after breakfast to get a fine view of the landscape. Beneath me, like a map, lay Lakes Zug, Lucerne, Sempach, and half a score of others, with their towns and villages; and in the distance the whole range of the Bernese Alps. The nearer view—now flecked with sun, now gloomed with shade—was a vision of delight, whose memory can never fade. The faint, far-tolling of the bells and lowing of the kine floated softly up, and all the beauty of the "incense-breathing morn" unfolded itself to the sight. One hundred and thirty mountain peaks are visible; within nearer view is Sempach, where Winkelried gathered a sheaf of Austrian spears in his arms, then buried them in his bosom, and "death made way for liberty." And there was the wild Morgarten fight in 1315, where 1,300 brave Switzers repulsed from their mountain vales 20,000 of the Austrian chivalry; and there is Cappel, where Zwingle, the great

Swiss Reformer, fell pierced by 150 wounds. His body lay all night upon the field of battle, and next day was tried for heresy, was burned, and the ashes mingled with those of swine, and scattered on the wandering winds. The view from Mount Washington, in New Hampshire, is more extensive, and in some respects more grand, but it is by no means so beautiful, and above all has not the thrilling historic memories.

Taking the steamer again, I soon reached Lucerne. Its ancient walls, and towers, and battlements climbing the slopes of the surrounding hills, and the dark background of Mount Pilatus, are very imposing. According to tradition, Pontius Pilate, when banished from Galilee, fled thither, and in the bitterness of his remorse committed suicide upon this desolate mountain. The ascent of the mountain was long forbidden by the government of Lucerne, lest the intrusion on the dark domain of the gloomy suicide, from whose soul not all the waters of the mighty deep could wash the damning guilt of his judicial murder of the Innocent One, should rouse the wrath of Heaven in storms upon the city at its feet. But the audacity of Napoleon invaded this mountain solitude, to procure a supply of timber for his shipyards. A trough eight miles long was made out of 30,000 trees, extending to the water's edge. Down this, logs and trunks of trees were shot, traversing, with a roar like thunder, the eight miles in six minutes. If one escaped from the trough it cut down the standing trees like a cannon ball.

Lucerne is a quaint old town of 15,000 inhabitants. Many of the houses are built of carved timber, with the upper stories projecting, and with broad overhanging eaves. Through it rushes with arrowy swiftness the River Reuss. The river is spanned by four bridges, two of which have long covered arcades, the spandrils in the roof being decorated with very strange paintings. One series of 154 represents scenes from the Scriptures and from Swiss history. The other series represents Holbien's celebrated " Dance of Death." The paintings are accompanied by descriptive German verses. Death is represented as a skeleton, masquerading in a variety of characters. He arrests a gaily-dressed gallant going to a festival, while the guests wait in vain ; he lays his bony hand on an infant in the cradle, while the mother, filled with trepidation draws near ; dressed in plumes and velvet doublet he confronts a warrior on his horse ; he appears as a spectre at a banquet ; he holds aloft an hourglass to a reveller ; he tears a banner from the grasp of a mail-clad warrior, and rides victorious through a battle-scene. With a wicked grin he holds the train of a queen walking in a procession, and acts the acolyte to a priest at the altar ; he appears suddenly to a king and his ministers at the council board, to a bride among her tire women, and plays on a dulcimer to a new-wed man and wife ; he snatches his spade and mattock from a gardener, and arrests travellers on the highway ; he comes to a goldsmith among his jewels, to a merchant among his bales ;

he mixes the colours of an artist; he greets a proud court dame in her state, a magistrate in his robes, a monk in his cell, and a gay pleasure-party in a carriage. He snatches the sceptre from a monarch, and his red hat from a cardinal. With a wicked leer he puts out the lights upon the altar where a nun is kneeling, while she turns her head to listen to a youth pleading at her side. In cap and bells he dances with a queen, and leads a blind beggar into an open grave. The sketches are full of character and expression, ranging from tragic to grotesque, yet all full of solemn suggestion. Underneath this great picture gallery of Death,

> Among the wooden piles the turbulent river
> Rushes impetuous as the river of life.

And through the long gallery, too, flows unheeding the stream of life—peasants, market-women, and school-children, who stood to watch me as I studied the pictures and jotted down the above notes.

The quaint carved Rath Haus, the arsenal, the Wein Markt, the walls and towers, the overhanging houses, and the queer old Schwann Hotel where I lodged, were objects of intense interest. The old town was gay with banners on account of the national Art and Industrial Exhibition, which continued for three months. It gave a very favourable impression of the skill of the Swiss in wood-carving, modelling, painting, and sculpture. The educational exhibit and collection of books was admirable, as were also the manufacturing exhibits. Diamond cutting and other-industries were in progress.

I was greatly impressed by the celebrated Lion of Lucerne, carved by Thorwaldsen in the face of a high natural cliff, in commemoration of the 26 officers and 760 soldiers of the Swiss Guard who fell in defence of the royal family of France during the Revolution. The dying lion, twenty-eight feet long, transfixed by a broken lance, endeavours, with a look of mournful majesty, to protect the lily-shield of the Bourbons with his paw. The rock is overhung with trees and creeping plants, and a spring which trickles down one side forms a dark pool, surrounded by shrubs, at the base, in which the colossal effigy is reflected. It is sublime in its simplicity, and touching in its tragic pathos.

In the evening I attended an organ recital in the venerable Hofkirche, an ancient building with two tall and slender spires. At the entrance is a rude relief of Christ in the Garden, arrested by black-faced soldiers, who carry real wooden staves and iron cressets.

During the travelling season, the Protestants are allowed the use of the church for worship after the Romish service is over. The same sacristan, who veils the altar, distributes the Protestant hymn-books, and from the same pulpit the doctrines of the two Churches are preached. The canton which owns the church, thus carries toleration to its extremest limit.

The organ performance I liked much better than that which I subsequently heard on the great instrument of Freiburg, or than any other I heard in Europe. A master hand was at the keys, and played with exquisite feeling and expression. First, clear flute-like notes came stealing on the ear, like the chanting of a far-off choir. Then came a burst of sound that shook the solid walls, dying away in the distance in deep tones of human tenderness, then swelling into an exultant pæan of triumph. Then came a pause of silence and another tempest of music, out of which warbled, like a human voice, a sweet air. It was like a dove gliding out of a thunder storm. Then soft echoes answered, faint and far. Slow and solemn movements followed—stately marches, and infinite cavalcades of sound. A lighter air was taken up and expanded, unfolded, and glorified, the organ rolling in thunder, but the sweet air singing on like a bird through it all. The closing performance was a famous storm-piece. The sighing of the wind and the moaning of the pines, grew louder and louder, then in a lull was heard the prayer of the peasants, which was soon drowned in the burst of rain and hail, and the crash of the loud-rolling thunder, shaking the solid ground. Then the storm died away, and a sweet hymn of thanksgiving, like the singing of a choir of angels, stole upon the ear. The twilight deepened into gloom, the vaulted arches receded into darkness, the tapers twinkled upon the altar, the figure of the dead Christ on the cross gleamed spectral through the shadows, and a group of tourists from many lands sat entranced and touched to deep emotion by the spell of that wondrous music.

CHAPTER IX.

THE BERNESE OBERLAND—BRUNIG PASS—MEIRINGEN—GRINDELWALD—THE JUNGFRAU—LAUTERBRUNNEN—INTERLAKEN—THE GEMMI PASS—LEUKERBAD.

I LEFT Lucerne in a pouring rain for my trip through the Bernese Oberland, most of which I made afoot.

The clouds hung low on Pilatus, and threatened a very dismal day. The lovely landscape loomed dim and blurred through a thick veil of rain. I went by boat and *diligence* to Meiringen. I could hardly find a dry spot for myself or knapsack on the little steamer. At Alpnach the boat-load of dripping tourists pattered about in the rain and mud, till assigned their places in the *diligences*. The local guides stood around, under the overhanging eaves of the houses, in a very disconsolate manner, each pulling away at a big pipe, like an overgrown baby at a sucking-bottle.

A rain-soaked and mud-bedraggled Frenchman who had that morning made the ascent of Pilatus, a Glasgow man, a Philadelphian, and a Canadian were the inside passengers. A pleasant-faced Swiss fraulein climbed on the step of the *diligence* as we rode along, and offered sweet wild strawberries, goat's milk, cheese, and cakes for sale. Her garrulous chatter wheedled each of the party into the purchase of her simple refreshments. I was charmed with the affable manners of the Swiss. Even the little children by the wayside would respectfully salute one with "*Gut Morgen*," or "*Gut Abend, Herr.*" If I made a trifling purchase they would say with a frank familiarity, "Dank you, goot-bye," or "*Merci, Monsieur;*

AIGUILLES.

au revoir." A pleasant-voiced landlady came out in the rain while we changed horses to invite me to take a glass of wine or *cognac*, and when I declined, bade me a kind "goot-bye." They all tried to speak English, however imperfectly. "I dinks it will be wetter," said one in a pouring rain which seemed to make the prognostic impossible.

SWISS CHALET AND OLD TOWER.

The rain soon ceased, however, and the ride through the Unterwald and Brünig Pass was very grand. We rattled through quaint villages with old churches crowned by bulbous spires, the houses covered with scale-work of carved shingles, often with a pious inscription or Scripture text engraved upon the timbers. The farm-houses looked comfortable, with broad eaves, outside stairs and galleries, but with very small lattice windows, and frequently with great stones on the roof to prevent the wind from blowing the shingles off. But, especially in the higher Alps, not unfrequently the lower story was occupied by the cows and goats, and the garret by the fowls.

The women wore short skirts of home-woven stuff, which made them look like girls, and the girls often had old-fashioned long dresses, which made them look like little women. The men wore jackets or short bob-tailed coats of coarse frieze, which, but for the inevitable pipe, made them look like big boys. At Sachseln is a large church, containing the bones of St. Nikolaus, a Swiss hermit who died five hundred years ago. He subsisted, says the legend, for twenty years on the elements of the sacrament, which he received every month. Scarce a house in the Forest Cantons is without a portrait of good Brother Klaus.

The road winds higher and higher, through solemn pine woods and beneath great precipices, till we reach the summit of the pass. Then it sweeps down in long curves, through sublime scenery, to the charming village of Meiringen. This quaint old village, nestling at the base of lofty mountains, is the most picturesque that I have seen. In the evening the Falls of the Alpbach were lighted up with coloured fires, with charming effect. They flashed against a background of dark rock and darker forest, like a cataract of diamonds, emeralds, sapphires, and rubies, as the vari-coloured light—now white, now green, now purple, now crimson—played on the snowy cascade with a wondrous beauty that words cannot describe. The effect was magical. The hotel people did not forget to put an item in the bill for the illumination, but it was well worth it.

Here began my Alpine tramp; and this, let me say, is the only way to see Switzerland properly—on foot. Behold me, then, starting out with knapsack on my back and long alpenstock in hand, just like the pictures of Bunyan's pilgrim faring forth on his eventful journey. For awhile all went well. But soon the knapsack grew intolerably heavy, and the sun very hot, and I was glad to engage a guide to carry my pack over the mountains to Grindelwald. (This is a method I would strongly recommend. It leaves one free to enjoy the scenery, instead of toiling like a pack-horse.) A faithful, obliging, intelligent fellow my guide proved. Our conversation was rather limited, for he could not speak a word of English, and I very little German. But I made the most of that little, and it is surprising how far a very little will go when one has no other medium of intercourse. The path winds steeply up some 2,000 feet to the Falls of the Reichenbach. It is only a bridle-path—no carriages can pass; the snowy Reichenbach leaps with headlong plunge down the mountain side, then strikes the rock, rebounds, and is lost in the deep and narrow gorge.

FALLS OF THE REICHENBACH.

The path then winds through flowery upland meadows and beneath balm-breathing pines, enlivened by chalets and herds. In the bright sunlight the whole region seems transfigured and glorified. All day the lofty peaks of the Oberland form the sublime background of the view—the Engelhorn, the Wetterhorn, the Shreckhorn, the Eiger, the Mönch, the Silberhorn, and, grandest of all, the Jungfrau. These mountain names are often very suggestive, as the Angel's Peak; peaks of Tempest, of Darkness, and of Terror; the Silver Peak, the Monk and the Virgin. Nearer at hand sharp aiguilles, or needles of rock, rise precipitously, as shown in the initial cut of this chapter. There, in a lateral valley, is the beautiful Glacier of the Rosenlaui. Like a huge gauntlet that Winter has flung down, as Longfellow remarks, it age after age bids defiance to the Sun. Or rather, like some mighty dragon with glittering scales and horrent crest, it creeps stealthily from its mountain lair as if to devour the valley and its flocks and herds. But the golden shafts of Phœbus Apollo pierce his icy mail, and baffle and defeat and drive back the truculent monster.

The snow peaks pierce wedge-like the deep blue sky, cloud pennons streaming from their summit. Up, up, the vision climbs, along sheer precipices of thousands of feet, so steep that not even the snow can find a resting-place. At many of the grandest points of view the traveller is waylaid by sturdy mountaineers blowing their Alpine horns, at whose challenge the mountain echoes shout back their loud defiance. The Alp horn is a huge affair, from six to eight feet long, of either wood or metal. Upon it quite a musical air can be produced by a skilful player. The echoes are often exquisitely sweet, growing fainter and farther and dying away in the lone mountain solitudes. They made me think of Tennyson's Bugle Song:

> "O hark, O hear! how thin and clear,
> And thinner, clearer, farther going;
> O sweet and far, from cliff and scar,
> The horns of Elfland faintly blowing!
> Blow, bugle, blow, set the wild echoes flying;
> Blow, bugle, answer echoes, dying, dying, dying."

I gave an old fellow half a franc to fire off his rusty cannon, and presently the mountain walls returned the cannonade, the echoes rolling and crashing in deep reverberations through the valley, like heaven's loud artillery. The traveller is beset by sturdy beggars, who pester him for alms. One rough-looking fellow dropped his axe as I came up and held out his hat with a whine. I demanded if he owned the mountain, and held out *my* hat asking alms for a foot-worn pilgrim, when the fellow rather sheepishly went back to his work.

The path lay over the Grindel Alp, along a narrow "hog's back" ridge, giving magnificent views of the mountain and valley. The Wetterhorn rises in a buttressed and pinnacled façade, three or four thousand feet high, that seems almost to overhang the path, and then sweeps up to the height of 11,400 feet.

The descent into the Grindelwald is very abrupt and fatiguing. I diverged from the path to visit the celebrated glacier. The splintered and pinnacled mass creeps down its rocky bed with a slow, grinding motion, torn and rent by crevasses, crushing and scratching the rock, and leaving a huge moraine on either side and in front. An artificial grotto has been hewn a hundred feet into the heart of the glacier. The ice roof rises a hundred feet thick above our head, of an exquisite crystalline texture, through which a faint light of a weird unearthly azure hue penetrates into the grotto. I placed my ear to the solid wall of ice and listened to the musical tinkling sound of the water trickling through its veins. The somewhat hilarious mirth of a gay tourist party caused a deep gurgling sound of laughter to run through the mass. One of the party fired off a pistol in the grotto, producing an extraordinary crashing noise.

Fair English girls were sketching by the roadside as I entered the village in the warm glow of sunset. Long after the twilight filled the valley, the snowpeaks burned with golden light, which deepened to a rosy glow, and then gleamed spectral white, like giant ghosts in the cold moonlight. My guide liked his service so well that he asked permission to accompany me the following day. To this I heartily agreed, and he went to sleep in a hayloft, and I to the comfortable repose of the quaint old Hotel du Grand Eiger. The midday luncheon of sweet mountain milk and home-made bread had been delicious;

but that did not lessen the appreciation of a substantial dinner after a hard day's work.

The next day, July 24th, was one of the greatest fatigue and greatest enjoyment of my life. I started early for a long hard climb to the summit of Mount Männlichen, 7,700 feet high. The mountains threw vast shadows

MOUNTAIN PASTURES.

over the valley, but out of these I soon climbed into the sunshine, which was very hot, although the shade was very cold. Soon I felt a difficulty in breathing the keen and rarified mountain air. The effort to loosen some stones to roll down the mountain side, where they went bounding from ledge to ledge, quickened painfully the action of the heart and lungs. I felt also an intense thirst, which I tried to allay by copious draughts at the frequent ice-cold springs, and by eating snow gathered from the snow-fields over which I passed.

But the sublimity of the view more than compensates for all the fatigue. There rises in mid-heaven the shining Silberhorn with its sharp-cut outline, like the wind-chiseled curves of a huge snow-drift. The Finster-Aarhorn towers 13,230 feet in air, bearing upon his mighty flanks the accumulated snow of myriads of years —suggesting thoughts of the great white throne of God in the heavens. But the sublime beauty of the Jungfrau —the Virgin Queen of the Bernese Oberland—is a revelation to the soul. In her immortal loveliness and inviolable purity she is like the New Jerusalem coming down out of heaven—adorned as a bride for her husband.

As I reached at length the crest of the Männlichen, there burst upon my sight a view unequalled elsewhere in Europe. There lay, half in deep shadow and half in bright sunlight, the narrow valley of the Lauterbrunnen, 5,000 feet deep, so near that it seemed as if I could leap down into it. On its opposite side could be traced, like a silver thread, the snowy torrent of the Staubach. The birds were flying, and light clouds drifting, far beneath my feet, and from that height of over 7,000 feet I looked up 6,000 more, to the snow-cowled Monk and silver-veiled Virgin, whose mighty sweep from base to summit was clearly seen across the narrow valley. Suddenly across the deep, wide stillness

> There comes an awful roar,
> Gathering and sounding on.

It swells into a prolonged roll like thunder, and dies slowly away. It is the fearful avalanche. Its whole course can readily be traced. It looks like a vast cataract, pouring for thousands of feet down the mountain side, leaping from ledge to ledge, and then swallowed up in the abyss beneath. The heat of the afternoon sun loosened several snow masses, weighing, I suppose, many tons, which swept, like a solid Niagara, into the depths. This sublime phenomenon is well described by Byron in his "Manfred," whose scene is laid on this very spot.

The descent into the valley was very steep, and almost more fatiguing than the climb up. The grassy slopes of the Wengern Alp were covered by hundreds of cows and goats, each with a large bell attached, and each bell seemed to possess a different note. Instead of the discord that might have been expected, the strange musical tinkling, at a little distance, was far from unpleasing. More cannon firing and Alp horns followed. On the latter are played the simple Swiss *Ranz des Vaches*, or cattle call, which, when played in foreign lands, awakens such intense home longings in the exiles from these Alpine valleys.

From a balcony, hanging like an eagle's eyrie 2,000 feet above Lauterbrunnen, watched over evermore by the snowy Jungfrau—and lovelier "Happy Valley" even Rasselas never beheld—a delightful bird's-eye view is obtained. Many of the Swiss have a very peculiar way of speaking French,—with a strange, expostulatory, almost whining accent. The keeper of this eyrie inquired very solicitously about *madame*, my wife, and *les enfants*, my children, and hoped that I would bring them to see his beautiful country, which I assured him I should very much like to do. I exceedingly admire the kindly, home-like ways of the Swiss peasantry. I found them extremely obliging and polite. Their life is one of austere toil, carrying great burdens up and down those steep mountain sides. Some of the herdsmen have a one-legged stool strapped on behind, so as to leave their hands free for climbing and milking. At a distance they look like a survival of a Darwinian *Homo Caudatus*.

The Staubach, leaping down the mountain's side, 980 feet in a single bound, gleams, to use the extraordinary figure of Byron, like the tail of the Pale Horse of Death, described in the Apocalypse. On nearer approach, the appropriateness of its name, "The Dustfall," is seen, as dissipated in vapour, it drifts away upon the wind. Or, perhaps it looks more like a bridal veil, woven of the subtlest tissue, waving and shimmering in the air. There are in the valley some thirty similar "dustfalls." It well deserves the name of Lauterbrunnen—"nothing but fountains." Twelve hours on foot had earned a night's repose, but so wondrous was the spectral beauty of the

Jungfrau, gleaming in the moonlight like a lovely ghost, that I could scarce shut out the sight. Here I met again, to our mutual surprise and pleasure, my travelling companion through Italy.

It is a charming ride of seven miles down the valley to Interlaken—a town of less than 2,000 permanent residents, with over a score of large hotels. Its position, between Lakes Brienz and Thun, gives it its name and importance as a centre of travel. In summer it rivals Baden-Baden in the number of its visitors. In winter, I suppose, the people hibernate on what they have made off their victims. Like Baden, it has its Kursaal, or public concert hall, for whose behoof each traveller is mulcted in his bill.

The popular excursion from Interlaken is that up the lovely Lake Brienz to the Giessbach Falls—the most picturesque in Switzerland. In seven connected cascades, framed by the dark green foliage of pines and spruces, the river leaps from a height of 1,148 feet into the lake. Romantic walks, bridges, and arbours, and at night an illumination of the falls, make the spot a fairyland of beauty. The hotel, like most of those in Switzerland, is sumptuous. Here is seen in perfection the pretty Bernese female costume—black laced bodice, or scarlet trimmed with black, full white sleeves, silver chains looped up over the shoulders, and a short striped skirt. The flaxen hair hangs down the back in two long braids. On the head is worn sometimes a jaunty velvet cap, but more frequently a broad-leafed straw hat, trimmed with their native edelweiss, or Alpine rose.

One of the grandest excursions in Switzerland is that over the Gemmi Pass. I left Spiez, on Lake Thun, by *diligence*, traversing a beautiful, chalet-studded valley, as far as Kandersteg, beyond which there is only a bridle path. The little hamlet lies amid a magnificent mountain panorama. I took a lonely evening walk up a gorge of wildest desolation. The overhanging crags, swept by the trailing fringes of the clouds, seemed as if they would inevitably topple down and crush the rash mortal who had dared to invade the solitary domain. A more intense sense of isolation and of brooding solitude I never felt. It seemed like some lone valley of the primeval world, before the creation of man.

In the hotel parlour on Sunday we had a thoroughly High Church service. Two clergymen in full canonicals —gown, surplice, and hood—officiated. A table draped in white, at the east end of the room, served as an altar. On it were two candles—not lighted, however. The service was intoned throughout—Creed, Lord's Prayer, and all. The congregation consisted of four ladies and one gentleman beside myself. Nevertheless, the simple beauty of the prayers, which have voiced the aspirations of successive generations, could not be marred by the puerilities with which they were accompanied.

Early on Monday morning, with guide and alpenstock, I started upon another mountain tramp. The zig-zag path was dreadfully steep, but the grand views of the Blümlis Alp gave an excuse for often stopping to rest. I joined a pleasant Quaker party from Philadelphia, to whom my recognition of a quotation from Lowell, by one of the ladies, sufficed for an introduction—so unconven-

AN ALPINE PASS.

tional is the etiquette of mountain travel. After a four hours' walk we reached the summit of the pass (7,553 feet high), when there burst upon the sight a magnificent view of the Rhone Valley and the Alps of the Vallais, including the huge Weisshorn, and the rugged pyramid of the

Matterhorn, the scene of so many fatal accidents. Under the glowing light it was a panorama of entrancing beauty, and, at a dizzy depth beneath, lay the Baths of Leuk. Down the face of an almost perpendicular cliff, 1,800 feet high, winds, in many ziz-zags, one of the most remarkable Alpine routes. The winding way—a groove blasted in the rock—resembles a spiral stair, the upper parts actually projecting over the lower. The old Quaker lady was carried down in a chair by relays of strong-armed guides, who sang a wild refrain, which was weirdly echoed from the opposite wall of rock. The young ladies walked down, which it requires pretty good nerve to do. Invalids borne down to the baths sometimes have their eyes blindfolded to avoid seeing the perils of the way. In 1861 the Countess d'Herlincourt, travelling with her husband on her bridal tour, fell over the precipice and was dashed to pieces. From the valley it is impossible to trace the route by which one has descended.

The hot baths of Leuk have been famous from the time of the Romans. To get the full benefit of them patients must sit in the hot water—from 93° to 123° Fahrenheit—for several hours a day. To avoid the tedium of solitary bathing they wear a flannel suit, and sit, immersed to their necks, in a common bath. Each bather has a small floating table for his book, paper, chessboard, or coffee, and the ladies for their sewing or knitting. I saw a young girl reading a letter, and children playing ball and swimming about; and one stout old gentleman in spectacles had a very comical look. Of course perfect decorum is observed. They looked like a lot of mermen and mermaids—one almost expected to see the fins. I could hardly bear my hand in the water it was so hot.

The eight miles' walk down the wild valley of the Dala to the Rhone, was one of the grandest of my life. At the bottom of a gorge, 900 feet deep, raves the brawling torrent. Above the pathway towers a lofty cliff, the only way to climb which to the village of Arbignon is by a series of eight rude ladders attached to the perpendicular rock. The villages looked like eagles' nests hanging on the steep slopes. The ever-varying views were so entrancing that I scarce could tear myself away. As a consequence I had to hurry down a rough short cut, like the dry bed of a torrent, to catch the railway train at Leuk. Never, I think, was the transition from foot-sore, weary pedestrianism, to the rapid travel of an express train, more grateful than to the rather demoralized individual who, that lovely summer evening, was whirled down the Rhone Valley to Martigny. In the valley are several picturesque old castles of the robber knights and fighting bishops of the middle ages; and some date from Roman times.

CHAPTER X.

Adventures on Mule-back—Chamonix—Mont Blanc—The Mer de Glace—Geneva—Chillon—Lausanne—Freiburg.

AUBERGE AT THE CHAPEAU, MONT BLANC.

MY experience as a "tramp" on the Wengern Alp and Gemmi Pass had given me enough of walking for awhile, so I resolved to ride over the mountains from Martigny to Chamonix. Repairing, therefore, to the "Bureau of Guides," I engaged a mule and attendant for the following day. The head guide urged me to take the easier route by the Col de Balme, but I insisted on the more rugged but vastly grander route by Salvan. The guide, therefore, wrote out an agreement in duplicate, which we both signed as formally as if the bargain were to go to the North Pole. It was quite a curiosity in its way, and ran thus : " Un guide et un mulet pour Chamonix, par Salvan et par Gorge du Trient, et source de l'Arveiron. Hotel Clerc à 7 heures matin. Prix 20f. et le pour-boire.—Le guide-chef, Rouville."

Mounting my mule, with knapsack strapped on behind the saddle, I rode down the broad Rhone Valley to the Gorge du Trient. Dismounting, I penetrated a narrow cleft in the mountain through which tears a foaming torrent. It is grand and gloomy, stern and savage—not beautiful. No ray of sunlight ever pierces the dark defile. Over the brawling torrent hangs a wooden gallery, suspended by a wire rope ; on either side rise, for hundreds of feet, walls of wave-worn rock, and through a narrow rift gleams down a riband of bright blue sky.

Remounting my mule, the guide turned to what seemed an almost perpendicular forest-clad cliff. No trace of path was visible till we reached its base. Then by over twenty zig-zags we wound ever higher and higher up the mountain side, crossing as often a foamy torrent. The valley of the Trient sank deeper and deeper, till it lay nearly three thousand feet beneath us. The mule-track wound along a narrow ledge, and the mule would persist in walking on its outermost verge. One of my legs overhung the very edge, which I could not see for the body of the stubborn animal, which I could not make walk nearer to the cliff. But the guide stalked ahead without

THE GORGE OF THE TRIENT.

concern, and the mule nodded his head and flapped his
ears in a very contemplative and sagacious manner, and
"you saw he was thinking, thinking much"—the mule,
not the guide—" though never a word did he speak." So
I suppose there was no very great danger, though it looked
really frightful. We seemed to hang on the very "brink
of forever." The poet's lines somewhat describe the situation:

> "And you, ye crags, upon whose extreme edge
> I stand, and on the torrent's brink beneath
> Behold the tall pines dwindling into shrubs,
> In dizziness of distance; when a leap,
> A stir, a motion, even a breath, would bring
> My breast upon its rocky bosom's bed
> To rest forever."

But no words can give an adequate conception of the
growing grandeur of the scene. Behind was the snowy
St. Bernard. In front came gradually into view the mighty
dome of Mont Blanc. There it gleamed against the deep
blue sky, like—so it seems to mortal thought—the great
white throne of God in the heavens. The winding path,
the deep ravine, the balm-breathing pines, the brilliant
sun-lighted foliage, the fragrant mountain flowers—violets,
harebells, anemones, and *les clochettes*, or fairy-bells, and
little blue forget-me-nots—that swing their sweet censers
in the perfumed air—it was like the Delectable Mountains
in Bunyan's vision; and the broad grassy valley of Chamonix gleamed in the distance like the asphodel meadows
of the land which the pilgrims saw afar off. At one

point of the Tête-Noire Pass, the road pierces through a tunnel, while far below brawls the raging torrent, clearly seen, but at this distance unheard.

The noon-day rest, at the summit of the pass, in full view of the highest peak in Europe, with the lunch of bread and goat's milk cheese, strawberries and cream, was an hour of deep delight. But the afternoon ride down hill into the Vale of Chamonix was one of excessive fatigue. Jolt, jolt, went that dreadful mule, till every joint seemed dislocated. I was glad to dismount and walk by way of rest. But the Monarch of Mountains, in his lonely majesty, rises every moment higher and higher. With a good glass—after sweeping up its successive zones of pine-forest, bare rock, glacier, and everlasting snow—I could see four black figures like emmets, which, I was told, were men climbing the mountain. But with all its grandeur, Mont Blanc will not compare with the immortal loveliness of the Jungfrau, the Virgin Queen of the Bernese Oberland.

ON THE TETE-NOIRE.

Never was more weary wight than he who dismounted from his mule at the Hotel des Alpes at Chamonix. Ben

Johnson cynically says that one's warmest welcome is always at an inn. It is amusing to witness the affectionate solicitude of the Swiss host for his guests' welfare. As they ride up to the door, a lackey in waiting rings a large warning bell. Then three or four waiters in swallow-tails, or valets in uniform, swarm out to assist the travellers to dismount, and the *maître d'hôtel* gives them most unctuous greeting, and assigns them rooms in turn, to which they are conducted by neat *femmes de chambre* in Bernese costume and snowy cap. At the dining table one's seat corresponds with the number of his room. At a signal from the head-waiter, his well-trained subordinates file in and out like automatic figures, with the several courses. These are almost invariably as follows: soup, fish, roast, vegetables alone, chicken and salad together, dessert and fruit. Dinner generally lasts an hour, but after a hard day's work one does not grudge the time, and it gives an opportunity to study the varied phases of tourist character, of many lands and many tongues, thus brought together. Some of my pleasantest recollections of travel are of the numerous charming acquaintances made at the *table d'hôte*. In the evening there is frequently a parlour concert of really good music by native performers—perhaps by Tyrolese in their picturesque costume, warbling their sweet mountain airs.

A party of Cook's American tourists had invaded the village, filled the hotels, and monopolized all the available mules. So next day I set out afoot to climb the Montanvert, cross the Mer de Glace, and return by the Chapeau. The weather was superb. After a climb of 3,000 feet there burst upon the sight a magnificent view of the motionless billows of the Sea of Ice, sweeping in a gigantic cataract down a lateral valley. One may trace its upward course for six miles—like a stormy sea frozen instantaneously into glittering ice. In its resistless onward glide it is rent into a thousand deep crevasses, descending to unknown depths. Just beyond this ice sea is a group of gigantic granite needles, one—the Aiguille Verte—piercing the sky to the height of 13,540 feet. No snow can rest upon their splintered pinnacles. Thunder-scarred and blasted, and riven by a thousand tempests, they seem, like Prometheus, to defy the very heavens; and in their awful and forever inaccessible desolation were, I think, the sublimest objects I ever beheld.

In company with an English gentleman I crossed the Mer de Glace without a guide. Leaving the beaten track, we strolled up the glacier, which rolled in huge ridges and hollows for miles up the valley. Many of the crevasses were filled with water—clear as crystal, blue as sapphire. I hurled my alpenstock into

ON THE MER DE GLACE.

one, and after an interval it was hurled back as if by the invisible hand of some indignant ice gnome from the fairy grottoes of his under-world. Others were empty, but we could not see the bottom. The large stones we rolled in went crashing down to unknown depths. Into one of these crevasses a guide fell in 1820 and forty-one years later his remains were recovered at the end of the glacier, brought to view by the slow motion and melting of the mass. His body was identified by some old men who had been the companions of his youth over forty years before. Along the margin of the glacier is a moraine of huge boulders, ground and worn by this tremendous millstone.

To reach the Chapeau one must pass along a narrow ledge, with steps hewn in the face of the steep precipice, known as the Mauvais Pas—the Perilous Way, or "Villanous Road," as Mark Twain translates it. The cliff towered hundreds of feet above our head, and sloped to a dizzy depth beneath our feet. This passage was once an exploit of much danger, but iron rods have been bolted into the face of the cliff, so that it is now quite safe. The view of the splintered pinnacles, "seracs," and ice-tables of the glacier was of wonderful grandeur and beauty.

I stopped for lunch at the auberge shown in the initial cut of this chapter, and found the place overflowing with a hilarious company of tourists. I joined their party to descend the mountain, entered a huge ice-cave, and got well sprinkled with the falling water. From a vast arch of ice in the glacier leaps forth the river Arveiron in a strong and turbid stream, soon to join the rapid Arve. As we sat gazing on the sight, an American lady quoted with much feeling Coleridge's sublime hymn to Mount Blanc:

> " O Sovran Blanc,
> The Arve and Arveiron at thy base
> Rave ceaselessly; but thou most awful form,
> Risest from forth thy silent sea of pines,
> How silently.
>   Ye ice-falls! ye that from the mountain's brow,
> Adown enormous ravines slope amain—
> Torrents, methinks, that heard a mighty Voice,
> And stopped at once, amid the maddest plunge.
> Motionless torrents! silent cataracts!
> Who made you glorious as the gates of heaven?
> And who commanded (and the silence came)
> Here let the billows stiffen and have rest?
>   Thou, too, hoar mount, with thy sky-piercing peaks,
> All night long visited by troops of stars,
> Or while they climb the sky or when they sink;
> Thou kingly spirit throned among the hills,
> Thou dread ambassador from earth to heaven—
> Great Hierarch! tell thou the silent sky,
> And tell the stars, and tell yon rising sun,
> Earth with her thousand voices praises God."

The sublimest aspect of Mont Blanc, I think, is when illumined with the golden glow of sunset. It seems converted into a transparent chrysophrase, burning with an internal fire. But, as the daylight fades, the fire pales to rosy red, and palest pink, and ashen gray, and ghastly white against the darkening sky. Through a strong telescope I could see the silhouette of a chamois goat sharply defined against the lighted window of the hut at Grands Mulets, five miles distant on the mountain slope.

Next morning I started with the six-horse *diligence* for the ride of fifty-three miles to Geneva. A score of passengers rode in the large open carriage, with a canopy overhead, affording an uninterrupted view of the magnificent scenery. Mont Blanc seemed to tower higher above the Titan brotherhood as we receded, and to reign in lonely majesty the monarch of the mountain world—" on his throne of rock, in his robe of cloud, with his diadem of snow." Yet amid these sublimities of nature the condition of the people was very abject. As we changed horses, hideous *cretins* came to beg. Their idiotic faces seemed to indicate only intelligence enough to hold out their palsied hands for alms. The women were toiling in the fields, and carrying on their heads, along steep mountain paths, great loads of hay, which made them look like walking haystacks. Their clothing was coarse, their cabins squalid, their food meagre and poor, and their rude life left its reflex on their rude and unintelligent features.

Few places in Europe possess greater historical interest than Geneva. For centuries it has been the sanctuary of civil and religious liberty, and its history is that of the Reformation and of free thought. The names of Calvin, Knox, Beza, Farel, the Puritan exiles, and later of Voltaire, Rousseau, Madame de Stael, and many other refugees from tyranny, are forever associated with this little republic, so small that Voltaire used to say that when he shook his wig he powdered the whole of it. Here too are the graves of D'Aubigné, Sir Humphrey Davy and many other world-famous men.

Geneva is the handsomest city for its size I have ever seen. It has less than 50,000 inhabitants, yet it abounds in splendid streets, squares, and gardens; public and private buildings and monuments; and its hotels are sumptuous. It lies on either side of the rapid Rhone, where it issues from the lake. The waters are of the deepest blue, and rush by with arrowy swiftness. It has many interesting historic buildings. As I was looking for the sexton of the cathedral, a Roman Catholic priest whom I accosted went for the key, and himself conducted me through the building and explained its features of historic interest. It seemed to me very strange to have that adherent of the ancient faith exhibit the relics of him who was its greatest and most deadly foe. With something of the old feeling of proprietorship, he looked around the memory-haunted pile and said proudly, yet regretfully, " This was all ours once," and he pointed in confirmation to the beautiful chapel of the Virgin and the keys of St. Peter sculptured on the walls. Then he led me to Calvin's pulpit, once the most potent intellectual throne in Europe, and to Calvin's chair—in which I sat, without feeling my Arminian orthodoxy affected thereby—and pointed out other memorials of the great Reformer.

Near by, I visited Calvin's house in a narrow street, but his grave is unknown, as he expressly forbade the erection of any memorial. I found, too, the house of the "self-torturing sophist," Rousseau. It bore his bust and the inscription, "Ici est né Jean Jacques Rousseau." On a shady island in the river is his monument—a fine bronze figure, sitting pen in hand.

In the old gothic Hotel de Ville is a singular inclined plane leading to the upper floor, up which the councillors used to ride. Here sat the international commission which conducted the Geneva arbitration between Great Britain and America. The arsenal hard by contains the ladders by which, in 1602, the Spaniards tried to scale the walls, their flags, and the armour of hundreds who fell into the fosse; weapons from Sempach; the lance of Winkelried, the martyr-patriot; captured Austrian trophies, and many other objects of intense interest. A garrulous old pensioner took infinite pains to explain everything. He asked me to try on one helmet, and I attempted to do so, but could hardly lift it from the floor.

A reminiscence of Voltaire is the Rue des Philosophes. Near by, at Ferney, is his villa and the chapel which, with cynical ostentation—" sapping a solemn creed with solemn sneer"—he built, bearing still the inscription, *"Deo erexit Voltaire."* The splendid monument of the Duke of Brunswick, who left his immense fortune to the town, is one of the finest in Europe. The university, museums, art galleries, and a splendid school of art, are proof of the high culture of the little republic. In the latter institution, professors in blouses were instructing students in sculpture, modelling, repoussé work, bronze casting, wood-carving, designing ; and were exceedingly courteous in their explanations of their methods. This great Dominion might learn a lesson in art culture from this little city.

In the evening twilight I walked down the Rhone to its junction with the Arve. The former flows clear as crystal from the pellucid lake ; the latter rushes turbid with mud from the grinding glaciers. For a long distance the sharp contrast between the two may be traced—"like the tresses," says the poetic Cheever, " of a fair-haired girl beside the curls of an Ethiopian ; the Rhone, the daughter of Day and Sunshine ; the Arve, the child of Night and Frost."

I called next day to see Dr. Abel Stevens, the well-known historian of Methodism. To my regret he was in London ; but I met Dr. Butler, the founder of American Methodist Missions in India and Mexico. I had met him before in Canada, and we had a pleasant talk looking out upon the lovely lake, whose beauty recalls the lines of Byron :

> " Fair Leman woos me with its crystal face,
> The mirror where the stars and mountains view
> The stillness of their aspect in each trace
> Its clear depths yield of their fair light and hue.
> There breathes a living fragrance from the shore
> Of flowers yet fresh with childhood. . . Here the Rhone
> Hath spread himself a couch, the Alps have reared a throne."

In the afternoon I sailed on the "Bonnivard" up the clear blue lake to the Castle of Chillon, at its upper end, stopping at these memory-haunted spots—Coppet, Nyon, "sweet Clarens," and many another famed in song and story. Splendid views were obtained of Mont Blanc, hanging like a cloud on the horizon. The sloping shores were clothed with luxuriant chestnuts, walnuts, magnolias, and vines, and crowned by tasteful villas, old castles, or magnificent modern hotels. Midway is Morges with its lofty donjon keep, built eleven centuries ago by Bertha of Burgundy, the beautiful spinner, who used to ride through the country on her palfrey with the distaff in her hand. Her example is still cited, like that of Solomon's virtuous woman, for the imitation of the Swiss maidens. At Chillon, in company with a German artist, I took a small boat for the Castle, which rises in sullen majesty from the waves. "A thousand feet in depth below their massy waters meet and flow." This gloomy tower has been used as a prison for over a thousand years. What bitter memories of wrong and sorrow could its rude walls tell! Over the gate are the mocking words, "*Gott der Herr segne den Ein- und Ausgang*"—" God bless all who go in and come out." An intelligent and pretty girl conducted us through its vaulted dungeons, the torture chamber, with its pulleys and rack, and the ancient Hall of Justice, with its quaint carving. She showed us the pillar to which Bonnivard, for six years, three centuries ago, was chained; the marks worn by his footsteps in the floor, and the inscriptions of Byron and Victor Hugo on the walls. As the afternoon light streamed through the narrow loop-holes on the arches and columns, and on the fair face of the girl, it made a picture in which Rembrandt would have revelled.

> " Chillon ! thy prison is a holy place,
> And thy sad floor an altar,—for 'twas trod
> Until his very steps have left a trace,
> Worn, as if the cold pavement were a sod,
> By Bonnivard !—may none those marks efface,
> For they appeal from tyranny to God."

I returned by rail to Lausanne, the road climbing the steep slope, and giving grand views of the lovely lake. Hither were brought in the sixth century the relics of St. Anne, hence the name, *Laus Annæ;* and here in 1479 were solemnly tried and excommunicated an army of locusts which devoured every green thing. The Hotel Gibbon, at which I stopped, was formerly the property of the great historian of the Roman Empire. I sat beneath the chestnut tree on the garden terrace, where he wrote the closing chapters of his history, and plucked an ivy leaf as a memento of the spot. In the great dining-room, with its gilt panelled ceiling and parquetry floor, he gave his state banquets and receptions.

But another memory of Lausanne is more lovingly cherished by millions of Methodists than that of the skeptical historian—the memory of the saintly Fletcher. After dinner, therefore, I visited the Fletcher Memorial College. This is a noble institution for the theological training of French-speaking candidates for the Wesleyan ministry. There were, at the time of my visit, eleven students in residence, and in the absence of the Rev. Mr. Cornforth, the English principal, one of them showed me the handsome chapel, Sunday-school, students' rooms, refectory, and parlours. It is, architecturally, one of the handsomest buildings in the town ; and is a worthy monument, not only of the great man whom it commemorates, but of the liberality and missionary zeal of English Methodism. My young *cicerone* returned with me to my hotel, and we sat long in the glorious moonlight, listening to the music in the public square, and conversing on the religious condition of the country. There was much rationalism in the Established Church, he said, which was the mere creature of the State. I witnessed a confirmation of the latter statement next day, as I saw a police office established in a church.

The old cathedral, built 1235–75, is in the massive early gothic style. It is on a hill, reached from the marketplace by a queer covered stairway of one hundred and sixty steps. The picturesque old stone saints, with their arms and noses knocked off by the image-breaking Reformers, looked quite pathetic. One of them, St. Denis, carried his head in his hand, as if for safety, and the sculpture was stiff, archaic, and grotesque. It is quite common to see figures of angels playing on violins, and I saw one firing an arquebuse. The mail-clad knights, lying in their tombs, keep, age after age, their lonely vigils in their shadowy shrines. The old stalls are wonderfully carved. The Lady Chapel of the old Roman Catholic times was fitted up as a Sunday-school for the children, with low seats and a queer little pulpit and organ.

The bishop's castle of the 13th century is more like a feudal baron's donjon than an episcopal residence. Those stern old bishops belonged to the Church militant, certainly. A low-browed arch, guarded by a portcullis, admits to a thick-walled barbican or broad squat tower with corner turrets. Loop-holes for cross-bows and arquebuses give it a more military appearance. The old bishop evidently meant to hold his own against all comers. It is now used as a council hall, and is as quaint within as without. Yet in this mediæval-looking old town, where almost everything and everybody seemed at least five hundred years old, I saw oxen dragging rude carts up the steep streets—just as one might see in the newest and rawest backwoods village in Canada.

From Lausanne to Freiburg is a delightful ride of forty miles, through a fertile, undulating country, with fine mountain views, and picturesque towns and villages, with ancient walls, watch-towers, and castles. Freiburg is a wonderfully quaint old town, on the high bluffs of the winding Sarine. Across this are two cobweb-looking suspension bridges, one 168 feet and the other 305 feet above the river. A waggon passing over makes them undulate in a manner rather discomposing to timid nerves. A steep road, the pavement of which serves as the roof of a long row of houses, leads to the lower town, where German is chiefly spoken, as French is in the upper town.

It must be rather odd for the persons living in these houses to hear the carts rattling over their heads. The old church of St. Nicholas dates from 1285. Its organ, with 67 stops and 7,800 pipes, some of them 33 feet long, is one of the finest in Europe. I attended an organ recital, but liked it far less than that at Hofkirche, at Lucerne. The organ is very powerful, but lacks the sweet flute-like notes of the latter. The deep bass shook the solid walls. The rising rage of the storm-piece was tremendous—like chaos come again. It was at the garish hour of noon, and the market square close by was filled with noisy and homely-looking peasants, in their odd and uncouth costumes. In the church was a singular Chapel of the Sepulchre, a dim grotto with angels, the Maries, and a sleeping soldier of Swiss physiognomy, on which fell strong beams of light through narrow loopholes. It was very realistic and Rembrant-like. The choir screen was a perfect thicket of iron thorns. There was a dreadfully haggard figure of Christ on the cross, the blood dropping from the thorns on His brow over His body—an object painful to contemplate. A "Last Judgment," over the west portal, is very grotesque. A devil with a pig's head is carrying off souls in a huge basket, weighing them in scales and casting them into a dragon-shaped hell's mouth, while a saint carries the souls of the saved to heaven in her apron.

Around the town were curious towers, very strong on the outer side, towards the enemy; but quite open on the inner side, so as to be untenable if taken.

CHAPTER XI.

BERNE—BASLE—FALLS OF THE RHINE—THE BLACK FOREST—
STRASSBURG—HEIDELBERG.

COURT-YARD, HEIDELBERG CASTLE.

BERNE, the capital of Switzerland, is a quaint old town of 40,000 inhabitants. It is, as its name signifies, the City of the Bear. That animal seems to be the tutelary guardian, as well as the heraldic emblem of the canton. It ramps upon its shield. Two gigantic granite bears are warders of the city gates. A whole troop of mechanical bears go through a performance every hour on the clock tower. On the neighbouring Bears' Fountain appears bruin, equipped in armour. Even in the stalls of the cathedral they are carved, in all manner of grotesque attitudes. In the Bears' Den—a large stone enclosure twenty feet deep—quite a menagerie of black and brown bears are maintained at public expense. When I saw them, a great lazy fellow lay on his back, with his four legs in the air, sleepily catching in his capacious mouth cherries thrown him by his visitors. He seemed half asleep, with his eyes nearly closed, but he watched the cherries close enough, with a strangly human expression, and caught them every time. In 1861 an English officer fell into the den, and was torn in pieces before he could be rescued.

The houses in the old town are build over arcades, under the arches of which the sidewalk runs. In the middle of the wide street are fountains and tanks, where the housemaids come for water, and to wash the table vegetables. One of these, the Fountain of the Ogre, has a hideous monster, with his capacious pockets full of children. He is at the same time devouring another, while below is the inevitable group of bears. Beneath the arcade are seats for wayfarers; that opposite the clock tower is like an old-fashioned square pew. Here, every hour of the day, a tourist group watches the procession of bears defiling before a seated figure, who turns an hour-glass and opens his mouth at every stroke which a harlequin gives a bell. In the shops are grotesque wood-carvings of bears masquerading in every sort of costume, and other fantastic subjects. Many of these wood-carvings are of remarkable artistic excellence—chamois hunting scenes, Alpine guides, and the like. One group of a chamois goat protecting her kid from the swoop of an eagle, was really pathetic in its expression. The Swiss *chalets*, cuckoo-clocks, and the like, were of wonderful delicacy of construction and carving. Musical boxes are concealed in many unsuspected places, and while you sit down on a chair or take hold of a watch case you are surprised by their pleasant tinkle.

The fine old cathedral dates from 1421. The sculptures of the west portal represent, in a singularly *naïve* manner, the Last Judgment and The Wise and Foolish Virgins. The only service on Sunday was a short sermon, and prayers at ten o'clock. During the rest of the day, the noble terrace of the church, one hundred feet above the river, was crowded with promenaders in their picturesque holiday garb, while at intervals a fine band played operatic selections. And this in the chief Protestant town in Switzerland!

The glory of Berne is its unrivalled view of the whole range of the Bernese Alps—the Mönch, Eiger, Jungfrau, and all the rest of the glorious company—considered by Humboldt the finest view in Europe. At sunset their serrated and pinnacled crests gleam and glow with unearthly beauty—golden and snowy and amethystine, like the crystal walls and pearly gates of the New Jerusalem. "Earth hath not aught to show more fair." Long after the evening shadows fill the valleys, the light lingers lovingly upon the rosy summits, as the parting day gives them her good-night kiss. Their strange spiritual loveliness speaks to the soul, like the voice of the angel to the seer of Patmos, saying, " Worship God."

From Berne to Basle is a magnificent ride of eighty miles, through a wild and picturesque region. A chattering Swiss school-girl would persist in talking bad English, while I wanted to enjoy the glorious scenery. I got a magnificent view of Lake Bienne, spread out like a map. Then the road plunged into the wild Munster Thal—a narrow cleft through the Jura range. An angry torrent raves through the deep defile, and the contorted strata rise in perpendicular walls on either side. One tunnel of the road passes underneath the old castle of Augenstein, and another beneath a natural arch, which was fortified by the Romans in 161. Fertile meadows and picturesque villages succeed this savage scenery.

Basle, a thriving town of 45,000 inhabitants, has played an important part in Reformation annals. It is mentioned in 374 as Basilea—hence its name. The minster, founded in 1010, a huge structure of red granite, is one of the finest Protestant churches in Europe. In a quaint relief of the Last Judgment, the risen dead—stiff archaic figures —are *naïvely* shown putting on their resurrection garments. Here was held the great Council of Basle, lasting from 1431 to 1448 ; and here is buried the great Reformer Œcolampadius, whose fine statue, with a Bible in its hand, stands in the square without. In the Council Hall are frescoes of Holbien's famous Dance of Death, like that at Lucerne. Kings, popes, emperors, lawyers, and doctors, lords and ladies are all compelled to dance a measure with the grim skeleton, Death. Quaint German verses enforce the moral, some of which have been rudely translated as follows:

> " O Queen, for joy there is no room,
> You must descend into the tomb;
> No gold avails nor beauty's sheen,
> To keep you from the world unseen.
>
> " My ladye, leave your toilette's care
> And for a dance with me prepare;
> Your golden locks can't help you here.
> What see you in your mirror clear?"
>
> " O horror! what is this? alas!
> I've seen Death's figure in my glass.
> His dreadful form fills me with fright,
> My heart grows cold and senseless quite."

In the museum is a large mechanical head, which, till 1839, stood on the clock tower of the bridge, and at every stroke of the pendulum rolled its eyes and protruded its long tongue in derision of the people at Little Basle, on the German side of the Rhine. A corresponding figure on that side returned the graceful amenity. I saw a similar clock still in operation at Coblentz.

The cloisters adjoining the cathedral are of singularly beautiful stone tracery, five hundred years old. In the grass-grown quadrangles sleep the quiet dead, unmoved by the rush and roar of busy traffic without. The Rathhaus, or town hall, is an exquisite bit of mediæval architecture, with its quaint gothic courts, stairways, and council chamber. An old church of the 14th century is used as a post office; high up among the arches of the vaulted roof is heard the click of the telegraph instruments; the chancel and solemn crypts are used to store corn and wine and oil; and beneath the vaulted roof which echoed for centuries the chanting of the choir, is now heard the creaking of cranes and the rattle of post waggons. The old walls which surrounded the city have been razed, and the ramparts converted into broad boulevards, lined with elegant villas. The quaint old gates and towers have been left, and form conspicuous monuments of the ancient times. I lodged at the Trois Rois Hotel, whose balconies overhang the swiftly-rushing Rhine. Just beneath my window were gorgeous effigies of the three Gipsy kings, Gaspar, Melchoir, and Belshazzar—one of them a Negro—who presented their offerings to the infant Christ.

Instead of going direct from Basle to Strassburg, which is only a few hours' ride, I made a long detour up the left bank of the Rhine, and through Wurtemburg and the Black Forest—a route which commands some of the finest river and mountain scenery in Europe.

The Falls of the Rhine at Schaffhausen are by far the largest in Europe, but they are not to be mentioned in the same day with our own Niagara. Nevertheless they are very picturesque and beautiful. The river makes three successive leaps over a ledge of rock. The whole fall, with the rapids above and below, is about one hundred feet. The surroundings are much more beautiful than at Niagara. The banks are high and rocky, and mantled with the richest foliage. The cliff overhanging the fall has a quaint old castle inn, and pavilions and galleries command superb views. Three huge rocks rise in mid-stream, against which the furious river wreaks its rage. Ruskin goes into raptures over this beautiful fall. He ought to see Niagara and the Yosemite. The old town, with its castle and minster dating from 1104, and odd architecture, is exceedingly picturesque. It is only an hour's ride from Constance, with its tragic memories of Jerome and Huss.

ISLAND AND CASTLE OF MAINAU.

Constance, now shrunken to a town of only 10,000, gleams, with its grey stone towers, surrounded by the waters of the Boden See, like a pearl set in sapphires. The beautiful island and castle of Mainau possess pathetic interest as furnishing a refuge for the hapless Empress Josephine.

At Singen I turned northward, through Wurtemburg

and the Black Forest, This wild mountain region—the famous Schwarzwald of German song and story—is a portion of the old Hercynian Forest, which once covered a great part of Central Europe, and later was known as the Swabian Land. Its grandest passes are now traversed by the new Black Forest Railway, one of the finest engineering works in Europe. Near Singen, rises on an isolated and lofty basaltic rock, the old Castle of Hohentweil, which held bravely out during a terrible siege of the Thirty Years' War. The spiked helmets and black eagles of Germany are everywhere seen, and German gutturals are everywhere heard. The country looks bleak and bare. The villages are crowded collections of rude stone houses, with crow-stepped gables or timbered walls, and the churches have queer bulbous spires. I asked the name of a pretty stream, and was told it was the Donau —the "beautiful blue Danube," which strings like pearls upon its silver thread the ancient cities of Ulm, Vienna, Presburg, Buda-Pesth, and Belgrade, and after a course of 1,780 miles, pours its waters into the Black Sea.

Now higher and higher winds our train. An open observation car is attached, affording an unobstructed view of the magnificent scenery. I was much amused at the travelling equipment of an English tourist, who was constantly consulting his pocket compass and aneroid barometer and watch, to see how rapidly we rose, and how frequently we changed our course. The road winds in great zig-zags and horse-shoe curves, and, crossing the watershed between the Danube and the Rhine, as rapidly descends. Leagues and leagues of dark pine-forest stretch beneath the eye. Deep valleys, with picturesque wooden villages, are at our feet, adown which bright streams leap and flash. The native costume is very quaint. The men wear queer-cut coats with red linings, and the women a green bodice, with gaily trimmed straw hats. At the pretty town of Offenburg, the last place in the world one would look for it, is a statue of the gallant English sailor, Sir Francis Drake, erected to his honour for having "introduced the potato into Europe, 1586." We sweep into the Rhine Valley, studded with grey old castles, and crossing the river on a magnificent iron bridge, behold, glowing in the rosy light of sunset, the mighty minster of Strassburg.

Nowhere has gothic architecture reached a grander development than in these old Rhine cities; and the two finest minsters in the world are, I think, those of Strassburg and Cologne. To the great cathedral, therefore, I first of all betook me in the morning. Beautiful without and within—it is a glorious poem, a grand epic, a sublime anthem in stone. Even the grandeur of St. Peter's wanes before the solemn awe which comes over the soul beneath those vast and shadowy vaults. The one represents the perfect triumph of human achievement; the other the deep religious yearning and the unsatisfied aspiration of the spirit: the one, the cold intellectual work of the Southern mind; the other, the awe and mystery, and sublime emotions, of the northern soul. These clustering columns ; these dim, forest-like vaults; these lone-drawn aisles ; the solemn gloom irradiated by glimpses of glory through the many-coloured robes of apostle and prophet, saint and angel, in the painted windows, so like the earthly shadows and the heavenly light of human life and history—these wake deep echoes in the soul, as no classic or renaissance architecture ever can.

As I entered the church, the deep-toned organ was rolling forth a sublime fugue, descriptive of the Last Judgment—the clear pealing of the archangel's trumpet, the deep thunder of doom, the wail of everlasting despair, the jubilant triumph of the saved. The pure, sweet, innocent voices of the white-robed choir boys, and the deep and solemn chanting of the priests, echoed through the vaulted aisles in cadences by turns tender and sublime. It was, I found, a mass for the dead. The coffin, covered with a velvet pall, lay on a catafalque before the altar, surrounded by burning tapers. The clouds of incense rose, and its fragrance filled the air. Then a procession of priests, in white surplices, and boys, " with tapers tall," passed into another chapel, behind an open screen, where more chanting and singing followed. However the judgment may condemn this dramatic sort of worship, it is certainly profoundly impressive to the imagination.

Not far off was a more striking display of Romish superstition. A statue of the Virgin and the dead Christ was tricked out with lace and flowers. Around it were a number of votive images in wax, of legs, arms, hands, and feet—a thank-offering for the cure of maladies of these members. Kneeling in the coloured light from a painted window, were a number of persons praying before the image, among them a mother with her sick child in her arms, seemingly interceding for its recovery. At the door was a stall where sat an old woman selling tapers for use in this semi-pagan worship.

From the time of Clovis, in the 6th century, a church has stood upon this spot, but the present structure was begun in 1179. The western façade, with its great rose window, forty-two feet across, its "stone lace-work," and canopied niches, is the work of the famous architect, Erwin Von Steinbach. Among the statues is an impressive group of the Seven Virtues trampling under their feet the Seven Vices. Two huge towers flank the façade. Between them is a large stone platform, two hundred and sixteen feet from the ground, from which is obtained a magnificent view of the town at our feet, with its storks' nests on the roofs, its walls and ramparts, and in the distance the Vosges Mountains, the Black Forest and Jura range. The stork seems a sacred bird. The townsfolk put up false chimneys for it to build on, and I saw one huge nest transfixed on a spire. From the platform rises the open stone spire, to a height of four hundred and sixty-nine feet—the highest in Europe.* The scars and

---

* That of Cologne, since completed, exceeds it by about thirty feet.

grooves made by the Prussian cannon balls, fired during the late ten weeks' siege, are plainly seen on the stone. The massive cross on the top is that which Longfellow in his Golden Legend represents the Powers of the Air as striving, in a midnight tempest, to tear down.

The pillars that support the tower and spire are enormous. I walked around one and found it thirty-two paces in circuit. At the south door is a statue of Erwin Von Steinbach and his daughter Sabina. They are thus commemorated by Longfellow:

> "The architect
> Built his great heart into these sculptured stones;
> And with him toiled his children, and their lives
> Were builded with his own into the walls,
> As offerings unto God. You see that statue
> Fixing its joyous but deep-wrinkled eyes
> Upon the Pillar of the Angels yonder.
> That is the image of the master, carved
> By the fair hand of his own child Sabina."

The "Erwinspfeiler" referred to is of great beauty. The stone pulpit, of 1485, is exquisitely carved. But many of the statues are painted in execrable taste, with black beards and coloured robes. A mob of tourists go gaping about after a liveried verger during the service, and gather every hour before the famous clock, where an angel strikes the quarters and a skeleton the hours, and a brazen cock flaps his wings and crows. I thought it a very paltry performance, and a desecration of the grand old church. In the cloisters is the tomb of Erwin and his wife, and near by his house, with the most exquisite gothic winding-stair in stone that I ever saw.

Germany holds with an iron grip her recent conquest. Sentries in spiked helmets were patrolling the streets, and here and there arms were stacked as if it were war time. The day I arrived, a feigned surprise of the city was repulsed ; cavalry galloped through the streets, and infantry massed in the squares. The day I left, a mock siege took place, and the heavy guns were firing from the citadel and ramparts, which have been made almost impregnable. One of the townsfolk told me that the thrifty German administration, which had introduced water-works and promoted the prosperity of the place, reconciled the people to their change of masters. In the narrow and crooked streets are many fine old mediæval houses, with gothic gables and elaborate wood-carving; and the old gates, watch-towers, and walls are delightfully quaint.

I went from Strassburg to Heidelberg, by way of Baden and Carlsruhe. Baden, which used to be the rendezvous for most of the titled and professional blacklegs of Europe, has lost much of its "bad eminence" since the abolition of its gaming tables. It is still a favourite resort of fashion on account of its mineral waters, its gaiety, and its beautiful scenery.

The great attraction of Heidelberg is the castle, once the finest in Europe, and now, next to the Alhambra, says Longfellow, the most magnificent ruin of the middle ages. Its older portions date from 1294, but it was frequently enlarged till it became of vast extent and extraordinary magnificence. It is a charming walk through the quaint old town and up the castle hill, now terraced into a stately pleasure-ground. The deep, wide moat, the massy walls and ivy-mantled towers—at once a fortress and a palace—have an air of stern feudal grandeur that I have seen nowhere else. After being the abode of kings and electors for four hundred years, it was captured by the French, consumed by fire, blown up by powder, and left the magnificent ruin we now behold. Beneath a grim portcullis, with its grate drawn up, we enter the great court-yard shown in the initial cut of this chapter, once gay with tilt and tourney, with martial array or bridal train. All around are stately façades of various ages and of splendid architecture adorned with exquisite arabesques, garlands of fruit and flowers, mouldings and fluting and lace-work admirably carved in stone. In niches on the wall stand rows of knights in armour, and on the front of the Rittersaal the heroes of Jewish history and classic fable; but all, alas! marred and dismembered by the iron mace of war. We are led through vaulted corridors; through roofless banquet halls, where kings once feasted; through a ruined chapel and up stone winding-stairs to the bower-chambers of fair queens and princesses—now open to the owls and bats. In the great kitchen is a huge fire-place, big enough to roast an ox, an evidence of the royal hospitality of ancient days. The *Gesprengte Thurm*, or "shattered tower," was, as its name signifies, blown up by the French. One-half of its cliff-like wall, twenty-one feet in diameter, fell into the moat, and, after two hundred years, still lies an unbroken mass. On the ruined "Elizabeth Tower," built for the daughter of James I. of England, grows a tall linden, and in her bridal chamber the swallows make their nests. An air of desolation mantles over all.

In an old gallery is preserved a collection of historic portraits, relics, and antique furniture, china, embroidery, ornaments, and weapons of former inmates of the castle. I was specially interested in the portraits of the fair English princess, Elizabeth, the hapless mistress of these stately halls; of Maria Theresa, of Luther and his wife, and in the wedding-ring with which he espoused the gentle nun.

From the castle terrace overhanging the valley, I enjoyed a glorious sunset view of the lovely Neckar, winding among the vine-clad slopes of the forest-billowed Odinwald—the ancient haunt of the "Wild Huntsman of Rodenstein"—and the more remote "blue Alsatian Mountains." Of course nobody leaves without seeing in the castle vaults the "great tun," which will hold eight hundred hogsheads of wine. It lies on its side, is as high as a two-story house, and one goes up a ladder to a platform, twelve by eighteen feet on the top, on which many a dancing party has been held. The hogshead shown in front of the tun, gives some idea of their relative sizes. In the foreground to the left is seen the guardian of this treasure, a gnome carved in wood, modelled after the old-time court fool of the castle. The tourist is invited to pull a cord by his side, when a hideous figure springs out of a box.

THE GREAT TUN, HEIDELBERG.

It was a students' fête day, the schloss garden was full of merry-makers, and at night the old castle was illuminated with coloured Bengal lights. Every window, which in daytime looks like the eyeless socket of a skull, and every loop-hole and cranny was ablaze, as if with the old-time revelry of the vanished centuries, or with the awful conflagration by which it was destroyed. A thunderstorm swept down the valley, and the firing of the old cannon on the castle ramparts blended with volleys of " heaven's loud artillery."

The famous university, with seven hundred students, dating from 1386, occupies a large plain building. The students wear a jaunty scarlet cap with a broad gold band. I saw on the cheek of one a great scar of a sabre slash, received in a student's duel, to which these golden youth are much addicted. The Church of the Holy Ghost is unique, I think, in this respect, that it is occupied in common by Catholics and Protestants. In 1705 a wall was built between the choir and nave, and the two Churches have ever since conducted their service under the same roof.

CHAPTER XII.

WORMS—LUTHER MEMORIES—MAYENCE—FRANKFORT—THE RHINE AND ITS LEGENDS—BINGEN—COBLENTZ—EHRENBREITSTEIN—BONN.

NO memories of the German Fatherland are more potent than those of the Great Reformer, Martin Luther. With no mightier name can one conjure up the spirit of the past. I made, therefore, a devout pilgrimage to Worms, as the scene of one of the grandest conflicts for human freedom that ever took place. Worms is one of the most ancient, and in the middle ages was one of the most important, cities of Germany. It was destroyed by Atilla, rebuilt by Clovis, and here Charlemagne and his successors frequently resided. Its population of 70,000 in 1815 had dwindled to 5,000. It is now about 15,000. The chief glory of Worms, however, is its memories of Luther and its famous Luther Monument, This is one of the finest in Europe. It cost $85,000, and was nine years in execution—finished in 1868. A massive platform, sixteen yards square, bears in its centre a large pedestal, and around its border seven smaller ones. On the central pedestal, twenty-eight feet high, stands a colossal bronze statue of Luther, eleven feet high. He wears his academic costume; in his left hand he holds a Bible, on which his right hand is placed emphatically, while his face, on which faith is admirably portrayed, is turned upward.

CATHEDRAL OF WORMS.

On the base are written the immortal words: "Hier stehe Ich: Ich kann nicht anders: Gott helfe mir. Amen!"—"Here I take my stand. I can do no other. May God help me, Amen!" Fine bas-reliefs on the base illustrate events in the life of the great Reformer: in front, the Diet of Worms; at the back, Luther nailing his Theses to the door of the Wittemburg church, the students cheering, and the monks scowling; at the right, Luther giving the cup to the laity, and his marriage; at the left, Luther preaching and translating the Bible. At the base are four sitting figures of the great Reformers before Luther—Waldus, Wycliffe, Huss, and Savonarola. At the four corners of the platform are majestic bronze figures, nine feet high, of four illustrious fellow-helpers of Luther—Frederic the Wise, Philip the Magnanimous, Melancthon, and Reuchlin. In the interspaces of the side are beautiful seated female figures, symbolical of the towns of Magdeburg, mourning the slaughter of her children; Spires, protesting; and Augsburg, with a palm branch, making confession. The whole makes one of the most impressive groups and finest monuments I have ever seen.

From the Luther-Platz I went to the old Romanesque Cathedral, begun in the eighth century, in which the condemnation of Luther was signed by Charles V. It is 423 feet long. The vaulted roof rises to the height of 105 feet, and four lofty towers are weathered with the storms of well-nigh a thousand years. It is one of the finest specimens of Romanesque architecture in Germany. The carvings are very quaint. In one the genealogy of our Lord is shown by a tree growing out of the body of David, from whose branches spring Christ's kingly ancestors, and from the top, as the consummate flower of all, springs the Virgin Mary. In this stern cradle of the Reformation, a mass for the dead was being sung. When the procession of priests and nuns filed out, I was left alone to moralize upon the memories of the past. I afterwards wandered through the narrow streets and bustling market-place and depopulated suburbs, and tried to conjure up the great world drama of the Diet of Worms, three centuries and a half ago.

From Worms I went to Mayence (in German Mainz), a strongly fortified town of 60,000 inhabitants, with a garrison of 8,000, at the junction of the Main and Rhine. Here a Roman fortress was built by Drusus, B. C. 14. The bastions of the citadel are still named after Tacitus, Drusus, and Germanicus; and the Eigelstein, a monument forty-two feet high, erected B. C. 9 by the Roman legions, to Drusus, is still shown. Here Boniface, the Apostle of Germany, in 751, set up his See. He was the son of an English wheelright, and assumed as his seal a pair of wheels. To this day, after twelve hundred years, these are still the arms of the city. The Cathedral, a huge structure of red sandstone, 522 feet long, is of several dates, from 978. It is filled with monuments of much historic interest, from the 13th century. Here lived Guttenburg, the German inventor of printing, 1440. His statue, house, and printing-office are shown.

On every side are evidences of a stern military domination. The largest buildings in the city—great stone structures—are barracks, full of soldiers. At the gates are sentry-boxes, painted with black and white chevrons. Infantry in spiked helmets, cavalry, and artillery parade the streets; massive ramparts, with a deep fosse, surround the city; and ancient gate-towers tell of its warful history.

The old Electoral Palace, a vast building, is occupied as a museum of Roman antiquities, the richest in Germany. Here are altars, votive slabs, and tombstones of the Roman legions; bronze swords, helmets, and other weapons and armour; torques, balistas, lamps, vases, coins, and even the piles of the old Roman bridge across the Rhine—taking one back to the very dawn of the history of central Europe.

The octagonal tower of St. Stephen's Church rises majestically to the height of 327 feet. At the top is a watchman, always on the look-out for fires. If one wishes to ascend he rings a bell at the foot of the tower, when the watchman throws down the key in a bag, and expects his visitor to bring it up. I was very tired, and did not know what might be the consequence if I failed to carry the key up to the top, so I did not ring for it.

It is an hour's ride from Mainz to Frankfort. The railway runs along the winding Main, commanding fine views of the Taunus Mountains. Frankfort is, after Rouen, the most quaint old city I saw in Europe. It dates from the time of Charlemagne, who held here a convocation of notables of the Empire in 794. It was a rallying-place for the Crusaders, and the trade emporium of Central Europe. Here, for centuries, the German Emperors were elected and crowned. Its great fairs, in which merchants from all parts of Europe assembled, have, through the growth of the railway system, lost their importance; but it is still one of the great money-markets of the world, with a population of 100,000.

I lodged at the magnificent Hotel Schwann, in which the final treaty of peace between France and Germany was signed by Jules Favre and Bismarck, May 10th, 1871. I was shown the handsome *salon* in which this historic act took place, the inkstand and table used, and Bismarck's room. The city abounds in splendid streets, squares, public buildings, art galleries, and gardens. But to me its chief attraction was its ancient, narrow alleys between the time-stained timbered houses, with their quaintly-carved fronts, each story projecting over the lower till the upper ones almost meet overhead, with grotesque figures supporting the projections and roof; the old historic churches and halls, and the mouldering gates and watch-towers of its walls; and the old inn court-yards, with huge, long-armed pumps.

One of the most picturesque of these streets is the Judengasse, or Jew's Quarter. Though much improved of late, it is still very crowded and squalid. Hebrew signs abound—I saw that of A. Rothschild, the father of the house—and keen-eyed, hook-nosed Shylocks were seen in the narrow shops. Till the year 1806 this street was closed every night, and on Sundays and holidays all day, with lock and key, and no Jew might leave this quarter under a heavy penalty. They had to wear a patch of yellow cloth on their backs, so as to be recognised. In the Römerberg, an ancient square, was the inscription: " Ein Jud und ein Schwein darf hier nicht herein"—" No Jews or swine admitted here." Such were the indignities with which, for centuries, the children of Abraham were persued.

I tried to get into the old Jewish Cemetery, a wilderness of crumbling mounds and mouldering tombstones, but after crossing a swine market and wandering through narrow lanes around its walls, I could not find the entrance, and could not comprehend the directions given me in voluble German gutturals. There are now 7,000 Jews, many of them of great wealth, in the city, and the new synagogue is very magnificent.

The most interesting building, historically, in Frankfort, is the Römer, or town hall, dating from 1406. It has three lofty crow-stepped gables toward the Römerberg. I visited the election room, decorated in red, where the Emperors were chosen by the electors, and the Kaisersaal, in which the newly-elected Emperor dined in public, and showed himself from the windows to the people in the square. On the walls are portraits of the whole series of Emperors for over a thousand years—from Charlemagne down—the Karls, Conrads, Seigfrieds, Friederichs, and many another, famous men in their day, long since turned to the dust and almost forgotten.

Among the more striking monuments of Frankfort is that of Guttenburg, Faust, and Schœffer, the German inventors of printing; with figures of Theology, Poetry, Science, and Industry sitting at its base—a noble tribute to a noble art. There are also fine monuments of Schiller, Senckenberg, and Gœthe; and the birthplace of the latter, a handsome timbered house with four projecting stories.

The Roman Catholic churches are decorated in a wretched florid manner, and everywhere we read, "Heilige Maria, bitt fur uns"—"Holy Mary, pray for us." Livid Christs, stained with gore, harrow the feelings and revolt the taste.

A handsome stone bridge, dating from 1342, crosses the Main. It is embellished with a statue of Charlemagne, and with a gilt cock perched on a crucifix. According to the legend, the architect vowed that the first thing that crossed the bridge should be sacrificed to the Devil, and a cock became the victim.

Of special interest to me was a very picturesque carved house in which Luther lodged, from whose window he preached when on his way to Worms. It bore a curious effigy of the Reformer. The quaint corner oriel was very striking.

The art treasures of Frankfort are numerous and important. Here is Dannecker's Ariadne, a lovely figure riding on a panther—a symbol of the triumph of beauty and innocence over brute ferocity. In the museum are several Dürers, Holbeins, and Van Eycks. But nothing impressed me more than Lessing's " Huss before the Coun-

LUTHER HOUSE, FRANKFORT.

cil of Constance." The scarlet-robed cardinals and the mitred bishops, all the pomp and all the power of the age, seek to crush the solitary, dark-robed man before them— his features wan and worn with long imprisonment. But in the calm high look upon his face, you read that, though they may burn him, they cannot conquer or harm him— that he is above and beyond their power. I never saw such profound dejection portrayed on canvas as in a striking picture of the Jews in Babylon.

In sailing down the legend-haunted Rhine, I travelled leisurely, stopping at the more interesting points—Bingen, Coblentz, Bonn, and Cologne. On my way to Bingen—" Sweet Bingen on the Rhine "—I passed Ingleheim, now a straggling village, once the site of a famous palace of Charlemagne, of whose splendour the chroniclers give fabulous accounts—scarce a relic of it now remains. At Bingen, a charming old town, I climbed a hill to an ancient castle on the site of a Roman fortress. A pretty young girl did the honours, showing the old banners, antique furniture and portraits of the dead mediæval barons, who held that eagle's eyrie against all comers ; and pointing out the glorious view of the lovely Rhine valley, with the vine-covered Neiderwald, Rüdesheim, Johannisberg, and other richest wine-growing regions in the world. Every vine removed in building the railway cost about $2.50. The famous Johannisberg Vineyard is only forty acres in extent, carefully terraced by walls and arches ; yet in good years it yields an income of $40,000. A bottle of the best wine is worth $9—enough to feed a hungry family for a week.

Between Bingen and Bonn lies the most picturesque part of the many-castled Rhine, whose every crag, and cliff, and ruined tower is rich in legendary lore. It winds with many a curve between vine-covered slopes, crowned with the grim strongholds of the robber knights, who levied toll on the traffic and travel of this great highway of central Europe—even a king on his way to be crowned has been seized and held till ransomed. When they could no longer do it by force, they did it under the forms of law, and, till comparatively late in the present century, trade had to run the gauntlet of twenty-nine custom-houses of rival states on the Rhine. In the whole of Germany there were 400 separate states, or, including baronies, 1,200 independent powers.

There are over 100 steamers on the Rhine, many of them very large, splendid, and swift. More than a million tourists travel on these steamers every season, not to mention those by the railway on each side of the river. A Rhine steamer, like a Swiss hotel, offers a fine opportunity to study the natural history of the genus tourist, of many lands and many tongues. The French and Germans are very affable, and are very fond of airing their English, however imperfect it may be. I was much amused in observing an imperious little lady, followed by a gigantic footman in livery, whose arduous task it was to humour the caprices of her ladyship and her equally imperious little lap-dog. There is also much freight traffic on the river by means of powerful tugs, which pick up and overhaul a submerged cable wire.

Just below Bingen, on a rock in the middle of the stream, is the Mausethurm, or Mouse Tower, a tall, square structure, which takes its name from the legend of the cruel Archbishop Hatto, of Mayence, which has been versified by Southey. Having caused a number of poor people, whom he called " mice that devoured the corn," to be burned in a barn during a famine, he was attacked by mice, who tormented him day and night:

> " I'll go to my tower on the Rhine," said he ;
> " 'Tis the safest place in all Germany ;
> The walls are high, and the shores are steep,
> And the stream is strong and the waters deep."
>
> But the mice have swum over the river so deep,
> And they have climbed the shores so steep,
> And now by thousands up they crawl
> To the holes and windows in the wall.
>
> And in at the windows, and in at the door,
> And through the walls by thousands they pour,
> And down through the ceiling, and up through the floor,
> From within and without, from above and below—
> And all at once to the Bishop they go.

The legend is a curious illustration of the growth of a myth. It undoubtedly arises from the name Mauth-Thurm, or Tower of Customs, for levying toll, which the old ruin bore in the middle ages. The Rheinstein is a wonderfully picturesque, many-towered old castle, dating from 1279, perched on a rocky cliff, accessible only by a narrow path,

It is the Vautsberg of Longfellow's "Golden Legend." The poet's lines vividly photograph the view of the Rhine valley from its crumbling ramparts:

> Yes, there it flows, forever, broad and still,
> As when the vanguard of the Roman legions
> First saw it from the top of yonder hill !
> How beautiful it is ! Fresh fields of wheat,
> Vineyard, and town, and tower with fluttering flag,
> The consecrated chapel on the crag,
> And the white hamlet gathered round its base,
> Like Mary sitting at her Saviour's feet
> And looking up at His beloved face !

The Falkenburg, a famous marauder's castle, was besieged by the Emperor Rudolph in the 13th century, and all its robber knights hanged from its walls. Near by is a chapel, built to secure the repose of their souls. The picturesque castle of Nollich frowns down from a height of 600 feet, whose steep slope the Knight of Lorch, according to legend, scaled on horseback, by the aid of the mountain sprites, to win the hand of his lady love. The name, Hungry Wolf, of one of these grim old strongholds, is significant of its ancient rapacity. So impregnable was the castle of Stahleck, that during the thirty years' War it withstood eighty distinct sieges. Pfalz is a strange hexagonal, many-turreted ancient toll-house, in mid stream, surmounted by a pentagonal tower, and loopholed in every direction. Its single entrance is reached by a ladder from the rock on which it stands.

The Lurlic Rock is a high and jutting cliff, on which is the profile of a human face. Here dwelt the lovely Siren of German song and story, who, singing her fateful song and combing her golden hair,* lured mariners to their ruin in the rapids at her feet. Two cannon on deck were fired off, and woke the wild echoes of the rock, which reverberated like thunder adown the rocky gorge. According to a veracious legend, the Neibelungen treasure is buried beneath the Lurlenberg, if the gnomes, offended at the railway tunnel through their ancient domain, have not carried it off. The fair daughters of the Schönburg, for their stony-heartedness, were changed, says another legend, into the group of rocks named the Seven Virgins.

The Rheinfels is the most imposing ruin on the river. It once withstood a siege of fifteen months, and again resisted an attack by 24,000 men. Two rival castles are derisively known at Katz and Maus—the Cat and Mouse—probably from their keen watch of each other. The Sterrenberg and Liebenstein are twin castles on adjacent hills, to whose mouldering desolation a pathetic interest is given by the touching legend of the estrangement and reconciliation of two brothers who dwelt in them 600 years ago. At Boppard, a quaint old timbered town, the lofty twin spires of the church are connected, high in air, by the strangest gallery ever seen. Marksburg, a stern old castle, 500 feet above the Rhine, is the only ancient strong-

---

* Heine's song on this subject is one of the most popular :—

Sie kammt es mit goldenem Kamme,	With a golden comb she combs it,
Und singt ein Lied dabei;	And sings so plaintively ; [cents
Das hat eine wundersame,	O potent and strange are the ac-
Gewaltige Melodei.	Of that wild melody.

hold on the river which has escaped destruction. Past many another grim stronghold we passed, where wild ritters kept their wild revels.

> And many a tower, for some fair mischief won,
> Saw the discoloured Rhine beneath its ruin run.
> There was a day when they were young and proud,
> Banners on high and battles passed below ;
> But those who fought are in a bloody shroud,
> And those which waved are shredless dust ere now,
> And the bleak battlements shall bear no future blow.

After a day of rare delight, I was glad when the steamer glided through the bridge of boats to the quay at Coblentz, a large town, whose fortifications will accommodate 100,000 men. It dates from the time of Drusus, B.C. 9, and during the stormy centuries since then has withstood many a siege. In the old church of St. Castor, founded A.D. 836, I found, at eight o'clock next morning, several hundred school children, boys and girls, with their teachers, taking part in a religious service. The choir and chancel were filled with flowers—those human flowers more fair than they. One boy chanted the responses to the priest at the altar, and the clear voices of the children joined in almost, I think, the sweetest singing I ever heard. In this Church of St. Castor, the sons of Charlemagne met to divide his empire in 843. The monumental effigies in the old churches of this Rhine valley are often characterized by an elaborate grotesqueness that seems very incongruous on a tomb. Of this, the figures on the tomb of Conrad Kurzbold are a striking example. The narrow streets and old gates and churches of Coblentz were also very queer. On the clock tower a bearded mechanical figure forever rolls his eyes and opens his mouth in a very ridiculous manner. A lovely walk amid trees and flowers leads along the Rhine.

TOMB OF CONRAD KURZBOLD.

Crossing the bridge of boats, I climbed by many a zigzag between frowning walls, to the famous fortress of Ehrenbreitstein, the Gibraltar of the Rhine. During the century, $6,000,000 have been spent on this impregnable fortress. Its garrison is 5,000. A soldier conducted me through barracks and bastions, declaiming volubly in gutturals which seemed to choke him, about I don't know what. From the summit, 400 feet above the river, one of the grandest views in Europe is disclosed. Below, the turbid stream of the Moselle joins the clear current of the Rhine, and the whole course of the latter, from Stolzenfels to Adernach, may be traced as in a map. Our own St. Lawrence, as seen from the citadel of Quebec, is as large as half a dozen Rhines. As I stood on the ramparts, a regiment of spiked helmets marched across the bridge of boats, the stirring strains of the "Wacht am Rhein" floating up in the morning air. They marched with a springing stride up the steep slope—large, well-built, blue-eyed, full-bearded Teutons—far superior in physique and intelligence to the average French soldier. One gigantic fellow bore the eagle standard, with several bells and horse-tails attached. The uniform looked coarse, the knapsacks were of cow's hide, with the hair on; and some of the men wore glasses—there are no exemptions for shortness of sight. While hundreds of soldiers were lounging about in enforced idleness, I saw women unloading army stores from a railway van. "Woman's rights" in Europe struck me as woman's wrongs. Better endure a little civil disability then encounter the fierce struggle for unwomenly work with man.

Taking the steamer again, we stop at Neuwied, a Moravian town; Andernach, with its ancient walls, gates, towers, and bastions, and its quaint legend of the carved Christ who came down nightly from the cross to do works of charity through the town; and Hammerstein, a place of refuge for the Emperor, Henry IV., who did penance three days in the snow at Canossa. The view of Rolandseck, the lofty summits of the Siebengebirge, or Seven Mountains, and the towering peak, 900 feet above the river, where

> The castled crag of Drachenfels
> Frowns o'er the wide and winding Rhine,
> Whose breast of water proudly swells
> Between the banks that bear the vine,
> And hills all rich with blossomed trees,
> And fields that promise corn and wine,
> And scattered cities crowning these,
> Whose far white walls along them shine,

is one of the richest in natural beauty and romantic association of any in this lovely land. Rolandsbogen is a solitary crumbling arch on a lofty hill, the sole relic of the castle of the brave knight Roland, the Paladin of Charlemagne, who fell at Ronceval. Another legend is that Count Roland, affianced to the peerless Princess Hildegunde, joined a crusade and was reported slain by the infidels. The inconsolable Hildegunde became a nun, and took refuge in a neighbouring kloster of Nonnenwerth. Roland, though desperately wounded, recovered and returned to claim his bride, only to find her lost to him forever. In his despair he built the castle of which only the crumbling arch remains, and there lived in solitude, catching rare glimpses of his lost Hildegunde passing to her devotions in the kloster chapel, or watching the gleam of her taper at the convent lattice. At length he missed the fair form and the faint taper ray, and soon the knelling of the kloster bell, and the mournful procession of nuns, told him that his beloved Hildegunde had passed away from earth forever. From that hour he never spoke again; his heart was with the dead; and one morning he was found rigid and cold, his death-filmed eye still turned, as in its last look in life, toward the convent chapel. This tender tale of love and sorrow still speaks to the heart across the centuries with a strange spell; and we gaze with a pathetic interest on the crumbling tower and on the kloster chapel which still looks forth from its embowering trees.

I stopped at the ancient town of Bonn, with a fine university, the largest in Germany, occupying the old electoral palace, 600 yards in length. On an old bastion is a bronze statue of Arndt, the author of the "Wacht am Rhein," pointing with his right hand to the storied stream that he loved so well. Here was born Beethoven, whose fine statue was inaugurated by Queen Victoria. It bears simply the inscription, "Ludwig von Beethoven, geboren zu Bonn, 1770"—nothing more. The mediæval cloisters of the Romanesque cathedral are very interesting. The suburbs are beautiful, and in the quiet "Gottesaker" sleeps the dust of Niebuhr, Bunsen, Schumann, Arndt, and other famous men, and here Lange lives. From Bonn, I was whirled down the Rhenish Railway to Cologne, and soon caught sight of the grandest gothic church of Christendom.

CHAPTER XIII.

Cologne—Aix-la-Chapelle—Brussels—Antwerp.

THE crown and glory of Cologne is its wonderful minster. Its mighty mass seems to dominate over the city—a brooding presence of sublime majesty. From the windows of my hotel, almost beneath its shadow, I looked up and up with insatiable gaze at its lofty spires, surrounded by a cloud of scaffolding.

> Unfinished there in high mid-air,
> The towers halt like a broken prayer.

Nevertheless, incomplete as it is, it more fully satisfies the eye and mind than any other building I ever beheld. Its spires, turrets, flying buttresses, gargoyles, foliaged capitals, and flamboyant tracery seem more like an organic growth than a work of man's device. For six long centuries the mighty structure has been slowly growing, year by year, and this very year it reaches its late completion. The work of the last forty years has cost about $4,000,000. Its vast and vaulted roof rises to a shadowy height of over 200 feet, and its sky-piercing spire springs, like a fountain in stone, over 500 feet in air. But no mere enumeration of dimensions can give any idea of the magnificence and beauty of its exterior, or of the awe-inspiring solemnity of its vast interior. Arch beyond arch receded in seemingly infinite perspective, the deep-dyed windows poured their many-coloured light over capital and column, and the deep chant of the choir and roll of the organ throbbed and pulsated like a sea of sound.

There are many other objects of interest in the ancient city—the *Colonia* of Roman times. Notwithstanding its open squares, many of its streets are narrow, gloomy, and redolent of anything but *eau de Cologne*. Its lofty walls, with their massive gate-towers, deep moats, and drawbridges, give it the appearance of a huge fortress—which it is, with a garrison of 7,000 soldiers, and 135,000 civilians. The Rathhaus, or town hall, a quaint structure, is built on the arches of an old Roman fort. I was shown the Hansa-Saal, or hall in which the Hanseatic League was formed in 1367. The Fest-Saal, or Banquet Hall, is very magnificent. I visited half a score of ancient churches—those of St. Martin's and St. Maria, splendidly restored. St. Gereon's, commemorating 318 martyrs of the Theban Legion, slain in 286 by Diocletian, said to be founded by the Empress Helena, is very odd. The nave is ten-sided, and the skulls of the martyrs are preserved in the choir, which is nineteen steps above the nave. The most notable relic-church, however, is that of St. Ursula, a dilapidated old structure, crowded with the skulls and bones of the 11,000 virgin attendants of the English Princess Ursula, martyred here by the Huns in the fourth or fifth century—the legends do not agree which. The whole story is told in a series of quaint old paintings on the walls. Rows of shelves are full of skulls wearing satin caps and tinsel coronets, and some of peculiar sanctity rest in be-jewelled velvet cases. Some are still crowned with soft flaxen-hair, which, as a special favour, one may touch. Others have their names written on their forehead. The rest of the bones are piled up by the cord, or strung on wires and arranged in grotesque arabesques. In the cathedral, I should have mentioned, you are shown the bones of the Magi, or three Kings, brought by the Empress Helena to Constantinople, and since then stolen and recaptured, and held at a king's ransom. Can anything be more degrading than this worship of dead-men's bones and all uncleanness, with its puerile imbecilities and its palpable frauds and lies!

A picturesque ride of forty miles brings one to the very ancient town of Aix-la-Chapelle. It was the favourite residence of Charlemagne; here he died in 814, and here, for 700 years, the German emperors were crowned. I stopped here chiefly to visit the tomb of the Great Charles, the grandest figure in the half-mythical history of the Middle Ages. It is situated in the odd old cathedral, begun by the Emperor in 796. In the gallery of the octagonal nave is the marble chair on which the mighty monarch sat enthroned in all the majesty of death for 350 years. The tomb was opened by Barbarossa in 1165; the remains were transferred to an antique sarcophagus, and subsequently to a jewelled reliquary; and the throne was used in the coronation of the emperors till 1531. On a plain slab is the simple epitaph of the grandest monarch for a thousand years—CAROLO MAGNO. Nor needs he more. His true memorial is written in the institutions and history of mediæval Christendom. As I entered the church, the deep tones of the organ were pealing in solemn cadence through the lofty vaults, and the chanting of priests and choir boys blended with the unearthly sweetness of the strain. And so, I thought, during the long ages of rapine and wrong that have swept over the land, the hymns and prayers which have voiced the aspirations, and hopes, and sorrows of the successive generations, have gone up to God; and age after age the storm of battle has desolated, in wars almost without number, one of the fairest regions of the earth.

In another church I saw a large-sized model of the Grotto of Lourdes, lit up with tapers, at which a number of men and women were devoutly praying. I took a drink at the famous warm sulphur springs from which the place takes its name, which were known in the times of the Romans, but I found the water excessively nauseous.

The ride of ninety miles to Brussels is one of great beauty. The Netherlands, though for the most part deficient in picturesque scenery, possesses historic memories unsurpassed in heroic and romantic interest by those of any country in Europe. The Protestant struggle against the despotism of Spain is one of the grandest episodes in the history of mankind. The provinces of Brabant, Flanders, Hainault, and Holland, recall many a storied page of Motley, Prescott, and Robertson. The industries, art and literature of the Walloons, Flemings, and Dutch, both pique and gratify the curiosity of the tourist. Here, as nowhere else, he sees the *chefs d'œuvre* of Rubens, Vandyck, Rembrandt, and other Flemish masters.

The route to Brussels winds down the lovely valley of the Maas and Meuse, and through the wild forest of Ardennes, with bold cliffs, ruined castles, bosky glades, rich pastures, thriving villages, and a country cultivated like a garden. Liège, Namur, and Louvain are populous and busy towns, rich in Flemish art and architecture.

Brussels, with a population of nearly 400,000, is another Paris, with its broad boulevards, its palaces, parks, and squares, and its cafés and gay out-of-door life. In constructing new streets, the city offered prizes, from $4,000 down, for the best twenty façades. The result is some of the finest architecture in Europe, characterized largely by the use of the human figure in caryatides and the like. The new Palais de Justice is to cost $1,000,000. Of the new, however, one can see enough in New York and Chicago. My own taste is for the old, and this was amply gratified. The ancient church of St. Gudule is of vast size and venerable majesty—one of the richest I have seen. In an artificial grotto was a figure of the Virgin, dressed like a fairy queen. The singing of the vespers at twilight was exquisitely sweet. The celebrated Hôtel de Ville is one of the noblest town halls in Europe. Its flamboyant façade and exquisite open spire, soaring like a fountain 370 feet in the air, once seen can never be forgotten. At the summit the Archangel Michael forever waves his glittering sword as if to guard the city at his feet. The fretted stone work looks like petrified lace. An intelligent young girl showed me the old historic rooms, including that in which the Emperor Charles V. is said to have abdicated his crown, 1556. The scene is represented with much vigour on a piece of old tapestry. From the windows I could see the spot where those noble patriots, Counts Egmont and Hoorne, died as martyrs to liberty. The old guild houses of the butchers, brewers, carpenters, and skippers are very odd. The gable of the latter represents the stern of a large ship, with four pretruding cannon.

In the art gallery I saw an admirable statue of Satan, which embodied the conception of Milton's "ruined archangel" in a most marvellous manner. A statue of Eve with a serpent creeping to her ear, was exceedingly pathetic, with its manifest foredoom of the Fall. The portrait of Alva shows, in the thin lips and cruel eyes, the cold, stern, remorseless persecutor. But the strangest collection in Europe, probably, is that of the mad painter Wiertz, which fills an entire museum, many of the pictures being of gigantic size, and exhibiting Titanic strength of imagination. He was an ardent hater of war and of the great war maker, Napoleon. One painting represents with painful realism its horrors, and another, Napoleon in hell, confronted by the victims of his unhallowed ambition. "The Last Cannon" and the "Triumph of Christ" exhibit the final victory of Love over Hate, Cross over Corselet, Peace over War. There is a wild weirdness about many of his pictures that makes one shudder. He is fond, also, of practical jokes. Here a fierce mastiff is bounding out of his kennel. There a figure stands in a half-open door, as if about to enter. You look through an eye-hole and see a mad woman slaying her child, and through another and behold a prematurely buried man bursting his coffin. It is a chamber of horrors. Yet the execution is marvellous, and the *motif* of the picture is generally patriotic and humane.

From Brussels to Antwerp I had the honour of riding in the train with a papal ecclesiastic of very high rank, if one could judge by the magnificence of his purple soutane, and the deference paid him by the officials of the railway. At Vilvorde, which we passed, 360 years ago the English Reformer, Tyndale, for translating the Bible, was burned at the stake by the predecessor of this same ecclesiastic. His last words were, "Lord open the King of England's eyes." The very next year—was it not an answer to his prayer?—the Bible was published in England by royal command, and a copy placed in every church.

Antwerp, a busy town on the "lazy Scheldt," was, under Charles V., the most prosperous city in Europe. But Spanish tyranny and the terrors of the Inquisition reduced the population to, at one time, 40,000. It is strongly fortified, and has stood many a siege. The glory of the town is its magnificent cathedral. Its lofty open spire Napoleon compared to Mechlin lace, and Charles V. used to say it should be preserved in a glass case. Its interior is unique in this, that it has three aisles on each side of the nave. The perspective of the arches, supported on 125 columns, is very fine. The glory of the church is Rubens' masterpiece—his wonderful "Descent from the Cross." I confess to a lack of apprecianion of Rubens. I can see little beauty in his figures, and they have often a vulgar coarseness that is offensive to good taste. Of course, the masterful life and rich colouring of his pictures indicate the consummate artist. But there is none of the poetic feeling of Raphäel, nor of the seraphic purity of Fra Angelico. Crowded around the venerable cathedral, like mendicants around the feet of a priest, are a lot of squalid old houses, that greatly mar its beauty. Beside the principal portal is an ancient well, covered by an intricate canopy of wrought iron, made in 1529 by Quentin Matsys, whom, as an inscription records, love of an artist's daughter transformed into a painter—"*Connubialis amor Mulcibre fecit Apellem.*"

The Hôtel de Ville, with a splendid façade 300 feet long, rising to the height of 180 feet, contains some fine historic halls, one with an immense chimney piece, with famous Bible reliefs. In a neighbouring church-yard is an artificial Calvary, forty feet high, crowded with statues of saints and angels. Beneath is a grotto in imitation of the Holy Sepulchre, and an iron-grated purgatory, in which carved figures in painted flames beseech alms for masses to procure their release. It has all the horror of Dante without any of the poetry.

The picture gallery is wonderfully rich in *chefs d'œuvre* of Flemish art; but none impressed me more than a dead Christ, by Matsys, whose deep pathos brings tears to the eyes. I confess I liked better than the old masters much of the work in the Septennial Exhibition of modern Belgian painters. Their mastery of technique is perfect, and their interpretation of nature very sympathetic. In the public squares are fine monuments of Rubens, Teniers, and Vandyck, and the streets bear the names of famous painters.

My most delightful memory of Antwerp is that of its sweet chimes. There are in all, in the cathedral tower, ninety-nine bells—the largest, at whose baptism Charles V. stood god-father, and gave his own name, weighs eight tons. Every quarter of an hour they ring out a beautiful *carillon*, and at the full hour they proclaim in more elaborate melody the flight of time. My hotel was in the Cathedral Square, and at night I lay awake listening to the exquisite strain and thinking of Longfellow's musical lines:

> As the evening shade descended,
> Low and loud and sweetly blended,
> Low at times and loud at times,
> And changing like a poet's rhymes,
> Rang the beatiful wild chimes.
> Then with deep sonorous clangour
> Calmly answering their sweet anger,
> When the wrangling bells had ended,
> Slowly struck the clock eleven;
> And from out the silent heaven,
> Silence on the town descended.
> Silence, silence everywhere,
> On the earth and in the air.

CHAPTER XIV.

HOLLAND—DUTCH CHARACTERISTICS—KERMIS AT ROTTERDAM—THE HAGUE—AMSTERDAM—GHENT—BRUGES—FETE OF THE VIRGIN—HISTORIC MEMORIES—ENGLAND AGAIN.

> A country that draws fifty feet of water;
> A land that lies at anchor and is moored,
> In which men do not live but go on board.—*Hudibras.*

THIS amphibious country is well named Holland—the hollow land. Its character is indicated by its heraldic cognizance—a swimming lion, with the motto *Luctor et Emergo*, which may be freely rendered, "I struggle to keep above water." Much of the country lies below the level of the sea. These fertile pastures have been reclaimed from the domain of the ocean by the daring industry of the Dutch, who have built great dikes, or embankments, to keep out the ravening sea, which, unlike the "ancient and unsubsidized allies of England" —an invulnerable defence—is an implacable enemy, perpetually besieging their earthen ramparts. In spite of ceaseless vigilance against its assaults, the ocean sometimes bursts its barriers and turns fertile meadows and smiling valleys into a stormy sea—*Verdronken Land* as it is called—literally, "drowned land." Over and over again the patriotic Dutch have opened the dikes and laid their country far and wide beneath the waves, as their sole defence against Spanish tyranny. In the terrible siege of Antwerp by the French in 1832, the dikes were cut, and the country for three years was flooded by the sea, and gun-boats cruised about the fields. The stratum of saline sand deposited almost prevented cultivation for many years.

The route from Antwerp to Rotterdam traverses a characteristically Dutch landscape—vast meadows, level as a floor and divided by trenches of water. Canals ramify everywhere, along whose silent highways stealthily glide the *trekschuits* or "drawboats," often dragged by men, or even women, harnessed like horses. Along the horizon, wherever one looks, are rows of picturesque windmills, ceaselessly brandishing their mighty arms, as if to challenge any over-valiant Quixotte to mortal combat. I have seen a dozen in a single view. The villages, country-houses, and gardens are scrupulously, almost painfully, neat and clean. At Broek, near Amsterdam, no horses are allowed in the streets, and no one may enter a house with his boots or shoes on. The town-houses are generally high and narrow, built of red brick with crow-stepped gables, each with a large crane for hoisting goods from the streets, or from the canals which flow below. The lazy barges creep along, and just as you want to cross a canal up swings the counterpoised drawbridge, and you envy the Dutch patience of the vrows and mynheers who quietly wait—the latter stolidly pulling at their porcelain pipes, as though it were life's sole concern—till the bridge falls again. The language too, has such a grotesque, half comic look—like English gone mad. For instance, on cellar doors you read, " Water en vuur te koop "—" water and fire to sell," where boiling water and hot turf are furnished the poor to prepare their tea and coffee. " Dit huis is te huur,"— " This house is to hire,"—and " Hier verkoopt man sterke dranken,"—literally, " Here a man may buy strong drinks,"—frequently occur.

The men and women one meets in the street seem built on the same principle as the Dutch boats in the canals— very broad and staunch looking craft. I saw, at last, where Rubens found the models for his very solid saints and angels, and for his exceedingly ample, not to say exuberant, allegorical figures. There happened to be in progress, when I was in Rotterdam, a *Kermis*—literally a " Church Mass," but practically a peasants' fair or Dutch carnival, when the whole city, thronged with the neighbouring peasantry, was given up to holiday making. A balloon was sailing overhead, and till it passed from view everybody was craning his neck to catch a glimpse of it. Posts were planted across certain streets to prevent the intrusion of carriages on the region reserved for the fair. This region was crowded with booths, tents, merry-go-rounds ; stages for harlequins, mountebanks, quacksalvers, and cheap theatricals; shooting-galleries, peep-shows, and stalls for selling all manner of toys, trinkets, pictures, fancy goods ; and more than all, and everywhere, luncheon booths and drink counters. Greater Babel I never heard.

The chapmen and venders were crying their wares, bands were discoursing brazen music in half a dozen places at once; not to mention the drums, trumpets, and vociferations of itinerant showmen inviting the gaping crowd to enter the enchanted palace or fairy bower whose beauties were portrayed on glaring canvas; and the proprietors of the learned pig, the tame snakes, the happy family of monkeys and parrots, or of the dwarf or giantess, setting forth the attractions of their respective shows. It was the most vivid realization of Bunyan's Vanity Fair I ever expect to see. The throngs of people consisted largely of peasants in their gala dress—the men in stiff high-collared coats with big horn buttons, and high-crowned hats; the women in stuff gowns with a white neckerchief, a lace cap and a broad gold band across the forehead with spiral horns projecting at either side, and large, clumsy-looking pendants in their ears. These must be of considerable value, but Dutch thrift secures to almost every peasant woman this singular and ugly head-gear.

The inn where I lodged was thronged with these holiday makers, evidently bent on having a good time. I was much amused, as I took my lunch, at a group at another table—composed, I surmised, of the parish priest and three or four of his male parishioners with their wives; and stout, florid, homely, hearty women they were. They ordered the waiters about, and talked all together with their mouths full, ate with their knives, and sat so far from the table that not a little of their food fell on the floor, and gnawed their bones in a voracious manner. The common conventions of table etiquette did not trouble them in the least. They seemed to be a simple-minded, honest, industrious people. In this prosaic country even the dogs have to work for their living, as seen in the cut, which represents a common street scene in Rotterdam.

STREET SCENE IN ROTTERDAM.

The town has little of architectural interest. The Groote Kerk, or Church of St. Lawrence, is a large, bare, ugly structure. The view of red roofs, flat pastures, windmills and canals, did not repay me for my weary climb up its lofty spire. A great dike runs through the town, along which stretches the Hoog Straat, or High Street. The busiest spot in the city is the Boompjes, a handsome quay planted with trees, from which a hundred steamers and innumerable other vessels sail to many Dutch and foreign ports. The art gallery is rich in homely Dutch interiors and still life, painted with exquisite minuteness; but the prosaic subjects seemed to me not worth the skill or patience bestowed upon them. In the Groote Markt is a fine statue of Erasmus, and on the small house, now a tavern, in which the great scholar was born is the legend, "Hæc est parva domus, magnus qua natus Erasmus." Just opposite is the "House of the Thousand Terrors," where, during the Spanish massacre in 1572, hundreds of persons took refuge. Having barricaded the doors and windows they killed a kid and let the blood flow over the threshold. Seeing the gory stream the Spanish soldiers thought the work of butchery complete and hastened to deeds of slaughter elsewhere. To-day the peaceful draper shop which occupies the site presents no trace of that dreadful day of terror.

It is only fourteen miles from Rotterdam to the Hague, and on the way we pass, first Schiedam, celebrated for its "Hollands" and "Geneva," in which baneful manufacture 220 distilleries are said to be employed; and then Delft, which gives its name to our common pottery, and from which the Pilgrim Fathers sailed for Plymouth Rock. A more painful interest attaches itself to the Prinsenhof, or palace, the scene of the assassination of William the Silent, the grand Protestant champion of Europe. The mark of the bullet is still seen. Here also Grotius was born.

The Hague, for centuries the capital of Holland, with a population of 100,000, is one of the most charming cities I have ever seen. Its handsome streets, spacious squares, quaint old houses, splendid park of stately elms and chestnuts, its fishponds and tree-shaded canals. have an air of unsurpassed quiet, comfort, and thrift. Its galleries and museums are exceedingly rich in treasures of art. Nor is it without stirring historic memories. It was with profound interest that I visited the spot where the grand old Arminian, Barneveldt, was executed in his seventy-second year, 1619. In the art gallery one may read the naval history of Holland in the famous battle pieces which illustrate the career of De Ruyter and of Van Tromp, who, with broom at masthead, swept up the Thames till his guns were heard in London streets. The splendid wig and aristocratic nose of our Dutch sovereign, William III., will also profoundly impress the hero-worshipping mind. The gem of the collection, however, is neither King nor Kaiser, but Paul Potter's far-famed bull—a magnificent animal, which seems about to step out of the canvas. When it was stolen by Napoleon, the Dutch offered for it 60,000 florins—over $20,000. The naval, municipal, and royal museums abound in objects of intense artistic or historic interest.

The railway from the Hague to Amsterdam, by way of Leyden and Haarlem, traverses the sand dunes of the Northern Sea, and a broad "polder" reclaimed from the ocean. Leyden is chiefly famous for its three months' siege by the Spaniards in 1574, when 6,000 persons died of famine rather than yield to the hated foe, of whose historic defence the story is so grandly told by Motley. The old town has almost as many canals as streets, and the sluggish water forms a complete double moat. Its university was long one of the most famed in Europe.

Haarlem, too, has its story of cruel siege and brave defence, in which even the women took an active part, and 10,000 of the people perished. But the Spaniards were, at last, victors, and the Protestant clergy and 2,000 citizens were ruthlessly executed. The great organ of the Groote Kerk is one of the finest in the world. This was the chief seat of the tulip mania of 1637, when a single rare bulb sold for $5,000. In a few months the price fell to $20.

Amsterdam, the Venice of the North, contrasts very unfavourably with the Queen of the Adriatic. It may be more thrifty, but it is far less poetic. The busy traffic of its canals continually perturbs their muddy waters, which have the colour and consistency of pea-soup, and the tall, dull, red brick houses, through the sinking of the piles on which they rest, lean at various angles as though they would topple over. Like Venice, Amsterdam has grown from a few fishermen's huts, built like seagulls' nests, on an oozy sandbank, to be a great commercial entrepôt. It has a thrifty population of 300,000. Its ninety islands are connected by 300 bridges, and, as in Venice, almost every house can be reached by water. The stately rows of elms, however, that border the canals have no counterpart in the fairer southern city. The finest building is the Palace, a massive Renaissance structure, built for a town hall, on 14,000 piles—hence the jest of Erasmus about the people living on the tops of the trees. Its interior is exceedingly sumptuous, and the Council Chamber of those merchant princes is one of the most magnificent in Europe.

The Rijks Museum is the finest gallery in Holland. Here alone can Rembrandt be seen at his best—in his famous "Night Watch," and "Syndics." Helst's "Arquebusiers" is also marvellously life-like and real. Teniers, Van Ostade, Dow, Cuyp, and other masters of the Dutch school are here in their glory; but their favourite subjects seem to me irredeemably prosaic—a tavern scene, a kitchen, a fish-market, which are not much to my taste, however artistically shown. I went to see the famous fish auction, and was glad to escape from its unsavoury crowds of sailors and fish-wives and their slimy merchandise. I lodged at the old Bible House, in which the first Dutch Bible was printed. I was shown a copy of the original edition of 1542—a massive black letter book with queer old cuts. The son of the printer opened an inn, and set up as his sign an open Bible inscribed with the text, "Take a little wine for thy stomach sake;" and there, above the door, it is to this day.

I returned from this famed city of the Zuider Zee by way of Utrecht, where was signed the important treaty which gave peace to Europe in 1713, and Gouda, famed for its stained glass, to Rotterdam. I shared the carriage with a very polite and intelligent Jew and his family, who gave me much information. The religious toleration of Holland made it a place of refuge for these persecuted Ishmaels and Hagars of mankind, and added to the wealth and thrift of the country. Amsterdam has nearly 40,000 Jews, with ten splendid synagogues. Here, in 1632, the celebrated Spinoza, the "father of modern philosophy," was born.

On my return journey to Brussels, I travelled with a German merchant of very radical sentiments. He bitterly denounced the domestic policy of his Government, especially its oppressive military system, which, he said, was crushing the life out of the trade and industry of the country; and he cited examples which went far to vindicate his antipathy. The people, he said, were ready to revolt, but for the iron hand that kept them down. If such sentiments widely prevail, it is an omen of ill augury for the future of the Empire.

I was sorry that I could not visit the far-famed field of Waterloo, where, by English valour, the liberties of Europe were secured and the greatest despot of history overthrown; but my time would not permit. Only one more day was left for me on the Continent, and I must make the best of it. Reaching Brussels at midnight, I left it early in the morning for Ghent, Bruges, Ostend, Dover, and London. The railway traverses a flat and fertile country, cultivated like a garden. My first pause was at the ancient town of Ghent, celebrated in song and story—the birthplace of our English John of Gaunt, of the Emperor Charles V., of the Van Arteveldes, and of many another famed in history. In the fifteenth century it was one of the most important free cities of Europe, boasting 80,000 citizens capable of bearing arms. Its chief prosperity arose from its industrial supremacy, its weavers alone numbering 40,000. When the bell was rung that summoned them to work, so great was the living stream that no vessels might pass the drawbridges, nor private persons enter the public ways. The same bell is still rung, but only to make more striking the contrast between its once surging throng and its now quiet and, in part, grass-grown streets. The old historic city has an air of fallen splendour, and of mouldering decay, that is almost pathetic. So great was its ancient prosperity that Charles V., playing upon the meaning of the name—from which we have the word gauntlet—said to Francis I.: "Je mettrai votre Paris dans mon Gand,"— "I will put your Paris into my glove."

The venerable Church of St. Bavon, unattractive and plain without, is exceedingly magnificent with the armorial bearings of the Knights of the Golden Fleece within. At the summit of its lofty spire is a golden dragon, captured in 1204 from St. Sophia at Constantinople. The chimes of its bells are wonderfully sweet, and ever and anon booms the great bell which bears the legend, " My name is Roland ; when I toll there is fire, when I ring there is victory in the land."* It was the fête of the Assumption of the Virgin, and the Church was crowded with worshippers. A procession of priests in crimson, purple and gold, accompanied by vergers with crosses, halberds, and maces, and peasants in blue blouses and wooden shoes, passed

---

* "*Mynen naem is Roland; als ik klep is er brand, and als ik luy is er victorie in het land.*"

through the aisles, while the deep-toned organ shook the solid walls. The Hôtel de Ville has an excellent flamboyant façade, fronting a square surrounded by Spanish houses, in which, in a conflict of stormy guilds, 500 men were slain 500 years ago. I visited the famous Beguinage, a little suburb surrounded by its own moat and walls, with 18 convents, containing 1,000 Beguines, an order of nuns of extreme antiquity. In the *salon* is a fine Raphäel, and specimens of the exquisite lacework of the nuns, some of which I purchased as souvenirs for dear ones far away.

I stopped at Bruges chiefly on account of Longfellow's fine poem on its ancient belfry. In the fourteenth century Bruges was the greatest commercial centre of Europe. The ministers of twenty foreign powers dwelt within its walls, and vessels from Venice, Genoa, and Constantinople bore the wealth of the Orient to its wharves. In the Church of Our Lady—*Onze Vrouw*—is the splendid tomb of Charles the Bold and Mary of Burgundy, and many art treasures. The chapel of the "Holy Blood" and a colossal image of "God the Father" attest the sacrilegious superstition of the people. Of this I had a further illustration in the procession in honour of the Virgin, which took place on this wise:

In a side chapel of the church a number of young men arrayed themselves in a sort of ecclesiastical dress, with facings of scarlet and gold. After much music and marshalling, the procession was organized :—priests, acolytes, choristers, in their most gorgeous robes, carrying crosses and crucifixes and burning tapers ; halberdiers in mediæval costumes, bearing battle-axes ; young girls in white veils, with gilt palms in their hands, and gilt wreaths on their heads, six of them carrying a richly adorned image of the Virgin, dressed in gold brocade ; a troop of children, all in white and crowned with flowers; young men bearing banners, gilt shrines, and jewelled reliquaries; and a long procession of citizens, and bands of music playing martial airs in the intervals of the chanting of the priests and choir boys, while the continuous clamour of the bells rang through the air. The principal feature was a gorgeous canopy borne by four leading citizens over the " Host," which was enclosed in a jewelled pyx and carried by a splendidly apparelled priest. Thurifers swung their censers ; young girls strewed flowers, fern leaves, and palm branches before the sacred shrine ; and the multitude of spectators fell down on their knees as the Real Presence of the Redeemer, as they imagined, passed by. Although some scowls were directed towards me as I stood erect, no one molested me. Candles were placed in the windows, and the houses were decorated with festoons and evergreens and wreaths of gilt ivy, as the pageant swept through the narrow streets, among mouldering monuments, and over an ancient bridge, in the placid waters beneath which the lilies floated, and stately swans dressed their snowy plumage, and an ivy-covered, ruined wall was reflected. It seemed more like an illuminated picture out of a mediæval missal than like an actual experience. I felt like rubbing my eyes to see whether I was dreaming or whether this strange pageant was a reality.

I then wandered into the Grand Place, a large square at one side of which rose the celebrated Belfrey of Bruges, of which Longfellow sings so pleasantly. I inquired for the Fleur-de-Blé at which he lodged, but found that it had been demolished. I lunched, therefore, at a little table in front of a café, and feasted my eyes meanwhile on the stately tower and listened to the musical chimes, pronounced the sweetest in Belgium; and mused upon the vanished splendours of the mouldering town. Near by was the beautifully carved gothic Hôtel de Ville, where the Counts of Flanders, on their accession to the throne used to fling largess to the people and swear to maintain the rights of the city. Longfellow thus recalls the associations of the scene :—

In the market-place of Bruges stands the belfry old and brown;
Thrice consumed and thrice rebuilded, still it watches o'er the town.

Not a sound rose from the city at that early morning hour,
But I heard a heart of iron beating in that ancient tower.

Then most musical and solemn, bringing back the olden times,
With their strange, unearthly changes, rang the melancholy chimes.

Like the psalms from some old cloister, when the nuns sing in the choir;
And the great bell tolled among them, like the chanting of a friar.

Visions of the days departed, shadowy phantoms filled my brain;
They who lived in history only seemed to walk the earth again.

I beheld the pageants splendid that adorned those days of old;
Stately dames, like queens, attended, knights who bore the Fleece of Gold;

Lombard and Venetian merchants with deep-laden argosies;
Ministers from twenty nations; more than royal pomp and ease.

I beheld the Flemish weavers, with Namur and Juliers bold,
Marching homeward from the bloody battle of the Spurs of Gold;

And again the whiskered Spaniard all the land with terror smote;
And again the wild alarum sounded from the tocsin's throat;

Till the bell of Ghent responded o'er lagoon and dike of sand,
"I am Roland! I am Roland! there is victory in the land!"

Then the sound of drums aroused me. The awakened city's roar
Chased the phantoms I had summoned back into their graves once more.

Bruges had an ancient reputation for the beauty of its maidens—"formosis Brugæ puellis"—but they had an unintelligent expression that, to me, was less attractive than the bright looks of our quick-witted Canadian girls. A blight and mildew—the effect of Romish superstition—seems to have overgrown the place; one-third of the population are said to be paupers—and very homely-looking ones they are—the women in long blue cloaks, and wearing clumsy wooden shoes.

In the fading twilight I took the train to Ostend, a famous fishing and watering place. Without stopping, I went on board the steamer, and soon left behind the row of glimmering lights of the seaside town. I was roused from my short slumber at two o'clock to climb a steep ladder to the pier at Dover, took an express train at four, and, getting a good view of Shakespeare's Cliff and of the grand old Castle, sped through the beautiful hop-fields of Kent, far surpassing in luxuriant beauty the fairest vineyards of Italy and the Rhine, and passing through Canterbury with its noble proto-cathedral of England, and Chatham with its famous docks, reached London at six o'clock, glad to see once more around me familiar English faces and to hear again the familiar English speech.

CHAPTER XV.

LONDON AND THE THAMES.

THE great city of London would demand a volume for itself. I can give it only a few pages. Next to Rome, Athens, and Jerusalem, probably no city in the world abounds more in historic and heroic memories. Almost every street and square is connected with some great event in English history, or some great actor in the mighty drama of the past. Their very names as we come upon them strike us with a strange familiarity, as of places that we long had known. Many a monumental pile—perchance a palace or a prison—has been the scene of some dark tragedy, or of some sublime achievement. In the darksome crypts or quiet grave-yards of its many churches sleeps the dust of many whose name and fame once filled the world. Undisturbed by the ceaseless roar and turmoil of the great city they calmly slumber on.

Daily the tides of life go ebbing and flowing beside them,
Thousands of throbbing hearts where theirs are at rest and forever,
Thousands of aching brains, where theirs no longer are busy,
Thousands of toiling hands, where theirs have ceased from their labours,
Thousands of weary feet, where theirs have completed their journey!

The most striking topographical feature of London is of course the winding Thames. Near its banks are grouped many of its most famous buildings, and on its bosom took place many of its most stately pageants. It will give a sort of unity to our short survey of the world-famous city to follow up this storied stream, glancing briefly at the memorable places which we pass. Perhaps we may as well begin as far down as Greenwich. Although we might well begin at Tilbury Fort, where Queen Elizabeth harangued her troops, and visit Woolwich with its famous dockyard and arsenal.

VIEW NEAR GREENWICH.

It was on a bright sunny day that I visited Greenwich Hospital and park. The famous old palace dates from 1433. Here Henry VIII. and his daughters, Mary and Elizabeth were born, and here Edward VI. died. The vast pile with its river front of nine hundred feet bears the impress of successive sovereigns down to the time of George III. when the royal palace became the home of two thousand seven hundred disabled sailors, with two thousand receiving out-of-door relief. It is now used chiefly as a naval college and picture gallery, in which the victories of England's wooden walls still stir the viking blood of the old salts, who bask in the sun and fight their battles o'er again. About a thousand boys in white and blue were training for the sea, drilling and swarming like monkeys over the rigging of a great ship, high and dry on land—protected against falls by a strong netting all around its sides. The park with its tame deer and old chestnuts, its sunny slopes and grassy glades and famous observatory is a favourite resort of hilarious holiday-makers from the town. Near by Jack Cade and Watt Tyler harangued the London mob before entering the city.

I gained the impression that Londoners are the most bibulous people I ever met. In the Thames steamers, not only was almost everybody drinking something or other, but a perambulating nuisance was pacing up and down the deck calling out, with detestable iteration "ale, brandy, gin, rum and stout," till I felt my temperance principles quite outraged.

Threading the forest of masts from almost every port, and passing the maze of docks on either hand, we reach the gloomy Tower, fraught with more tragical associations than any other structure in England, perhaps than any other in the world. Here the soil drank the blood of Fisher, More, Cromwell, Queen Anne Boleyn, Queen Catharine Howard, the Countess of Salisbury, Lord Admiral Seymour, the Earl of Essex, Lady Jane Grey,

John Dudley, Earl of Warwick, Lady Shrewsbury, Protector Somerset, Sir Thomas Wyatt, Guilford Dudley, Strafford, Sir Harry Vane, Stafford, Algernon Sidney, Laud, Monmouth, Lord Lovat, Russell, and many more of England's princes, warriors, statesmen and nobles. Erected by the Norman Conqueror to overawe the turbulent and freedom-loving city, it was for centuries the grim instrument of tyranny, and here was wreaked many a cruel deed of wrong. These stern vaults are a whispering gallery of the past, echoing with the sighs and groans of successive generations of the hapless victims of oppression. Such thoughts haunt one while the garrulous beef-eater is reciting his oft-told story of the arms and the regalia, of the Bloody Tower and Traitors' Gate, and cast their shadow of crime athwart the sunlit air.

I threaded my way through the maze of vast warehouses in Thames Street, where Chaucer lived five hundred years ago, and lunched at a little den not much larger than a packing-box, much frequented by warehouse clerks. Passing the Custom House, which employs two thousand men, and Billingsgate, the greatest fish market in the world*, we reach the Monument, which with its crest of gilded flames, commemorates the Great Fire of 1666.

---

* At the Billingsgate market a wretched old woman, begging fish offal, aroused my sympathy, but a policeman told me he had seen her go into a neighbouring tavern thirty-five times in a single day. The drink problem of England is the most difficult one with which social philanthropists have to grapple.

To the left is London Bridge, across which pass one hundred thousand persons and twenty thousand vehicles every day—an everflowing tide of humanity which seems to know no ebb. The skill of the London Jehus and police are taxed to prevent a blockade of the immense traffic. Across the bridge stood Chaucer's Tabard Inn, and to the right is Eastcheap, the site of Falstaff's "Boar's Head Tavern." Further on is that wonderful square in which stand the Bank, Exchange and Mansion House— the very heart of London's civic and commercial life. Traversing the old historic Cheapside, probably the most crowded thoroughfare in the world, we reach St. Paul's, five times burnt down and rebuilded, and associated with many of the chief events of English history. Its mighty dome dominates the entire city with a majesty surpassing even that of St. Peter's at Rome. Of all its monuments, I thought the most impressive, that of England's greatest sailor, Horatio Nelson, in the solemn crypts, and that of her greatest soldier, Arthur Wellesley, in its lofty aisle; the latter a magnificent sarcophagus beneath a marble canopy.

> Under the cross of gold
> That shines over city and river,
> There he shall rest forever
> Amongst the wise and the bold.
> In streaming London's central roar
> Let the sound of those he wrought for,
> And the feet of those he fought for,
> Echo round his bones forever more.

From the golden gallery, four hundred feet in air, one gazes upon a denser mass of humanity and its abodes than is elsewhere seen on earth. The crowded streets, the far-winding Thames, the distant parks and engirdling hills, make a majestic picture, whose impressiveness is deepened by the thought that the pulsations of the heart of iron throbbing in the mighty dome vibrate upon the ears of more persons than people the vast extent of Canada, from sea to sea. I was surprised to see in the churchyard, near the site of the famous St. Paul's Cross, an old fashioned wooden pump, which seemed to have done duty from time immemorial. The strange names of Amen Corner, Ave Maria Lane and Paternoster Row commemorate the ancient sale of religious books, which still makes up much of the local trade.

Passing down Ludgate Hill, we enter Fleet Street, the heart of newspaperdom, and enter the purlieus of the law, Lincoln's Inn, and the secluded chambers and gardens of the Temple. The Temple Church, a thick-walled, round Norman structure, dating from 1185, is like a fragment of the middle ages in the busy heart of London. Here once preached the "judicious Hooker." On the paved floor lie stone effigies of the old Knights Templar, in full armour, with legs crossed, in token that they had fought in Palestine.

> The knights are dust,
> Their swords are rust,
> Their souls are with the saints we trust.

Beside a simple slab in the church-yard, every visitor pauses with feelings of peculiar tenderness. It bears the brief, yet pregnant inscription, "Here lies Oliver Goldsmith." An old gardener showed me a tree which he said was planted by Henry VIII., under which Goldsmith and Johnson used to sit.

Passing through Temple Bar and following the Strand, so named from its skirting the bank of the river, we pass the Savoy Church, half under ground, where Chaucer was married, and the vast Somerset House, on the site of the Protector's palace, where languished three unhappy Queens. It is now used as public offices, employs nine hundred clerks, and contains, it is said, 3,600 windows. At Charing Cross is a copy of the stone cross erected where the coffin of Queen Eleanor was set down during its last halt on the way to Westminster, six hundred years ago. Opposite is Trafalgar Square, and the noble Nelson's Monument, with Landseer's grand couchant lions at its base. On this grandest site in Europe is one of the ugliest buildings in existence, the National Gallery— the home of British Art!—with its paltry façade and absurd flat domes, like inverted wash-bowls. Right opposite is Whitehall—named from England's once grandest palace. Only the Banquetting Hall now remains. Here Wolsey gave his splendid fêtes; here the Royal voluptuary, Henry VIII., fell in love with the hapless Anne Boleyn; and here Charles I. stepped from the palace window to the scaffold. Here the bard of Paradise Lost wrote Latin despatches for the Great Protector who died within these walls; here Charles II. held his profligate court, and here he also died. The Hall is now a Royal chapel. I arrived late for service and found it locked; a little persuasion induced the guardian to open the door; but the haunting memories of the grand old hall, I am afraid, distracted my mind from the sermon.

Across the street is the Horse-Guards, with its statue-like mounted sentries, and the splendid new Government Offices flanking each side of Downing Street, from whence has been ruled for a hundred years a Colonial Empire vaster than that of Rome in its widest range.

Passing through a narrow street, we come upon one of the grandest groups of buildings in the world—the venerable Westminster Abbey, St. Margaret's Church, and the new Palace of Westminster. Of course the Abbey first challenges our attention. Grand and gloomy and blackened by time without, it is all glorious within—a Walhalla of England's mighty dead. A very courteous and clerical looking verger, wearing a much be-frogged gown, escorted our party through the chapels. I only discovered that he was not the Dean or Canon by the promiscuous manner in which he dropped his h's. After he had parroted his piece, I asked permission to stroll through the chapels alone. It was kindly accorded, and for hour after hour I mused amid the mouldering effigies of the kings, and queens, and princes, and nobles who slumber here. The exquisite stone fretwork of Henry VII.'s chapel can scarcely be over praised. But its chief interest is in the tombs of two women, " not kind though near of kin"—the proud and lonely Queen Elizabeth, who found her crown but a gilded misery; and the beautiful and unhappy Mary Stuart, who even in prison and on the scaffold commanded the homage of thousands of leal hearts. Here, too, are the tombs of many of England's sovereigns from the time of Edward the Confessor, who died eight hundred years ago. Beneath those moth-eaten banners and their fading escutcheons and crumbling effigies they keep their solemn state in death. Above the tomb of Henry V. hangs the armour which he wore at Agincourt, the helmet still exhibiting the gash made by a French battle-axe. The Coronation Stone, affirmed to have been Jacob's pillar at Bethel, is geologically identical with the Scottish stratum at Scone, whence it last came.

But a yet stronger claim upon the homage of our hearts have the kings of mind who still rule our spirits from their sceptred urns. I stood with feelings strangely stirred before the tombs or cenotaphs of the genial Chaucer, father of English verse; of Spencer, "the prince of poets of his tyme," as his epitaph reads; of Johnson, "O rare Ben;" of Cowley, Dryden, Addison, Southey, Campbell, Newton, Wilberforce, Macaulay, Lytton, Thackeray, Livingston, and many another whose written words have often given instruction or delight.

The Chapter House of the Abbey, a large and lofty octagonal room, from 1282 to 1547 was the Commons Chamber of England—the cradle of Constitutional Government, and the scene of some of the stormy conflicts by which were won the civil liberties we now enjoy.

From this chamber it is an easy transition to the New Palace of Westminster, where the great council of the nation is royally housed. The architecture is, I think, the finest civil gothic in the world, a little overladen with ornament, perhaps, and already crumbling beneath the gnawing tooth of the great *Edax rerum*, but grander than aught else I ever saw. Parliament had risen, so I could only see the empty seats of the great athletes who fight the battles of the Titans in the grandest deliberative assembly in the world.

CHELSEA, FROM THE RIVER.

The adjacent great Westminster Hall, with its open oaken roof six hundred years old, was the scene of some of the most important events in the history of the nation. Here many of the early parliaments were held; here Charles I. was condemned to death; and here Cromwell, throned in more than royal state, was saluted by the proud name of Protector. Among all the statues of the kings, princes and nobles in Westminster Abbey and Palace there is not found one of the peer of the mightiest of them all—the man who found England well nigh the basest of kingdoms and raised her to the formost place in Europe. In the Abbey I saw the spot from which the embalmed body of Cromwell was rifled, and then the pinnacles of this same Hall on which his head was exposed to sun and shower for thirty years. At length in a storm it was blown to the ground, picked up by a sentry, concealed in his house, and is now—strange irony of history—preserved, it is said, at Sevenoaks, in Kent.

Diverging to the right from the river we may pass through St. James, Green and Hyde Parks to the wilderness of fashionable west-end squares and the historic royal

OLD WIND-MILL, BATTERSEA.

residences of St. James, Buckingham and Kensington Palaces. But continuing to follow its pleasant windings we at length escape from the din of the great city to the quiet of its rural surroundings. A string of pleasant villages are strung upon the stream, like pearls upon a necklace. The first of these is Chelsea, now a suburb of the city, with its hospital for invalid soldiers, shown in our cut on page 306. Chelsea has many potent memories ;— here dwelt Pym, More, Locke, Addison, Steele, and Swift; and here still lives the venerable sage, Carlyle. In the quaint old church is a memorial slab of the luckless minister of Henry VIII. and near by the tomb of Sir Hans Sloane.

SIR THOMAS MORE'S MONUMENT.

Battersea with its handsome park, slender bridge and quaint windmill, lies on the opposite side of the stream. The tomb of Bolingbroke, near by, is the chief memoral of one of the most brilliant and profligate of English writers.

Fulham has been for six hundred years the country residence of the Bishops of London. To the left of the picture is seen the palace and church. Here Richardson wrote the tear-compelling story of Clarissa Harlowe.

At Putney, famous in boating annals, Gibbon was born, and the younger Pitt died. "England shall moult no feather of her crest," declared the great commoner, and he made good his proud boast.

Chiswick House, a splendid Palladian Villa, with fine park and gardens, witnessed the last hours of Charles Fox and George Canning.

SIR HANS SLOANE'S MONUMENT.

Drop on Fox's grave the tear,
'Twill trickle on his rival's bier.

FULHAM.

In the churchyard is the grave of Hogarth, the great moralist of art, bearing the inscription by Garrick—

If genius fire thee, reader, stay;
  If nature move thee, drop a tear;
If neither touch thee, turn away,
  For Hogarth's honoured dust lies here.

Gliding past the terraced lawns, and splendid gardens of Kew, an account of which I reserve for another page, we reach

HOGARTH'S TOMB.

PUTNEY.

Richmond, which I also describe elsewhere. Near by is the quaint village of Twickenham, with its memories of Pope and Walpole.

CHISWICK HOUSE.

Passing by for the present the stately halls of Hampton Court, and still following up the narrowing stream, we reach at length the picturesque old town of Staines, deriving its name from the "Stones" which once marked the limits of the jurisdiction of London in this direction. The sluggish stream, traversed by its slow moving barges, and its venerable parish church, are shown in the cut on page 312.

We have now reached the limits of our upward journey,

and are almost in sight of the ancient towers of Windsor, which must receive more ample treatment in another chapter.

STAINES CHURCH.

CHAPTER XVI.

Windsor—Richmond—Kew.

ONE of the most delightful excursions from London is that to Windsor and Eton. When weary of the rush and the roar, the fog and the smoke of the great city, a half-hour's ride will take one through some

WINDSOR CASTLE FROM ETON.

of the loveliest pastoral scenery of England to the quiet and ancient royal borough, where everything speaks only of the past. I spent the rainy days in the galleries and museums, and took advantage of the rare sunny ones to run out to Windsor, Hampton Court, the Sydenham Palace, and other suburban excursions. When the sun does shine in England, it lights up a landscape of richest luxuriance and most vivid verdure. Nowhere have I seen such magnificent oaks and elms, such stately beeches and chestnuts, as in Windsor and Bushy Parks; nor such soft, springy, velvet-looking lawns. "How ever can I get such a lovely lawn as you have?" said an American lady to an Oxford Fellow. "Nothing is easier, madam," he replied; "you have only to roll it and mow it for a couple of hundred years."

Before one enters on the rural paradise that surrounds London, he must pass through a dreary region of hideous deformity. For some distance the railway passes on a viaduct over the suburban streets. Anything more ugly than the hundreds of acres of blackened chimney-pots and red-tiled roofs and narrow alleys and crowded dwellings of London's poor, in the manufacturing district on the south of the Thames, it would be hard to conceive. But soon we emerge from this Arabia Petræa of London's stony streets to the Arabia Felix of her engirdling parks and villas and hedgerows and gardens. Soon the mighty keep and lofty towers of Windsor Castle, one of the largest and most magnificent royal residences in the world, come in view as we skirt its noble park. The most striking feature is the great round tower, dominating from its height on Castle-hill, like a monarch from his throne, the grand group of lower buildings. Dating back to the days of William the Conqueror, what a story those venerable walls could tell of the tilts and tourneys, and banquets and festivals, marriages and burials of successive generations of English sovereigns! And over it waved in heavy folds on the languid air that red cross banner which is the grandest symbol of order and liberty in the wide world. Here

NORMAN GATE AND ROUND TOWER, WINDSOR.

to this winding shore—whence, say the antiquarians, the name Windleshore, shortened to Windsor—came, eight hundred years ago, the Norman Conqueror, and during all the intervening centuries here the sovereigns of England have kept their lordliest state—the mighty castle growing age by age, a symbol of that power which broadens down from century to century, firm as this round tower on its base, when thrones were rocking and falling on every side.

I obtained a ticket of admission to the Castle from the comely saleswoman in a bookstore. She made no charge for the ticket, but offered for sale a book of plates, which forms a very pleasant souvenir of my visit. One enters first through a frowning gateway in a massive

ETON COLLEGE, FROM NORTH TERRACE, WINDSOR.

tower into an irregular quadrangle, flanked by the lovely gothic St. George's Chapel, and the Dean's Close—a delightfully quiet and sequestered group of buildings with timbered walls in the old English style—and a long range of "knights' apartments." The chapel dates from 1474. In the chancel are the stalls of the Knights of the Garter emblazoned with their arms, and overhead hang their dusty banners. Adjoining the chapel is the royal mausoleum, in which, surrounded by the splendours of their palace home, repose the remains of Henry VI., Edward I., Henry VIII., Charles I., George III., George IV., William IV., and other royal personages—a perpetual reminder that *sic transit gloria mundi*. The deathless love of the sorrowing Queen has made this chapel an exquisite memorial of the virtues and piety of the late Prince Consort.

ETON COLLEGE AND CHAPEL.

The Upper Ward is a large and rather gloomy quadrangle, entered through a Norman gateway, surrounded by the state chambers and the Queen's private apartments. The former only may be seen. Visitors are conducted in groups by a rather pompous attendant, who feels to the full the dignity of his office. The state-rooms contain some fine paintings, but the barriers of cord leave only a narrow passage, and the guide hurries one through in a rapid and perfunctory manner, so that the visit is rather unsatisfactory. It is quite a shock to one's susceptibilities also to hear such a faultlessly attired gentleman drop his h's in such a promiscuous manner. We are led in succession through the Queen's audience chamber, and presence chamber, and guard chamber, and many another, filled with elegant tapestries and the like. St. George's Hall, in which state banquets are held, is 200 feet long, and is gay with the gold and gules and azure of royal and knightly arms. The Vandyck room is rich in royal portraits, that almost speak, by that great painter. The noble terraces—one is a third of a mile long—command lovely views of the royal gardens and park—rich in flowers, fountains, statuary, and stately trees. Herne's famous oak, celebrated in Shakspeare's " Merry Wives of Windsor," a few years ago blew down, but the Queen planted another in its place.

One climbs by a narrow stair in the thickness of the solid wall to the battlements of the ancient keep, long used as a castle palace, then as a prison—here James I. of Scotland was confined. From the leads is obtained one of the finest views in England, extending, it is said, into twelve counties. At the base is the deep moat, once filled with water, now planted with gay beds of flowers. Like a map beneath us lie the many suites of buildings, the Royal Gardens, the Home Park, the Great Park, and the

Long Walk and Queen Anne's Ride—two magnificent avenues, nearly three miles long, of majestic elms. Under the bright September sunlight it was a grand symphony in green and gold.

ELMS NEAR THE HERONRY, WINDSOR PARK.

The English are wonderfully fond of horses and dogs. One of the things, therefore, which one must not fail to do at Windsor is to visit the royal "mews," or stables—so called from the " mews " or coops in which the royal falcons were kept, three hundred years ago—such is the persistence of names in this old land. Grooms in very glossy hats, and with eyes keenly expectant of fees, do the honours of the splendid establishment, built at the cost of £70,000, which is, of course, kept scrupulously neat. Many of Her Majesty's lieges would be only too happy to be as well cared for as Her Majesty's horses and hounds.

The Thames, here a meagre stream, is converted into a canal, by means of locks, many of which are favourite subjects for the artist's pencil.

LOCK AT WINDSOR.

A few minutes' walk from Windsor is Eton College, the most famous of English public schools. The young

Etonians, who represent the very bluest blood in England, swarm about Windsor—there are 900 in attendance—in turn-over collars and stove-pipe hats, and are an odd combination of frolic and precocious dignity. "It is not fine clothes that make a gentleman," said a mother to her Eton boy. "No, mamma, I know it; it's the *hat*," was his reply. But see these boys at cricket when the "stove-pipes" are tossed aside, and a more manly set of lads you will not often find. "It was here," the Duke of Wellington used to say, "that Waterloo was won." And here for over 400 years the proudest peers of England have been trained.

Near Windsor is the sequestered church-yard of Stoke-Pogis, rendered memorable for ever by Gray's pensive elegy. This beautiful "God's acre" now contains the poet's grave, as also that of his brother-poet Waller, and of the eloquent Burke.

HORTON CHURCH.

In the same vicinity is Horton, the early home of a mightier genius, John Milton. In its ivy-mantled church is the tomb of his mother, *ob.* 1637. Here were written his sweetest poems—Lycidas, L'Allegro and Il Penseroso. And here is shown the pear tree beneath whose shade he used to woo the muse. Beaconsfield, a quaint village near by, with a fine old church, gave a home to Burke and a title to Disraeli.

I took the train to Richmond, and then walked down the winding Thames to Kew. Nothing in England surprised me more than the size of the parks in and near the great city, where land is more precious than elsewhere in the world. Here is Richmond Park of 2,255 acres. Windsor Park is still larger. Bushy Park, near by, has 11,000 acres. Epping Forest, in the suburbs, contains 3,000 acres. Hyde Park and Regent's Park, in the heart of London, comprise nearly 1,000 acres.

Richmond is a charming town, climbing the slopes which overlook the winding Thames. It has that comfortable air of finish and maturity which shows that it has long ago reached its majority—so unlike our restless, growing Canadian towns. The comfortable villas, lovely lawns and gardens have such a delightful air of repose, as if here the eager rush of life was never known. From the summit of the hill is one of the loveliest conceivable prospects of stately park, majestic trees, quaint old ivy-covered churches and placid reaches of the Thames, gay with white-winged pleasure-barks and joyous boating parties. This scene forms the subject of one of Turner's finest paintings in the National Gallery.

Bluff King Hal and Good Queen Bess often held their court in the old palace, and here, in 1603, the latter died —clinging pitifully to the last to a life which had been to her little else than a gilded misery.

CLAREMONT.

A little further on rise " Claremont's terraced heights," haunted with painful memories of Clive, the Government clerk who " founded an empire where the foot of Alexander had trembled," and then returned to gnaw his heart at the ingratitude of his country, and seek rash refuge in self-slaughter. Hither, too, Leopold of Belgium brought his bride, the Princess Charlotte, the pet and pride of the

British nation—to mourn, after one brief year of wedded bliss, her untimely fate. And hither, in later times, fled Louis Philippe, a refugee from the anger of his revolted subjects. What a lesson the stately halls and broad fair acres of the grand old park read of the vanity of earthly fame and glory!

RICHMOND BRIDGE.

After a pleasant lounge on the old stone bridge at Richmond, I walked down the Thames side as far as Kew, with its old palace and famous gardens. The gently sloping lawns and charming villas and old historic seats recalled Mrs. Hemans' lines:

> The stately homes of England,
> How beautiful they stand
> Amid their tall ancestral trees
> O'er all the pleasant land.

One of the most notable of these, Zion House, is an imposing pile. In the fifteenth century it was a nunnery, but is now the property of the Duke of Northumberland. The famous lion which used to ramp upon the top of Northumberland House, in Trafalgar Square, London, was removed hither when the town house of the proud race of the Percys gave place to a modern hotel.

ZION HOUSE.

Near by is Isleworth, with its ivy-mantled old church tower; and a little further on, the palace of Kew, an unpretending, large red-brick house, in old-fashioned grounds, the residence for many years of George III.

The glory of Kew is its Botanic Gardens—the finest in the world. They comprise over 300 acres, laid out with sylvan walks and drives, charming lakes and fountains, and magnificent gardens and conservatories. The palm-house is 362 feet long and 100 feet high, and beneath its lofty roof rise the feathery fronds of majestic oriental palms. I viewed with special interest the splendid Victoria lilies, with blossoms a foot in diameter, and great raft-like floating leaves five or six feet across. The strange whimsical-looking cacti, all prickles and knobs and brilliant blossoms, were very remarkable. Here are three museums, rich in the curious vegetable products of every clime—a collection of nature's freaks, and an object lesson in botany unequalled elsewhere in the world. I was glad to see the woody wealth of Canada so well represented. Huge cross sections and thick planks of British Columbia pine, about eight feet in diameter, and polished specimens of the rich woods and other native growths, give a very favourable impression of the resources of England's greatest colony.

I rode back to London on the top of an omnibus, in the deepening twilight, through miles of elegant suburban streets, and then through miles of brightly-lighted crowded city thoroughfares, weary but delighted with a day of rich instruction and pleasure.

CHAPTER XVII.

Hampton Court—Oxford—Kenilworth.

GARDEN GATEWAY, HAMPTON COURT.

AFTER Windsor Castle, no palace in England possesses more historic interest, or seems a more fitting abode for its sceptred line of sovereigns than Hampton Court. It is reached in three-quarters of an hour from the heart of London, and the sudden transition from the din and turmoil of the great city to the cloistered seclusion of these quiet courts and galleries, and the sylvan solitude of these bosky glades, is a most delightful experience.

I left the railway train at the little town of Teddington,

with its many gabled church that I might enjoy the approach to the palace through the majestic avenues of Bushy Park, a royal demesne of 11,000 acres. It was a glorious day. An early shower had washed the air and brightened the verdure of the grand old park. Its chief glory is a magnificent avenue of limes and horse-chestnuts, six rows of them, extending in straight lines for over a mile. Such splendid masses of foliage I never saw elsewhere, except, perhaps, the grand old elms and chestnuts of the Hague. They were planted by William III., and for well-nigh two hundred springs and summers have flushed with the pink beauty of their blossoms, and gleamed with the russet hue of their prickly fruit. Our engraving gives some idea of the fine vista of the main avenue, seen reflected in the broad and placid pool in the foreground.

BUSHY PARK, CENTRE AVENUE.

Near the court end of the avenue is a curious basin with carp and gold fish, in the centre of which rises a singular structure, half monument, half fountain, weathered with age and overgrown with moss and lichen. The residence of the "ranger," a sombre red brick house screened off by railings, blends harmoniously with the quiet beauty of the scene.

The lowing of kine, the faint tinkling of sheep-bells, and the swift whirr of the pheasant or rustle of the hares through the ferns, are all the sounds that meet the ear. Through the distant forest glades sweep the antlered deer, or pause in their browsing to stand at gaze as undismayed as their ancestors in the days of merrie Robin Hood and Littlejohn. Here the grim Puritan, Oliver Cromwell, when he could lay aside for a time the cares of state, used to doff his steel hauberk and buff jerkin, and don a coat of Kendal Green for a swift gallop through the park after the flying deer or hares.

Reaching Hampton Court, we enter first the sequestered park known as the Wilderness, and every one on his first visit tries his skill in penetrating the famous labyrinth—" a mighty maze, but not without a plan "—that has bewildered generations of young and old children since the time of its creator, William of Orange. It is a narrow pathway winding backwards and forwards, and round about between quick-set hedges, leading to an arbour in the centre. If you once make a wrong turn you are lost, and may wander for hours without reaching the goal. I had no difficulty, by following the simple clue suggested by my guide-book, in finding my way in and out. A sturdy urchin was perched on a high seat overlooking the maze, to give directions, for a consideration, to those who had lost their way.

The palace not yet being open, I strolled through the spacious grounds in company with a gentleman from Norway. The gardens are laid out in the symmetrical Dutch

BUSHY PARK.

manner brought over by William III. from the Hague—broad walks, pleasant alleys, trim rectangular parterres, decked with flowers and foliage plants and statuary, and studded with noble masses of chestnuts, holly, and yew, the latter sometimes cut into fantastic forms. The views up and down the winding Thames, with its villas, its gray ivy-mantled churches, its quaint old inns, and its gay pleasure parks, are worthy of a Ruysdael's pencil.

The palace itself was originally built by the celebrated Cardinal Wolsey, the haughty minister of Henry VIII. The proud prelate was then in the zenith of his glory, and built and banquetted more like a sovereign prince than like a vassal of the Crown. The palace was successively occupied by Henry VIII., Mary, Elizabeth, James I., Charles I., Cromwell, Charles II., James II., William III., Anne, George I., and George II. Since the reign of the last

ON THE THAMES, NEAR HAMPTON COURT.

of these sovereigns it has ceased to be a royal residence, and is now occupied by certain noble but reduced pensioners of the Crown.

The building is of red brick, the older part in the Tudor gothic style, with battlemented parapets. The newer portions are in the renaissance style. Over the entrance to the central court are seen the arms of Wolsey, with his motto, "*Dominus mihi adjutor*"—"God is my helper."

On the walls are terra-cotta medallions of the Roman Emperors, presented to Wolsey by Pope Leo X.

Passing beneath the Tudor arch of Wolsey's Tower, with its fan-traceried ceiling, we ascend a broad stone stairway to a splendid baronial hall, whose open timber roof, stained windows, rich with gules and gold, gaily blazoned banners

HAMPTON COURT—WEST FRONT.

and gleaming armour, recall the stately mediæval pageantry of which it was the scene. Here are the ciphers and arms of the royal Bluebeard and his wife, Jane Seymour, and near them those of the fallen Cardinal. Here, in 1558, Philip and Mary held their Christmas banquet—with Elizabeth as their guest, or prisoner—the great hall blazing with a thousand lights. Here, it is said, Shakespeare's self played before good Queen Bess a part in the splendid drama which commemorates the glory of Henry and the fall of the proud founder of these halls. But of all this gorgeous pageantry only a shadowy memory remains. Our cut shows the quaint costume of the last century.

ENTRANCE TO WOLSEY'S HALL, HAMPTON COURT.

The colonnade of coupled Ionic pillars running across the middle quadrangle, as shown in the engraving on page 334, is a later addition by Sir Christopher Wren, and is quite out of keeping with its gothic surroundings.

The great attraction of the palace now is its splendid gallery of over a thousand paintings, many of them by distinguished masters. Conspicuous among these are the famous historical portraits by Vandyck; and the court beauties, by Sir Godfrey Kneller and Sir Peter Lely. The portraits of these fair frail creatures, once the pride of courts and cynosure of every eye—all dead and turned to dust two hundred years ago—are suggestive of stern

MIDDLE QUADRANGLE, HAMPTON.

moralizings to an austere mind. We cast no stone. *Requiescant in pace.* We pass through guard chambers, presence chambers, royal closets and bedrooms, chapels and banquet halls—all lined with paintings of much historic or artistic interest. Here were preserved, till recently, the famous cartoons of Raphäel, now in the Kensington Museum, which are so familiar from engravings. Originally prepared by the great painter, at the request of Leo

X., as designs for tapestry, "they were slit into strips for the guidance of piece work for a Flemish loom, tossed, after the weavers had done with them, into a lumber room; then, after a century's neglect, disinterred by the taste of Rubens and Charles I., brought to England, the poor frayed and faded fragments glued together, and made the chief decoration of a royal palace." They are among the very finest work of Raphäel. Before leaving the palace we pass

HAMPTON COURT—LOOKING UP THE THAMES.

through the stately gateway shown in our initial cut, into the private garden, and see the famous vine, under glass, of course, planted in 1769. Its stem is thirty inches in girth, its branches extend a hundred feet, and yield from 2,000 to 3,000 pounds of grapes. These are sent, by the Queen's command, as presents to her private friends.

Returning to London, we pass through the pretty town

of Hampton, possessing little of note except the memory and house of Garrick. Hither the great actor, sated and weary with the mimic life upon the stage, retired to spend his closing days in quiet, or in the society of a few favoured friends. The house and picturesque grounds are well shown in the accompanying engraving.

GARRICK'S VILLA.

One of the chief charms of rural England is the ancient church in almost every parish—often hoary with extreme age, and mantled with a venerable growth of ivy green. In the quiet God's acre in which they stand heave the mouldering mounds beneath which

>Each in his narrow cell for ever laid,
>The peaceful fathers of the hamlet sleep.

The old Walton Church, by the Thames side, shown in the cut, is a typical example of these monuments of the piety of our ancestors.

WALTON CHURCH.

My visit to Oxford was made under unpropitious circumstances. It had been raining for days, I might almost say weeks, and the whole country was flooded. The uncured hay was drifting about the fields, and the prospects for harvesting the grain were very gloomy. If you wait for fine weather in England, you may wait for a long time ; so I stayed not for storm or shine. Amid a pouring rain I visited the Colleges, the Bodleian Library, the Museum, new Keble Hall and Chapel, and the stately St. Mary's and Christ Church.

This venerable seat of learning, dating from the time of Alfred, the ancient Oxenforde—its cognizance is still a shield with an ox crossing a stream—has a singularly attractive appearance as seen from a distance, its many towers and spires, and the huge dome of the Radcliffe Library rising above the billowy sea of verdure of its sylvan surroundings. A nearer approach only heightens the effect of this architectural magnificence. Probably no city of its size in the world presents so many examples of stately and venerable architecture as this city of colleges. Look in what direction you will, a beautiful tower, spire, or gothic façade will meet the eye.

The general features of the Oxford Colleges, of which there are no less than twenty, are similar. They consist, for the most part, of one, two, or three contiguous quadrangles, carpeted with a turfy lawn of exquisite verdure, and surrounded by long rows of collegiate buildings, containing lecture rooms, library, refectory, students' rooms, and kitchen. Frequently there are quaint carved cloisters, as at Magdalen, or pleasant gardens, shady alleys, and daisy-tufted lawns. The outer quadrangle is entered by an arched gateway from the street, where a porter peers out from his den, and touches a well-trained forelock to strangers. As I passed beneath the archway of Christ Church, through Wolsey's "faire gate," well worthy of the name, I asked the porter which were the rooms that had been occupied by John and Charles Wesley. Somewhat to my surprise, the answer I received was : "I don't know. Never heard of them. That must have been a long time ago." I concluded that this ignorance must be an idiosyncracy of the porter mind, for at Pembroke College near by, of which Blackstone and Whitefield were

VIEW OF OXFORD.

students, is pointed out the room occupied by Samuel Johnson; and the name of Addison is still linked with one of the pleached alleys of Magdalen. I climbed the old tower from which "Great Tom," weighing 17,000 pounds—twice as much as the great bell of St. Paul's—every night tolls a curfew of 101 strokes, as a signal for closing the college gate.

The large dining-hall of Christ Church College, next that of Westminster, is the grandest mediæval hall in the kingdom. The open timber roof, of Irish oak, 350 years old, with gilt armorial bearings, is as sound as when erected. On the walls are paintings by Holbein, Lely, Vandyck, Kneller, and Reynolds, of distinguished patrons or students of the College, from Wolsey down to Gladstone, whose portrait occupies an honoured place. Here, at remarkably solid tables, the students dine. Here Henry VIII., Elizabeth, James I. and Charles I. banquetted and witnessed dramatic representations ; and here, in 1634, the latter monarch held his last Parliament when driven from Westminster.

Beneath the stone stairway is the passage leading to the great baronial kitchen, with its high, open roof. A white-aproned, rubicund old head cook did the honours of his important domain. He showed me a monster gridiron on wheels ; the huge turnspit, on which they still roast, before an open grate, thirty joints at once ; and the treadmill where the unhappy turnspit dog keeps up his unprogressive march on the sliding platform of his mill. Observing my admiration of a huge elm slab, about six inches thick, used for a kitchen table, "Fifty years ago," he said, laying his hand upon it, " I helped to bring that table into this hall." For half a century he had been cooking dinners for successive generations of " undergrads," and seemed hale and hearty enough to last for half a century more.

RADCLIFFE LIBRARY, OXFORD.

I went then into the venerable chapel, whose massive columns and arches date from 1180. It is also the cathedral church of the diocese. The sweet-toned organ was pealing, and the collegiate clergy were chanting the choral service, which has been kept up ever since the Reformation.

Oxford is such a crowded congeries of collegiate buildings, often connected by narrow and winding streets, that it is only by obtaining a bird's-eye glance that one can take in a comprehensive view of the city and its many colleges. Such a view may be had from the Radcliffe Library, shown on the preceding page. To the left may be seen the front of Brazenose College, said to be named from the *brazen-hus*, or brew-house, of Alfred's palace. Over the entrance—as a play upon the word—is a huge brazen nose, very suggestive of brew-house potations. Near by is the Bodleian Library. A sacred stillness seems to pervade the alcoves, laden with the garnered wisdom of the ages, of many lands and many tongues. One speaks involuntarily in tones subdued, and steps with softened tread. It was an agreeable surprise to find a book by the present writer in such good company. Among the objects of interest are a MS. copy of Wycliffe's Bible—the true charter of England's liberties, and MSS., by Milton, Clarendon, Pope, and Addison; the autographs of many English sovereigns; historic portraits, including one of Flora Macdonald, not at all pretty; Guy Fawkes' lantern, a very battered affair; a chair made of Drake's ship, in which he, first of English sailors, circumnavigated the globe; Queen Elizabeth's gloves, and a seal worn by Hampden, with the legend:

> "AGAINST MY KING I DO NOT FIGHT;
> BVT FOR MY KING AND KINGDOM'S RIGHT."

The ceiling is studded with shields bearing the University crest, an open Bible, with the pious motto, "DOMINVS ILLVMINATIO MEA."

It struck me as rather an anachronism to be shown as "New College" a building erected by William of Wykeham in 1386. Amid the religious silence and solemn beauty of its venerable cloisters—"a dainty relic of monastic days"—seems to slumber the undisturbed repose of five long centuries.

The ivy mantled gateway of St. Mary's Church, is an object of strikingly picturesque beauty. The image of the Virgin, above it, gave great offence to the Puritans, and was one of the causes of the impeachment of Archbishop Laud. It seemed to me a desecration to see civic placards about gun licenses and dog taxes affixed to the doors and gateways of the churches.

The air of complete seclusion from the din of life of many of these colleges, is one of their chief charms. Not more sequestered was the leafy grove of Academus, than the gardens of Magdalen, or "Maudlin," as it is locally called. Within a stone's throw of the busy High Street, deer are quietly browsing under huge old elms, with their colonies of cawing rooks, as though the haunts of men were distant and forgotten. Here, in a beautiful alley which bears his name, Addison used to walk and muse on high poetic themes. In the cloisters are a group of

GATEWAY OF ST. MARY'S CHURCH, OXFORD.

strange allegorical figures, the origin and meaning of which no one can explain. One of the Fellows with whom I fell into conversation, interpreted them as symbolizing the seven deadly vices and their opposite virtues—an admonition as necessary to the scholars of five hundred years ago as to those of to-day. On May morning a Latin hymn is sung on the tower, a relic, it has been suggested, of the May-day Baal worship of pagan times. The persistence of these old customs, amid the changefulness of modern life, is remarkable. Another singular one, of unknown origin, at Queen Philippa's College, is that on New Year's the Bursar gives each member a needle and thread, with the words, " Take this and be thrifty." The scholars here have, time out of mind, been summoned to dinner by the sound of a trumpet, instead of by bell, as elsewhere. Here, too, is the Boar's Head Carol sung at Christmas, to commemorate the deliverance of a student who, attacked by a wild boar, thrust into its throat the copy of Aristotle that he was reading, and so escaped. Of this College, Wycliffe, the Black Prince, and Henry V. were members.

St. Mary's Church is invested with some of the most memorable associations of the Reformation. From its pulpit Wycliffe denounced the Romish superstitions of his day, and maintained the right of the laity to read the Word of God, the true palladium of their civil and religious liberty. Two centuries later, when Romish influence was in the ascendant at the University, the martyr bishops, Cranmer, Ridley, and Latimer, were cited here for trial before Cardinal Pole, 1555 ; and hither the following year the venerable Archbishop Cranmer was brought from prison for the purpose of publicly recanting his Protestant opinions. "Soon," says Foxe, " he that late was primate

ST. MARY'S CHURCH, OXFORD.

of all England, attired in a bare and ragged gown, with an old square cap, stood on a low stage near the pulpit.'

After a pathetic prayer, stretching forth his right hand, instead of the expected recantation, he said : "Forasmuch as my hand offended in writing contrary to my heart, my hand therefore, shall be first punished, for it shall be first burnt." Having thus "flung down the burden of his shame," he was dragged from the stage, with many insults, to the place where he glorified God in the flames, after having been compelled to witness the martyrdom of Latimer and Ridley. On the scene of their death now rises the beautiful Martyrs' Memorial. The effigies of the martyrs are of remarkable expressiveness ; that of Latimer, bending beneath the weight of four score years, seems to be uttering his dying words, " Be of good comfort, Master Ridley, and play the man ; we shall this day light such a candle, by God's grace, in England, as I trust shall never be put out."

Additional pathetic interest is given to this St. Mary's Church, by the fact that in the choir, in a brick vault, lie the remains of the lovely and ill-fated Amy Robsart, the heroine of Sir Walter Scott's "Kenilworth." Her body was brought from Cumnor Hall, only four miles distant, to Oxford, and lay in state in Gloucester College.

After a hard day's work, I went to an old fashioned inn to refresh the hungry inner man. Instead of being sent into a great bleak dining-hall, in which one's individuality is completely lost, I was led up stairs to a small and cosy parlour. Here a tasteful repast—tasteful in two senses—was served by a neat-handed Phyllis, and I enjoyed the homely English comfort of "taking mine ease in mine inn."

The same night I took train for Stratford-on-Avon, on pilgrimage to the spot—

> "Where his first infant lays sweet Shakespeare sung,
> Where his last accents faltered on his tongue,"

and was whirled through the darkness at a speed surpassing that of even Herne the Hunter. I found lodgings at the Red Horse Inn, and slept in a great bed of state, with a huge four post canopy that might have come down from Shakespeare's time. Next morning—still in the rain—I found the sexton of the venerable parish church, which is approached through a beautiful avenue of limes, and is surrounded by cypress and yew trees, and soon stood above the plain stone slab in the chancel floor, which covers all that was mortal of the greatest poet of all time.

As I strolled along the banks of the gentle Avon, I thought : " Here the boy Shakespeare chased the butterfly, and plucked the buttercups, and hunted thrushes' nests, and sported in the crystal stream ; and across those meadows the love-sick swain sped to the cottage of sweet Anne Hathaway ; beneath those trees they held their tryst, and on their beechen bark he carved her name." I next visited the old Grammar School, of Edward the Sixth's time, where the immortal bard learned the mysteries of that English tongue which he has rendered classic for ever. I then proceeded to the house in which the future poet first saw the light. It is a quaint two-storied timbered house, which has successively been used as a butcher's shop and as an inn. The front door is cut in two, so that the lower part might be kept closed—to shut out the dogs I was told. The stone floor has also been badly broken by the chopping on the butcher's blocks. Passing up a winding wooden stair, we enter the room in which the wondrous babe's first cry was heard. Across this rough floor he crawled on his first voyage of discovery, and through this lead lattice he caught his first glimpse of the great world-drama, whose thousand varied scenes he has so marvellously painted for all time.

Here is his desk from the Grammar School, notched all over with his school-boy jack-knife. Here is his signet ring, and the chair in which he sat. What a potent spell of poetry to bring to this dull Warwickshire town, from all parts of Christendom, ten thousand pilgrims every year, to pay their homage at the shrine of genius ! Among the noted names etched on the lattice pane, I saw those of Walter Scott and Washington Irving.

The comely hostess of the Red Horse, notwithstanding her almost rustic-seeming simplicity, well knew how to charge for the bed of state and the toothsome viands so daintily served in the cosy breakfast-room. It was the dearest place—I mean in cost—at which I stopped in England.

I took the train—still in a pouring rain—to Warwick, said to be the oldest town in the realm—built by the British king Cymbeline, destroyed by the Picts, and rebuilt by Caractacus—the Caerleon of ancient times. The first Earl of Warwick was a knight of King Arthur's Round Table. The famous hero, Guy of Warwick, was a giant nine feet high, who performed prodigies of valour before he became a hermit and retired to the caves of Guy's Cliff, where he died. His tremendous sword and armour, in confirmation of the story, are shown at the castle. Warwick, the Kingmaker, maintained 30,000 vassals on his estates, and was the last of the turbulent barons who set up and put down sovereigns as they pleased. The famous old castle is declared by Sir Walter Scott to be the finest monument of ancient and chivalrous splendour which remains uninjured by age. Its massive walls rise like a cliff in air, and dominate the whole town—a monument of the stern feudal tyranny of " ye olden time." As the family were at home, I had to be content with an outside view.

The parish church is said to be the finest in England. The sepulchral monuments of the Earl of Beauchamp, and the Earl of Leicester, the unhappy favourite of Queen Elizabeth, read their impressive lesson of the vanity of earthly glory.

I engaged a carriage to take me around the quaint old town, and across the country to Kenilworth, one of the most charming drives in England. As the rain had ceased, I gave up the dignity of the coupé to ride on the box with the driver, that I might better enjoy the scenery and his conversation. He was the son, I found, of a Wesleyan local preacher; but he himself had sought fame and fortune as a jockey, only to meet with broken bones and an empty purse. The quaint villages, with their timbered houses, and the well-kept parks and fine granges, were a perpetual picture of rural beauty.

Kenilworth Castle is the finest ruin in England. Tradition refers its origin to the time of King Arthur; but the present structure dates from the time of Henry I., with extensive additions by Elizabeth's favourite, the Earl of Leicester. Here were celebrated the splendid pageants which accompanied the visit of the Virgin Queen to her high-born subject. But their chief interest is given to those crumbling ruins by the tear-compelling story of the fair Amy Robsart. I climbed the massive Cæsar's Tower, matted with the densest growth of ivy I ever saw; and lingered in the roofless banquet hall, that often rang with the sounds of wassail and revelry; and roamed through the pleasaunce and field of tourney where in the pride and pomp of chivalry, gallant knights in ringing armour, sought to win the prize of valour at the hands of beauty. But most I loved to muse amid the broken arches of Mervyn's Bower, which the Wizard of the North represents as the scene of the wretchedness of his hapless heroine. Strange that his enchanter's wand can cast such an undying spell over these mouldering ruins—all that the cannon of Cromwell have left of the once stately castle. At the bookstore of the little town I bought a copy of Scott's "Kenilworth" as a souvenir of the place, and learned from the comely saleswoman, who seemed to enter thoroughly into the romance of the story—as what woman's heart will not ?—some local traditions of the castle.

A rapid ride over the London and North-Western Railway,* through Coventry, with its strange legend of the fair Lady Godiva and the "low churl, compact of thankless earth," Peeping Tom ; past Rugby, dear to the heart of many a schoolboy ; past Olney, with its memories of Cowper, and Berkhamspstead, where he was born ; past Harrow, with its famous school, where Byron, Peel, and Palmerston were scholars ; and past Willesden Junction, through which pass four hundred trains a day, brings me to the splendid Euston Square Station, in time to take the Underground Railway *en route* for Sydenham Palace, to see the grand display of fireworks and the illuminated fountains. So much may one crowd into a single day in this land of rapid transit.

---

* This railway conveys 100,000 passengers and 73,000 tons of freight per day. It runs 29,000,000 "train miles" per year, has 10,000 miles of rails, 560 stations, 40,000 employees, and the annual consumption of coal is 600,000 tons.

CHAPTER XVIII.

CAMBRIDGE — YORK — EDINBURGH — MELROSE — ABBOTSFORD — STIRLING—THE TROSSACHS—GLASGOW— STAFFA—BELFAST—DUBLIN—WALES—CHESTER—"HOME AGAIN."

SCOTT'S MONUMENT.

ON my way to Scotland I stopped at Cambridge, Peterborough, and York, to see the colleges and cathedrals of those old ecclesiastical towns. The ride through the Fen country is tame and uninteresting, save for its historic associations. Yet, even this flat and amphibious region has its poetic aspects, as described for us by Milton, Tennyson and Kingsley. It was on the first of September that I visited Cambridge, the one day of the year when the college quadrangles are closed to the public, so as to maintain, I was informed, the control of the grounds. But a judicious fee is an "open sesame," almost everywhere ; and I was allowed to reach the *penetralia* of most of the colleges. At Christ's College, Milton "scorned delights and lived laborious days." I was shown his mulberry from which I plucked a leaf. His own melodious lines in "Il Penseroso" etch with an artist's skill the scene and its associations.

> But let my due feet never fail
> To walk the studious cloisters pale,
> And love the high embowèd roof,
> With antique pillars massy proof,
> And storied windows richly dight,
> Casting a dim religious light ;
> There let the pealing organ blow,
> To the full-voiced choir below.

In traversing the fat grazing lands of Huntingdonshire, memories of Cromwell and his Ironsides would assert themselves. At St. Ives, famous in nursery rhyme, a cattle fair was in progress, and bucolic graziers, with ruddy faces, top boots, and "horsey" dress, abounded. In England you can almost always tell a man's rank by his garb. In Canada you cannot, except that the master is generally a little worse dressed than the man.

The old Cathedral of Peterborough, on the site of an abbey founded by the Mercian Kings in 660, is of severe and majestic simplicity. The storms of seven hundred years have stained and weathered those Norman arches to a grim and hoary aspect, with which they frown down upon the ephemerides of to-day. Here that "most poor woman," Queen Katharine of Arragon was buried, and for a time also, the unhappy Queen of Scots.

But of all the cathedrals of England which I saw, the most impressive is the mighty minster of York. How it symbolizes the profound instinct of worship of the human soul, its yearnings after the unseen and eternal! The sweet and solemn chanting of the choir seemed to me the litany of the ages, the echo of the prayers of the dead and buried generations crying out for the living God. The great east window Pugin thinks "the finest in the world." The Monkish rhyme at the portal, we feel is no vain boasting : VT ROSA FLOS FLORVM, SIC EST DOMVS ISTA DOMORVM.

The ruined Abbey of St Mary's, founded 800 years ago by William Rufus, reminds us of the cowled brotherhood whose worship or wassail once filled those shattered vaults, now open to rain and wind. The old walls, the quaint "Bars," or gates and the stern old castle, celebrated in Scott's "Ivanhoe," are grim relics of the stormy feudal times. But these seem but as of yesterday compared with the older Roman ruins, dating back to the first century. Here the Emperors, Severus and Constantius died ; here Caracalla and Constantine were crowned, if indeed the latter was not a native of the place.

Through the bolder scenery of the North Riding ; past Durham with its grand cathedral crowning a lofty slope, where, as a legend reads, " HAC SVNT IN FOSSA BEDÆ VENERABILIS OSSA;" through Newcastle with its famous High Bridge, its grimy colliers and its eight hundred year old castle, which gives it its name ; between the far-rolling Cheviot Hills, and wild sea coast for ever lashed by the melancholy main; passing in full view of Holy Isle, the storm-swept Lindisfarne, and the grim prison of the Covenanters, Bass Rock, and near the scene of the hard-fought battles of Flodden-Field, Dunbar and Preston Pans, we glide by the grim couchant lion of Arthur's Seat into the Athens of the North, the memory-haunted city of Edinburgh.

THE NORTH BRIDGE.

No city in Europe occupies a grander site, and few cities in the world are invested with more heroic or romantic associations. My first visit was to the noble Scott monument, shown in the initial cut of this chapter, where I had a bird's-eye view of the scene, over which he has cast such an undying spell. Beneath the arch is a marble statue of the great enchanter, and filling the many niches are the figures that he called from the realm of fancy, and enbreathed with life forever. The deep ravine of the North Loch, now a charming public garden, crossed by lofty traffic-crowded bridges, separates the picturesque and historic old town and the handsome new city.

The lofty narrow crow-stepped buildings of the former rising tier above tier, especially when lit up at night, have a strangely picturesque appearance. It was like a dream, or like a chapter from the "Heart of Midlothian" to walk up the Cannongate, the High Street, the Lawn Market, between the lofty and grim-featured houses. My garrulous guide pointed out the Tron Church clock, which he said "was aye keepit twa minutes fast, that the warkmen might na be late;" and the old St. Giles Church, where Jenny Geddes flung her stool at the prelatic hireling "wha would say a mass in her lug."

OLD EDINBURGH BY NIGHT.

Here are buried the Regent Murray and the great Earl of Montrose, and without, beneath the stone pave-

ROOM IN WHICH KNOX DIED.

ment of the highway, once part of the churchyard, lies the body of John Knox. A metal plate with the letters,

"I. K., 1572," conjecturally marks his grave—the exact position is not known—and all day long the carts and carriages rattle over the bones of the great Scottish Reformer. Near by, the site of the old Tolbooth is shown by a large heart marked in the stones of the causeway.

In the High Street is Knox's house, a picturesque old place with a steep outer stair. It was with feelings of peculiar reverence that I stood in the room in which Knox died, and in the little study—very small and narrow —only about four feet by seven, in which he wrote the History of the Scottish Reformation. I sat in his chair at his desk, and I stood at the window from which he used to preach to the multitude in the High Street—now a squalid and disreputable spot. The motto on the house front reads, "LVFE. GOD. ABVFE. AL. AND. YI. NYCHTBOVR. AS. YI. SELF." There are many such pious mottoes, as: "MY. HOIP. IS. CHRIST;" "WHAT. EVER.ME.BEFALL.I.THANK. THE.LORD.OF.ALL;" "LAVS. VBIQVE. DEO;" " NISI. DO-

JOHN KNOX'S STUDY.

MINVS. FRVSTRA;" "PAX. ENTRANTIBVS. SALVS. EXEVNTIBVS." A garrulous Scotch wife, with a charming accent, showed a number of relics of the great Reformer, including his portrait and that of the fair false Queen, whose guilty conscience he probed to the quick, and the beautiful Four Maries of her court. In the Museum I saw Knox's old pulpit where, says Melville, "he was sae active that he was lyk to ding it in blads and flee out of it."

The grim old castle rises on an isolated crag, four hundred feet above the Forth—half palace and half prison—a memorial of the stormy days of feudal power. In a little chamber about eight feet square, James VI., only son of Mary Stuart, and future King of England, was born, and it is said he was let down in a basket from the window to the Grass Market, three hundred feet below. On the ceiling is a quaint black letter inscription:

Lord Jesus Christ that crowned was with thorne,
Preserve the bairn quha heir is borne.

At the other end of the long and narrow street—the most picturesque in Europe—is the Royal Palace of Holyrood, with its memories of guilt and gloom. Here is the chamber in which Knox wrung the Queen's proud heart by his upbraidings; the supper room—very small—in which Mary was dining with Rizzio and her Maids of Honour, when Darnley and his fellow-assassins climbed the winding stair, and murdered the unhappy wretch clinging to his royal mistress's skirts, and then dragged his body

THE CASTLE AND ALLAN RAMSEY'S HOUSE.

into the Queen's bedchamber, where the blood stains are still shown upon the floor. The Queen's bed with its faded tapestries, her private altar, the stone on which she knelt, her meagre mirror, her tiny dressing room, and the embroidered picture of Jacob's Dream, wrought with her own fair fingers, make very vivid and real the sad story of the unhappy sovereign, who realized to the full the words,

"Uneasy lies the head that wears a crown."

RIDDLE'S CLOSE, WHERE HUME COMMENCED HIS "HISTORY OF ENGLAND."

The Abbey Church, now an exquisite ruin, dates from 1128, and still affords a sanctuary to insolvent debtors.

The wynds and closes of the ancient town, once the abodes of the Scottish nobility, are now the squalid lairs of misery and vice. Once high born dames and knightly men, banquetted in carved chambers now the degraded purlieus of poverty and crime. Some of these have still interesting historic associations, as the houses of the Duke of Gordon, of Earl Moray, Hume, Boswell, Walter Scott, and others of distinguished name and fame. I penetrated some of the grim closes, which surpassed aught I ever saw of squalidness, and was glad to find myself safely out again.

The church yard of old Gray Friars is an epitome of Scottish history. On the broad flat stone shown in the cut on page 366, the Solemn League and Covenant was signed, 1638, and on Martyrs' Monument one reads, "From May 27th, 1661, that the most noble Marquis of Argyll was beheaded, until Feb. 18th, 1668, there was executed in Edinburgh about one hundred noblemen, gentlemen, ministers and others, the most of whom lie here." Nourished by such costly libations, the tree of liberty took root and flourished strong and fair. The tomb of "Bluidy Mackenzie," of sinister memory, still exerts its malign spell upon the belated urchin as he slinks past.

BUCCLEUGH PLACE, WHERE THE "EDINBURGH REVIEW" WAS PROJECTED.

While visiting the antiquarian museum, I had the great and unexpected pleasure of meeting a fellow-towns-

COLLEGE WYND, WHERE SCOTT WAS BORN.

man, Mr. John Macdonald, of Toronto, with his two charming daughters—the only persons that I had ever seen before that I met in a four months' tour. I gladly accepted the cordial invitation to join his party, and we drove again to Holyrood, the Canongate, the Cemetery in which lie the bodies of Drs. Duff, Candlish, Chalmers, Guthrie, Hugh Miller, and many other of Scotland's greatest sons; and Calton Hill, with its magnificent panorama of cliff and crag, and strath and frith, and

WHITE HORSE INN, CANONGATE.

ANCHOR CLOSE.

its noble group of monuments. A grizly blue-bonneted *cicerone* pointed out, with broad Doric comments, St. Leonard's Crags, the home of Davie Deans, the moss hags of Jennie's midnight tryst, St. Anthony's Chapel, and Arthur's Seat, like a grim couchant lion, one of the most majestic objects I ever saw.

It is a delightful excursion to Melrose and Abbotsford, through lovely scenery, over which is thrown the nameless spell,

> The light that never was on sea or shore,
> The consecration and the poet's dream.

The heather and the broom mingled with the gorse and gowans on the green slopes of the Tweed side, and the names of Eskdale, and Gala Water, Cockpen and Eildon Hills, recall many an ancient ballad or legend.

The old Abbey, dating from 1136, is one of the finest relics of gothic architecture extant. The image-breaking zeal of the Reformers, and the cannon of Cromwell have left only a picturesque ruin. It was quite pathetic to see the roofless aisles, the broken windows, the crumbling columns, and the grass-grown chancel where once the cowled brotherhood chanted their matins and even-song.

The battered saints looked down reproachfully from their ivied niches, and the effigies of the knights seemed to keep watch over the tombs, where, through the long ages their bodies "await the resurrection." I noticed

STONE ON WHICH THE COVENANT WAS SIGNED.

the touching inscription, "CVM VENIT JESVS CESSABIT VMBRA"—" When Jesus comes the darkness shall fly away." Here is the tomb of the arch wizard Michael Scott, whose awful apparition is recorded in the Lay of the Last Minstrel, and here was buried at last the fiery heart of Bruce. I sat in Sir Walter's favourite seat and gazed where "the darkened roof rose high aloof," and on the lovely eastern oriel with its slender shafts of foliaged tracery, of which he sings,

> "Thou would'st have thought some fairy's hand
> 'Twixt poplars straight, the osier wand
> In many a freakish knot had twined ;
> Then framed a spell when the work was done,
> And changed the willow wreaths to stone."

Was ever ruin so sad and fair? I lingered for hours in the legend-haunted spot, and then walked along the green Tweed side to Abbotsford where still wields his spell a mightier wizard than even Michael Scott. It is a large and rambling house with fantastic, yet picturesque groups of chimneys, gables and turrets. Over the door is the pious legend,

By night, by day Remember aye, ye goodness of ye Lord, And thank His name whose glorious eis spread throughout ye world.

The house is full of old armour—targes and claymores, helmets and hauberks; antique furniture and relics—the keys of the Tolbooth, Queen Mary's cross and purse, historic portraits and the like. Of especial interest was the stately library, and the small writing room, with the desk and books just as the master left them, and the effigy of faithful Maida. Then I stood with hushed spirit in the room in which he died, and through the open window heard the murmur of the distant Tweed, which in life he loved so well. I was ferried over the brawling stream by a stout-armed damsel with a pleasant face and strong Scottish accent, and was soon whirled by rail back to Auld Reekie again.

Next morning I left early for Glasgow by way of Stirling and the Trossachs. The royal borough of Stirling with its famous castle, perched upon a lofty crag, is delightfully quaint and picturesque. The view from the ramparts of the lovely valley of the Forth, and the purple-vested Ben Voirlich, Ben Lomond, Ben Ledi and the rest of the Titan brotherhood was unsurpassed even by that from Calton Hill. Queen Mary's View is a small opening in the wall where the "fair mischief" watched the tilts and tourneys in the jousting yard below. Here is a quaint old hall, adorned with strange mythological figures, where the ancient parliament of Scotland used to meet. In a gloomy chamber of the palace, James V. slew with his own hand his guest the Earl of Douglas; below is the monument of bold Wallace wight, and hard by the world-famous field of Bannockburn. But the chief spell of the scene is that cast by the filial piety of fair Ellen of the Lake. As I marched down Castle Hill I was preceded by a company of kilted and plaided pipers, skirling the wild music of their mountain pibroch on the air.

From Stirling the route skirts the Ochil Hills, passing Dumblane, where dwelt the "sweet Jessie" of the song, and "Bonny Doune," with its banks and braes to Callander, where first we hear the Gaelic speech. Here we take open coaches for the ride through the Trossach pass. The whole region is rife with associations of the winsome Lady of the Lake, and the scarlet-coated guard points out with effusion the scenes where took place the varied incidents of the poem. The scenery I must confess, after the loveliness of Como, and the grandeur of Lucerne, seemed bleak and tame; but the genius of the poet has invested it with an undying charm. We would hardly be surprised to hear the winding of a hunting horn and to see Fitz James and Roderich Dhu start up from the hazel thickets of the deep and tangled glen.

Reaching Loch Katrine—was ever seen " so lone a lake, so sweet a strand " ?—we traverse its mountain-girdled expanse—past fair Ellen's Isle, floating double on the wave and the Silver Strand where she met King James ; and again take coaches, and in a pouring rain reach Inversnaid, grandly situated on the steep slopes of Loch Lomond. Here Wolfe was once quartered to repress the depredations of the wild Highland clans under Rob Roy, whose cairn and birthplace and grave are shown. The sail down this many-isled lake gives glimpses of stern Ben Lomond frowning through his misty shroud. Passing in view of the majestic Dumbarton Rock—flung by the fiends after St. Patrick, when he fled from their persecution to Ireland, says the legend—we reach the crowded port and busy mart of Glasgow.

The chief glory of Glasgow is St. Mungo's church, dating from 1123. Its stained glass is the finest I saw in Europe. Its vast and majestic crypts are celebrated in " Rob Roy." The Reformers were content with destroying the images, so that it is, as Bailie Nichol Jarvie expressed it, " as crouse as a cat wi' the flaes kaimed aff." The large church-yard is literally paved with gravestones. Among the notable names in the adjacent Necropolis, I noticed those of Motherwell, Sheridan Knowles, Alexander Smith, Dr. Eadie, Dr. Wardlaw, and the ceno-

x

taphs of Knox, and of Hamilton and Wishart, burned at St. Andrews, 1528 and 1546. The chief relics of the

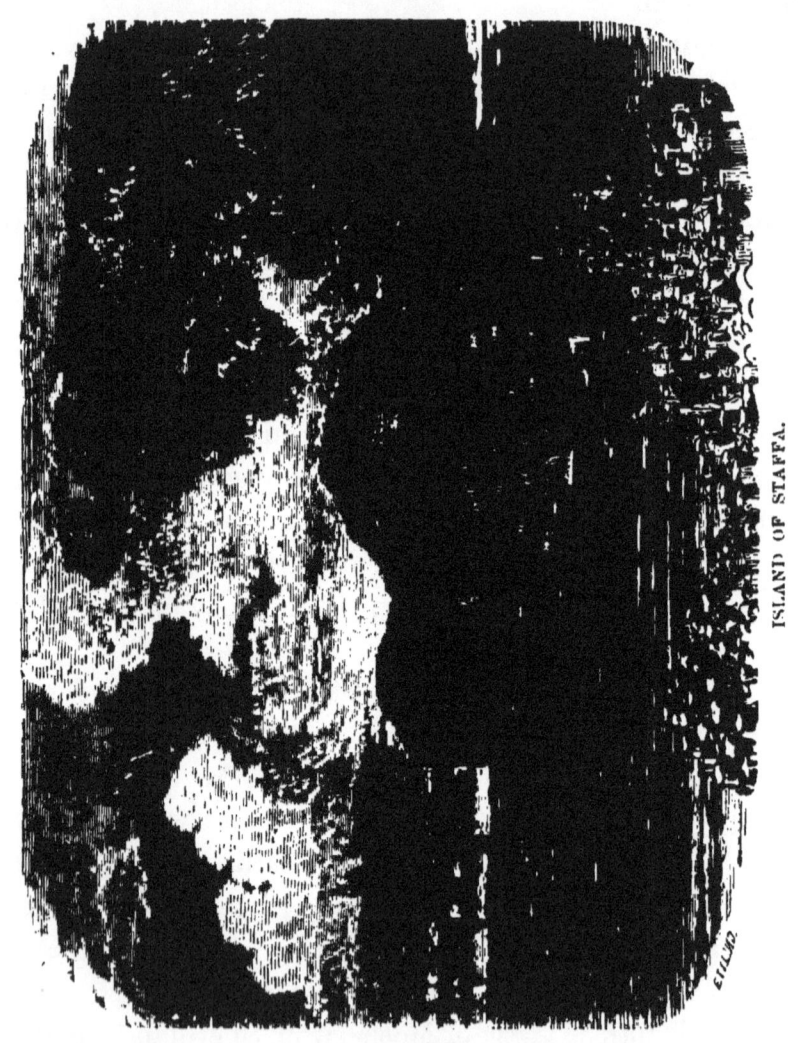

ISLAND OF STAFFA.

old city are the Trongate and "Saut Market," where dwelt the honest Bailie. The region is now the purlieus of poverty and vice. Nowhere have I seen greater squalor and wretchedness. Hundreds of idle men with grimy faces and greasy clothes glowered at me as I passed. A day or two later in a bread riot they rifled a baker's shop. Yet in this poorest region the gin-shops most abounded, and wretched creatures,—frowsy men and bareheaded, barefooted women—swarmed in and out " like bees about their straw-built citadel."

It is a short sail from Glasgow through the grand scenery of the Western Isles to Scotland's greatest natural curiosity —Fingal's cave in the Isle of Staffa. Staffa is only a mile in circumference, but its entire façade, and the arches and flooring of the caves strangely resemble architectural designs. The special wonder however is Fingal's Cave; the sides and front of which are formed of perpendicular basaltic columns. The arch is 70 feet high and supports a roof 30 feet thick. The chasm extends in length 230 feet. Mere dimensions however can give no idea of the weird effect produced by the twilight gloom, half revealing the varying sheen of the reflected light; the echo of the measured surge as it rises and falls, and the profound and fairy solitude of the whole scene. Our engravings give remote and near views of this remarkable cave. The columnar structure of the rocks and the tesselated pavement of the floor will be observed.

I crossed by night from Glasgow to Belfast. It rained all the time I was in Ireland, so I have rather depressing recollections of the country. Belfast seemed thriving and active much more so than Dublin. In spite of the rain the people whom I met seemed determined, like Mark Tapley, to be

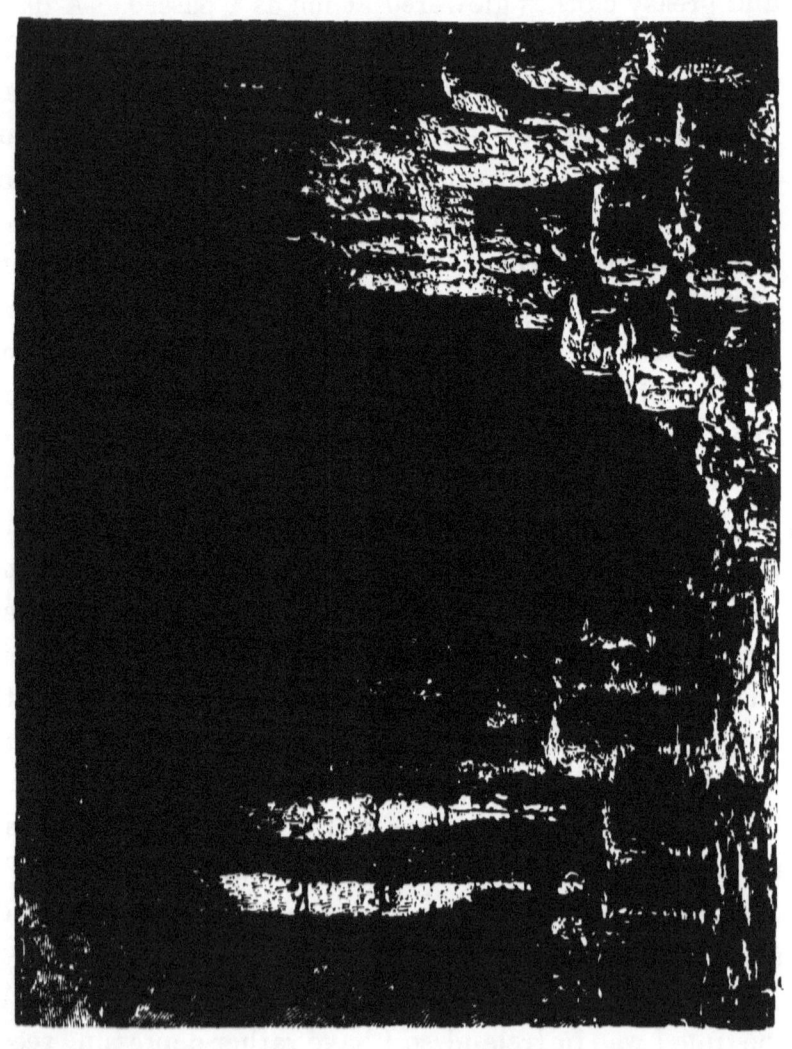

FINGAL'S CAVE.

as jolly as possible under adverse circumstances. "I'm the man kin tell ye all about it," said a tram-car conductor of

whom I asked some question. "It's ten years in the police force I was," and he gave the history of every noteworthy house that we passed. He seemed to know everyone. He would tip a wink to a pretty nursemaid in a window, and a nod to a friend in the street, and a merry jest to the passengers as they entered the car.

My route to Dublin traversed an amphibious region, where "the foinest pisantry in the woruld, sorr," were striving, in the month of September, to harvest their crop of hay which was drifting about the fields. Their little crofts and glebes and thatched cottages looked very poverty-stricken. The country is well called the Emerald Isle. Vegetation of such vivid green I never saw. But this was by no means characteristic of the people, who were anything but verdant—bright, witty and cheerful in spite of their poverty. The men wore superannuated beaver hats and long ulster coats, some of which, as specimens of patching, were works of art. One could hardly tell the original fabric, and, like Joseph's coat, they were of many colours. Anything more dreary than the water-soaked, black turf bogs it would be hard to conceive. At Drogheda, an ancient town which has had more than its share of Ireland's woes, I crossed the Boyne in full view of the battlefield on which the star of the Stuarts set for ever.

The finest thing I saw in Dublin was Trinity College. Indeed not even Oxford has as large and wealthy a foundation. In "College Green," so called, I suppose, *more*

Hibernico, because it has not a blade of grass, stands the most preposterous equestrian statue in the world—that of William III. One would think the man who made it never saw a horse in his life. As I strolled through the old Parliament House, now a bank, I asked a servant if he would like Home Rule again. "Some might, belike," he said, " not I ; shure, what's the differ ?" which cheerful philosophy I did not seek to disturb. St. Patrick's Cathedral is said to have been founded by its patron saint, A.D. 448. If that be so, it has done little for its environment in those 1400 years, for it has around it the most squalid purlieus of the town, which is saying a good deal.

The Liffy, the Four Courts, Nelson's Monument, and the "Phaynix Park" provoke the pride of every patriot, and not without due cause. The Castle, a stern feudal tower, is characterized by strength rather than beauty. The carving in the Chapel Royal is superb. The *custode* looked just like Dickens, and was such an eloquent gentleman that I had to double my intended fee. A ride in wind and rain over stony streets, in a jaunting car—it should be spelled j-o-l-t-i-n-g car—does not make one long for a repetition of the experiment. I had to hang on, metaphorically, " with tooth and nail." I suppose it is a little better than riding on a rail, but I am not sure.

Next day I crossed to Holyhead in one of the swift mail steamers which are subject to a penalty of 34*s.* per minute if the mails are delayed. The bold Welsh coast presents a rugged front, but few lovelier views than that of Menai Straits and Bridge can meet the eye. The scenery of North Wales is bold but bare. The country is almost treeless, and is divided into small fields by stone fences. The villages are clumps of low-walled, small stone houses, and the mountains roll away in purple billows to the cloudy distance. The towers and castles built to overawe the Welsh, are grim memorials of a bygone age. Especially fine are Conway and Denbigh Castles. Some of the mines have been worked from the times of the Romans. I saw acres of slates stacked up, enough, it seemed, to roof all the houses in the world.

The old city of Chester deserves a longer visit than I could give it. Its walls "grey with the memories of two thousand years," mark the camp of the Roman legions, and much of their work still remains. I walked all around the lofty ramparts. From one of the towers Charles I. watched the defeat of his army on Bolton Moor. Cromwell's cannon have left his bold sign manual upon the walls. The new bridge across the Dee has a span of 200 feet, the widest stone arch in the world. The most curious feature of the city is its Rows, or double terraces of shops, the upper one fronting on a broad arcade. The old timbered houses have quaintly-carved fronts, galleries and gables, like those in Frankfort, often with some Biblical or allegorical design. Of special interest is one which bears the legend,

God's Providence is mine Inheritance. mdclii.

said to be the only house which escaped the plague in that year. To reach the town house of an old Earl of Derby —a handsome place during the civil wars—I had to pass through an alley only two feet wide. It is now a sort of junk shop—so fallen is its high estate. A young girl showed me the hiding place in the roof where the Earl lay concealed for days till he was discovered, taken to Bolton and executed for his fidelity to his king.

It is a ride of only sixteen miles to Liverpool, and next day I found my old quarters on the S.S. *Dominion, en route* for Canada. One of the pleasures of going abroad, to speak Hibernically, is that of coming home again ; and one of its most important lessons is that no land under the sun furnishes for the average mortal happier conditions of existence than our own beloved Canada. Many of those old historic lands of Europe are charming places to visit, but they are also excellent places to leave. The struggle for a bare livelihood is more keen, the chances of success are less assured, and educational and social advantages are less easily attainable than in our own favoured land. Untrammelled by the fetters of the past, with almost boundless extent and inexhaustible resources, it offers to its sons a fairer heritage than is, I think, to be found elsewhere on earth. Land of my birth,

"WHERE'ER I ROAM, WHATEVER REALMS TO SEE,
MY HEART UNTRAVELLED FONDLY TURNS TO THEE."

THE END.

www.ingramcontent.com/pod-product-compliance
Lightning Source LLC
Chambersburg PA
CBHW020308240426

43673CB00039B/739